Designing and Delivering Effective Online Instruction

How to Engage Adult Learners

Linda Dale Bloomberg

Teachers College Press
TEACHERS COLLEGE | COLUMBIA UNIVERSITY
NEW YORK AND LONDON

Published by Teachers College Press,® 1234 Amsterdam Avenue, New York, NY 10027

Copyright © 2021 by Teachers College, Columbia University

Cover design by Rebecca Lown Design. Artwork by Gala / Shutterstock.

All rights reserved. No part of this publication may be reproduced or transmitted in any form or by any means, electronic or mechanical, including photocopy, or any information storage and retrieval system, without permission from the publisher. For reprint permission and other subsidiary rights requests, please contact Teachers College Press, Rights Dept.: tcpressrights@tc.columbia.edu

Library of Congress Cataloging-in-Publication Data is available at loc.gov

ISBN 978-0-8077-6528-9 (paper)
ISBN 978-0-8077-6529-6 (hardcover)
ISBN 978-0-8077-7953-8 (ebook)

Printed on acid-free paper
Manufactured in the United States of America

For Israel Lippert (1902–1974)
Julia Esther Lippert (1906–1997)
Rosalind Ann Diamond (1947–1978)
All a constant source of energy,
inspiration, and strength.
Their spirit lives on.

And for my three children
Carla, Brent, and Adam Bloomberg.
In the hope that they will strive to realize
their individual strengths.
And always follow their dreams in the pursuit of
fulfillment, peace, and happiness.
And for little Bella, for staying at my side always.
My love for you all is never ending.

Contents

Preface	ix
Purpose and Function of This Book	xi
Organization of This Book	xv
What Sets This Book Apart?	xviii
Additional Defining Features of This Book	xxii
Introduction: Going the Distance—An Overview of Online Learning	1
The Landscape of Online Learning	1
The Role of the Online Instructor	7
PART I: THE ART OF THE START—DESIGN AND DEVELOP ONLINE INSTRUCTION	13
1. **Develop Course Learning Outcomes**	17
Outcomes Are Aligned with Your Vision for the Course	18
Outcomes Are Sequenced	22
Outcomes Are Specific and Measurable	24
Course Content is Aligned with Outcomes	24
Chapter Summary and Synthesis	27
Reflection Checkpoint	27
2. **Plan for Assessment of Learning**	29
Assessment Instruments and Methods	30
Formative and Summative Assessment	35
Guidelines for Effective Assessment	37
Chapter Summary and Synthesis	39
Reflection Checkpoint	39

3.	**Create Course Content**	**41**
	Adult Learning Principles	42
	The Multimedia Principle	44
	Transforming Teaching Material into Audio and Video Content	51
	Organization and Presentation of Material	53
	Collaborative Learning Opportunities	58
	Scaffolding	63
	Inclusion, Equity, and Accessibility	65
	Chapter Summary and Synthesis	72
	Reflection Checkpoint	73

Part I Synthesis   **75**

PART II: TRAVELING THE EDUCATIONAL JOURNEY— DELIVER ENGAGING AND EMPOWERING LEARNING EXPERIENCES   **81**

4.	**Onboard and Welcome Learners**	**85**
	Learner Engagement and Teaching Presence	85
	Prepare for the Online Learning Experience	90
	Strategies for Onboarding Engagement	91
	Support Learners to be Successful	96
	Strategies for Ongoing Supportive Engagement	99
	Monitor and Address Progress and Development	103
	Strategies for Effective Monitoring	103
	Chapter Summary and Synthesis	104
	Reflection Checkpoint	105
5.	**Establish and Build Teaching Relationships**	**107**
	Benefits of Positive Working Relationships	108
	Develop Your Working Relationships	108
	Engage Through Presence	110
	Foster a Growth Academic Mindset	112
	Power and Positionality	116

Contents   vii

       Chapter Summary and Synthesis   119
       Reflection Checkpoint   120

6. **Multimodal Teaching Strategies to Engage and Empower Learners**   122
       Respect Diversity and Strive for Inclusion   122
       Culturally Responsive Teaching   123
       Address Unequal Access to Technology   124
       Develop a Learning Community   126
       Facilitate Group Work and Collaboration   127
       Feedback as the Medium of Instruction   130
       Prepare to Provide Feedback   135
       Guiding Principles for Substantive and Engaging Feedback   139
       Multimodal Teaching   146
       Assessment and Grading   151
       Chapter Summary and Synthesis   153
       Reflection Checkpoint   154

Part II Synthesis   157

PART III: TAKING STOCK—A REVIEW OF MULTIMODAL ENGAGEMENT   165

7. **Revisiting Your Engagement Strategies**   167
       Engagement Indicators   167
       Ensure Teaching Presence   170
       Nurture Working Relationships   171
       Apply Effective Facilitation Practices   174
       Create a Sense of Community   176
       Address Diversity and Inclusivity   178
       Embrace Learner Autonomy and Empowerment   180
       Support Learners' Use of Technology   182
       Establish and Maintain a Culture of Trust and Transparency   183
       Chapter Summary and Synthesis   186

8. Instructor as Reflective Practitioner	**187**
Reflective Practice	187
Implicit Bias	189
Final Reflection	190
Glossary	**193**
References	**216**
Index	**224**
About the Author	**234**

Online Appendixes

    Appendix A: Bloom's Taxonomy

    Appendix B: Accessibility Resources

    Appendix C: Sample Welcome Letter

    Appendix D: Learner Support Resource: How to Benefit from Feedback and Critique

    Appendix E: Sample Learning Contract

    Appendix F: Guidelines for Conducting Peer Review

    Appendix G: Guidelines for Implementing Peer Dialogue Journals

    Appendix H: Satisfactory Versus Unsatisfactory Written Feedback Samples

    Appendix I: Samples of Feedback Commentary

    Appendix J: Sample Grading Rubric

    Appendix K: Sample Grade Justification Rubric

    Appendix L: Engagement Evaluation Rubric

    Appendix M: Annotated Research Resources: Engagement in Online Learning

    Appendix N: Online Support Resources

    Appendix O: Applications to Support and Enhance Online Teaching and Learning

The appendixes can be viewed by scanning this QR code:

Preface

Online learning is currently the most rapidly growing subsection of education and has become entrenched in business and higher education, offering access and opportunities to learners worldwide. In 2006, a rule that restricted U.S. colleges and universities from offering more than 50% of their courses online was eliminated from the Higher Education Act. For-profit and adult-focused public universities swiftly launched online programs that proved popular among adult learners who wanted a flexible program that fit their busy lives. These pioneering schools were soon followed by entrepreneurial nonprofit colleges and universities, often seeking to reverse stagnant or declining enrollments. Their strategy for introducing online programs was simple: "If you build it, they will come." Learners came to these programs in droves. Once online programs proved profitable, a wave of schools entered the market, including both for-profit and nonprofit institutions. The U.S. Department of Education approved a major overhaul of regulations relating to **distance education,** and by 2016, only 10 years after the 50% rule was eliminated, 32% of college students took at least one online course, and 17% were enrolled in fully online programs (National Center for Education Statistics [NCES], 2016). At that time, 72% of public schools and 50% of private, nonprofit schools offered fully online programs (Xu & Xu, 2019). The National Center for Education Statistics Integrated Postsecondary Education Data System (IPEDS) data shows that in 2017, 3.1 million higher education students were enrolled in courses that were exclusively delivered via distance education across a variety of **synchronous** and **asynchronous** delivery technologies (NCES, 2019a, 2019b). Moreover, an increasing number of hybrid or **blended learning** programs had emerged, which included a significant distance learning component. As the percentage of college students rises and access to broadband increases, it has been predicted that online enrollments will undoubtedly follow suit (Learninghouse, 2019). According to an Inside Higher Ed and Gallup poll of 2,000 U.S. faculty members in October 2019—that is, well before the COVID-19 pandemic—39% fully supported the increased use of education technologies, up from 29% in 2017. And a national survey of more than 4,000 faculty members in early 2020 found that 45% had a better opinion of online learning since the pandemic began; fewer than one in five (17%) had a more negative perception (McKinsey & Company, 2020b). Online learning was clearly a rapidly emerging educational market.

Fast forward to the spring of 2020, when the field of online learning was revolutionized as the world suddenly faced an unprecedented emergency situation due to the COVID-19 pandemic—a watershed moment for education systems around the world, and possibly leading to the largest teaching intervention ever. This occurrence accelerated a rapid, radical, and far-reaching shift across colleges, universities, and organizations to online teaching models, with face-to-face courses and programs being taken out of the physical classroom and thrust head-first into virtual formats and domains. For those not already engaged in online learning, this change was abrupt, disruptive, and jarring. The massive shift brought with it some significant challenges, including an overtaxed technological infrastructure, learners' disorientation, and instructors' own learning curve. Most instructors had no previous online teaching experience, and there was very limited time for preparation and limited support, thus leaving them scrambling to adapt their teaching plans, tools, and techniques to fully online as well as blended and hybrid platforms. With the ongoing pandemic and widespread closures and reorganization, there has been a significant and continuing need for "reskilling and upskilling" as a result of disruptive change in the job market (McKinsey & Company, 2020a; World Economic Forum, 2020, 2021). According to the World Economic Forum's survey data, in order to match workers to new roles and activities, employers are expected to lean primarily on internal capacity to deliver training, supplemented by online learning platforms and external consultants. The trend toward the use of online reskilling has accelerated due to the restrictions on in-person learning since the onset of the pandemic. Current data provided by the World Economic Forum (2020) signals a substantial and rapid expansion of online learning, with increases in the numbers of individuals seeking opportunities for learning online through their own initiative, in employer provision of online learning opportunities to their workers, and in enrollment of learners seeking access to online learning through government programs.

While online learning represents an expanding and ever-increasing phenomenon that offers many benefits, studying at a distance does raise questions about the difficulties of isolation and **motivation**, with the sense of **exclusion** and detachment becoming potential **barriers to learning**. The theory of **transactional distance**, developed by Moore (1997), explains the perceived "psychological and communication space" in the online learning environment, often causing learners to participate minimally, disengage, or completely withdraw. This theory defines distance as pedagogical and social, rather than merely physical and geographical, and emphasizes the need for structures that foster dialogue and **collaborative learning**. **Teaching presence**, a key component of the **Community of Inquiry model** developed by Garrison et al. (1999, 2001, 2003), relates to instructors developing collaborative working relationships and interacting with learners in order to bridge transactional distance and generate greater engagement. Research supports a clear link between instructor engagement, learner engagement, and learning. Furthermore, the evolution of online technologies enables **interaction** among instructors and learners to shift from individual approaches to multiple forms of collaborative learning, and as this technological transformation takes place, teaching presence and its influence on engagement has become even more prominent.

It is important to remember that technological advances offer not "promises" but "possibilities," and there is no guarantee that these advancements will necessarily translate into benefits for learners, especially if the focus is on a mechanistic rather than a relational teaching approach. Being an engaged instructor starts with understanding what engagement and **presence** imply and how you can proactively and intentionally develop authentic interactions and meaningful working relationships with your learners. While online learners are typically adults who prefer **self-directed learning** experiences, online learning should not be viewed as "alone learning." To mitigate the experience of transactional distance, it is essential that multiple support structures be put in place to supplement learners' self-directed pathways, building their capacity as they strive to achieve their goals. Whether the online learning environment is blended, hybrid, or entirely online, instructors must be committed to ensuring a learning experience that promotes and facilitates deep learning. The challenge becomes *how we craft the experience* for our diverse learners, engaging them in meaningful interactions and learning experiences within a virtual environment.

PURPOSE AND FUNCTION OF THIS BOOK

Online learning continues to expand across diverse education settings and contexts, creating a high demand for quality online instructors at all levels. As colleges, universities, schools, and organizations around the world adopt large-scale technologies, and as traditional class models merge with online environments, critical insights are needed regarding the implications for planning and **pedagogy**. In the recruitment of online instructors, the most important consideration is *the ability to teach online* (Bigatel et al., 2012; Bloomberg, 2014, 2020a, 2020b, 2020c; Bloomberg & Grantham, 2018; Cutri & Mena, 2020; Khan, et al., 2017; Martin et al., 2019; Roddy et al., 2017). Moreover, not all instructors may be ready and willing to learn new pedagogical skills, and many instructors feel significantly unprepared for what lies ahead (Gratz & Looney, 2020). While it is acknowledged that face-to-face teaching **competencies** such as **knowledge** of curricula and pedagogy do transfer to online contexts, it is also important to recognize the specific and unique competencies required for online teaching success, and the role of institutions in setting instructor duties and responsibilities. The shift to online learning, which is typically multimedia based, requires adjustments to the teaching practices associated with traditional learning environments, thereby placing new (and increased) demands on instructors. Core competencies for online teaching include organizational and time-management skills and the ability to facilitate **collaboration** and teamwork, build community, pose questions effectively, and present and engage fully with learners in virtual environments. Indeed, understanding the pedagogy of online education is foundational.

As the **online teaching** environment has continued to advance and evolve, instructors have not always managed to keep pace, often demonstrating a tendency to rely too heavily on **technology** to form connections with their learners or to revert to conventional teaching practices that are more suited to traditional classrooms. Being an experienced instructor and possessing advanced technological skills does not necessarily lead to effective **online instruction,** and even those who are experienced may often find themselves at a loss when their traditional pedagogical methods do not necessarily translate to an online setting. Moreover, with the continual introduction of technological advancements and improvements, training and professional development for novice online instructors has not always been able to adequately keep up with the fast pace of the field of online learning to ensure that instructors acquire the necessary competencies to successfully teach online. Given the prevalence of technology in education, there has been a trend toward developing professional training courses that focus on expanding technological knowledge through informal learning, in-service training, or structured certificate programs (Wasserman & Migdal, 2019). While useful, this technical training and support does not necessarily assist instructors with some of the effective pedagogical practices and their application in the online environment (Bloomberg, 2020a, 2020b, 2020c; Karchmer-Klein, 2020; Ko & Rossen, 2017).

The implication of this gap in training becomes even more critical with the massive shift to online learning given the start of the pandemic in spring 2020 when educators found themselves having to solve the problems of course design, delivery, and quality assurance without sufficient time to think about, plan, and prepare for all the aspects of technology and pedagogy. Most of 2020 and going into 2021 was less about distance learning, and more about crisis teaching. Going forward, we have the opportunity to be much more purposeful and intentional in our approach, and this is where *Designing and Delivering Effective Online Instruction: How to Engage Adult Learners* will prove indispensable. This book curates decades of research in adult learning and education to focus specifically on those evidence-based strategies and practices that apply best to an online environment. As online modes of study continue to expand and diversify, especially in the post-COVID era, there is increasing awareness that developing institutional competence for online instruction will require a thoughtful and purposeful approach to training online instructors and a significant investment in staff training and development. With the ongoing expansion of online learning, it is therefore crucial that instructors are provided with initial and ongoing support to enhance their teaching practice and better meet the needs of their learners through engaging, meaningful, and personalized instruction.

A key motivator for developing this book is to go beyond the typical standards that meet minimum requirements for online teaching, toward a more dynamic and robust approach in addressing the need to design and deliver education to a diverse body of learners, while at all times ensuring access and equity for all. Intended to be a practical and useful resource, this text incorporates and highlights effective practices for online course design and teaching that are grounded in principles of adult learning, and illustrates how to understand and adopt pedagogical techniques and approaches that are targeted specifically for online learning environments. Considering the workload that may be encountered in working with multiple learners at any one time, which could become overwhelming if not efficiently managed, there are also a number of skills and strategies that can be learned and used to streamline teaching without diminishing the quality thereof. Whether you are an instructor who is contemplating teaching online, are relatively new to online teaching, or have been engaged in the field for some time and seek to enhance your practice, this book offers key principles for understanding the **online learning experience** as well as actionable strategies for engaging and supporting your learners. The approach that is presented in this book will also be of interest to administrators responsible for the training and support of online instructors (including instructional designers, technologists, program directors, program or discipline chairs, and instructional deans), as well as to learners in **instructional design** and technology programs. Moreover, the book's content is readily applicable across disciplines and institutional types.

Precipitated by the COVID-19 pandemic, which accelerated the shift to online learning, and as more and more programs and courses at every level have transferred to online platforms, many instructors remain overwhelmed and are struggling to rapidly expand their skill sets to become proficient in technologies that they have never, or perhaps only briefly, explored. One concern has been what instructors will do to ensure that they are indeed able to meet a much higher set of expectations for quality instruction and learning, especially with schools remaining closed in the foreseeable future—either wholly or partially. Many questions still remain: Is this pedagogical transformation just a "blip," or will this become the "new normal"? Was this a catalyst for a more significant disruption to education more generally? What are the longer-term implications of this disruption? What are the emergent opportunities for teaching and learning? What are the advantages and the challenges inherent in the online environment, and what are the lessons learned? While we cannot be certain what our post-COVID future holds, what we can do is seize the moment to be intentional in applying effective practices and working toward continuous improvement to offer optimal online learning experiences that will engage and empower our learners. The transition to an online teaching and learning format may be unfamiliar, but the necessary skills and techniques *can be learned and mastered* to serve the current and ever-expanding need and ensure high-quality learning experiences. Although the impact on schools has been and will continue to be disruptive and difficult, through crisis comes opportunity. This forced and abrupt move to online learning may provide institutions with the prospect of innovating and piloting new approaches, thereby helping to create positive and enduring changes, including ways to integrate remote teaching capabilities with on-site instruction. What lies ahead are valuable learning opportunities to achieve the following:

- leverage technologies to create strong, authentic learning experiences, not simply replicate the traditional classroom environment;
- develop **learner-centered** curriculum that helps leverage interest and passion to learn
- support learners as they develop 21st-century skills and practices that will prepare them for navigating an uncertain future; and
- focus on mentoring learners by facilitating **multimodal learning** experiences that will foster deep learning and empowerment.

The forced shift to online learning that occurred as a result of the pandemic has heightened the significant disparities that exist at both the individual and institutional levels. The focus going forward will certainly be on increasing access and increasing learning opportunities. Institutions will hopefully emerge with an opportunity to reflect on and evaluate how they were able to implement effective teaching practices to maintain continuity and quality of instruction, and what key lessons were learned. Since there cannot be one online program or practice that will serve all learners' needs equally well, it is imperative to ensure that instructors are focused on being engaging and inclusive in their teaching approach to meet the needs of all learners—including those who are most vulnerable. As educators, we have an opportunity to build and improve communities; both locally and globally. It is the author's hope that this text will add value to the ongoing discussion regarding the roles and competencies of online instructors in the rapidly ever-expanding online environment so that all learners can be maximally successful. If instructors are appropriately supported, the COVID pandemic crisis can result in sustainable change to online instruction! Are YOU ready to teach online?

ORGANIZATION OF THIS BOOK

The book addresses in detail all of the components that make up the online learning experience, and provides an in-depth overview of the knowledge and skills needed to engage with, support, and teach an increasingly diverse online learner population. The focus throughout is conceptual understanding as it relates to the practical aspects of online instruction. A key component of the book is to encourage instructors to view themselves as **reflective practitioners** who are invested in their own development as teachers. Because reflection is a cornerstone of deep learning, reflective questions are included throughout the chapters, serving as prompts to think more deeply about the impact of your teaching, thereby opening the way for new insights and awareness regarding improved practice.

Introduction: Going the Distance—An Overview of Online Learning

Designing and delivering high-quality online learning experiences requires instructors to help learners persist, learn deeply, and experience transformation as a result of their learning. This requires some awareness of the challenges of online education. It also takes skill development, thoughtfulness, planning, and caring. The introduction provides an overview of some of important contextual information to familiarize you and get you started. To begin, you will need to develop an understanding of the total *online learning experience,* including the current landscape of the online learning environment, the challenges inherent in online learning, and methods of online instruction. Additionally, details are provided regarding the demographics and attributes of online learners, as well as the role of the online instructor, including competencies and pedagogical strategies not necessarily applicable to traditional educational contexts. Knowing all of this will foster a greater appreciation of the factors that contribute to effective teaching and learning, including learner skills and learner supports.

Part I: The Art of the Start—Design and Develop Online Instruction

A positive culture for online learning begins with excellence in preparation of instructional design and development. Instructors want and need practical strategies; access to and ease in using the technology; and the ability to design, develop, and customize instructional materials. The first part of the book addresses all aspects of course design and development throughout planning and implementation.

Chapter 1: Designing and developing an online course that addresses diversity and inclusion, and that engages and empowers all learners, does not just begin with selecting the very best in technology and technical details. Front and center should be the importance and applicability of what learners will *actually learn,* and *how you are going to get them there.* The success of any course is determined by how well it is planned and built prior to its delivery. At the outset, you learn how to determine and establish strong and viable course learning outcomes that will shape and drive the overall course design.

Chapter 2: Having defined your course learning outcomes, you will need to know how to plan for assessment of learning to ensure the alignment of course objectives and critical course components. Monitoring learning through regular assessments is an integral element of an instructor's role. By making our expectations for learning explicit, clearly articulating course and program outcomes, and providing purposeful opportunities for learners to achieve, we create opportunities to gather, analyze, and interpret assessments of their learning. The results of those assessments are used to make informed decisions about learning, and to implement the necessary improvements with regard to teaching and instruction.

Chapter 3: With a clear set of course learning outcomes and an assessment plan, you will move to create course content that will foster deep (as opposed to surface) learning by helping learners engage with the material at the level that is most meaningful to them. As you develop your content and work toward sustained learner engagement, you are constantly reminded of two key considerations: diverse content options and diverse **communication** options. Equal access to **education** is mandated by law and is grounded in the hope that all learners will indeed have equal access. Designing a course means being cognizant of building in **accessibility** from the start; making sure that all content supports all learners and ensures **equity** and **inclusion**; and that the content provides multiple opportunities for engagement, interaction, and deep learning.

Part II: Traveling the Educational Journey—Deliver Engaging and Empowering Learning Experiences

Online instructors will face new and often unexpected challenges when delivering online instruction. Whether one is teaching in fully online or hybrid environments, instructors must master the tools of technology, and serve as content specialist and **facilitator** of learning. Moreover, instructors will work with an increasingly diverse population of learners. A central aspect to promoting learner engagement, and in turn ongoing success, is the establishment of **teaching presence**. In this part of this book, readers will explore best practices to intentionally enhance teaching presence in order to deliver engaging and empowering learning experiences.

Preface   xvii

Chapter 4: Educational institutions are charged with the responsibility of graduating all learners, and making sure that they are equipped with the essential knowledge and skills necessary for success in their chosen fields. Instructors are responsible to do their best to retain as many of their learners as possible. Whether readers are experienced instructors or new to online teaching, meeting this expectation may require developing or revising their strategies to ensure that all learners remain engaged. This chapter provides strategies for onboarding, preparing, and supporting learners for the online learning experience, and planning ways to continually monitor and address their progress and development.

Chapter 5: We begin to work toward a more inclusive educational experience when we take the time to understand our learners' contexts and unique needs through building meaningful and supportive relationships with them. The instructor's role is "guide on the side," "learning partner," or mentor. This chapter covers the benefits of positive working relationships, and how to go about developing working relationships that will facilitate and sustain learning. The implication is that instructors remain visible, approachable, and available through the collaborative and supportive working relationships that they establish with their learners.

Chapter 6: Instructors are expected to offer guidance throughout a course by employing instructional methods that are engaging and inclusive, and that encourage critical reflection and a growth academic mindset. Every institution has its own culture and expectations regarding best teaching practices. There is no one-size-fits-all approach to teaching, and customization is essential. Included in this chapter are a number of skills and strategies that you can learn to use in order to streamline your teaching without diminishing the quality thereof. In the online environment, the primary instructional delivery mode includes written, audio, or video feedback, which creates the foundation for constructive and meaningful learner–instructor interaction. Because online learning can certainly be a lonely and isolating experience, a key goal is to make the learning environment conducive to active participation by implementing strategies that will increase learner engagement not only with the course content and with the instructor, but also with peers, thereby building a learning community. Throughout this chapter, there is a strong focus on respectfully addressing diversity and inclusion, and ensuring that this is intentionally infused throughout your teaching practice.

Part III: Taking Stock—A Review of Multimodal Engagement

As the growth of online programs continues to rapidly accelerate, there has been an increased concern about quality, success, and retention. While models for understanding persistence in the face-to-face learning environment are well established, there is a need for establishing effective frameworks or taxonomies for evaluating online learning experiences in light of the unique characteristics of the online environment and the online learner. Ongoing and current research indicates that attrition rates are significantly higher than in face-to-face programs. As such, the development of models to explain and assess learner engagement in the online environment is imperative so that progress can be appropriately monitored and addressed.

Chapter 7: Engagement has been presented as a central multimodal construct throughout this book. In this chapter, eight sets of engagement indicators serve as a practical model to determine the extent to which engagement has been established and maintained throughout a course. These indicators are based on and derived from the essential drivers of success that apply to the online learning context, and which have been detailed in previous chapters. Indicators include teaching presence, positive working relationships, application of effective teaching and facilitation practices, creation of community, diversity and inclusivity, learner autonomy and empowerment, technology support, and culture of trust and transparency. Each of these sets of engagement indicators is accompanied by reflective questions to stimulate deeper insights and awareness.

Chapter 8: The idea that has been emphasized throughout this book is that engaged online learning is "instructor facilitated and learner owned." Having read this book, you will clearly understand the complex challenges and barriers to learning that exist in the online environment, and know more about facilitating meaningful online learning experiences. Engaging in **self-reflection** or **self-reflexivity**, as recommended by leaders in the field of adult education, can become an ongoing best-practice. Just as we encourage our learners to reflect on their learning, so is it important for instructors to reflect on their own learning for purposes of ongoing development and improved practice. **Reflection** checkpoints are built into each of the chapters, which serves as a summary of the knowledge gained in each chapter for purposes of facilitating practical application. In this concluding chapter, the final reflection checkpoint allows you to think about lessons learned, and consider more deeply your role as an online instructor and how and in what ways you will continue working to ensure instructional excellence and impact.

WHAT SETS THIS BOOK APART?

Some books on teaching online explain the process either too simplistically or, conversely, in overcomplicated or densely theoretical language; the classic textbook scholarly writing style that tends to mystify or overwhelm the reader. Other books on the subject make assumptions that by following a set of instructions, the reader will somehow know how to proceed, and do not account for the inherent nuances involved in teaching online. Still, others include too many unrelated examples and fail to provide sufficient detail of the key underlying elements that characterize effective online teaching and what is needed to ensure a successful learning experience. This book's approach is to foster the deepest learning possible, by helping learners engage with the material at the level that is most meaningful to them. The idea that education is about the "transmission" of knowledge or information from an expert to a novice is problematic for multiple reasons. Rather, knowledge is *constructed* when we bring prior understanding to interact with new ideas, experiences, and environments. Online learning is about the interactions among learners and instructors, and the ways in which learners and instructors interact with learning spaces and tools. Although online models may support some of those interactions, they only scratch the surface when it comes to offering diverse, rich, and multimodal educational experiences. This responsibility is ultimately that of the instructor.

In the same way that we want our learners to understand the reasons for doing things a certain way, the pedagogical strategies presented in the book are backed by relevant and appropriate principles and practices, thereby offering instructors the "why" behind the "what" and "how." It is worth noting that while this book is grounded firmly in research, theory, and cutting-edge practices (the "science"), great care was taken in how to best incorporate this. In preparing the book, the author was very mindful that readers will be looking for readable and useful material that can actually be used and directly applied in practice, and that teaching is certainly a creative activity too (the "art"). As such, without running the risk of becoming too theoretical, *the main focus is on practical application and accessibility*, with the prominent emphasis throughout on five cutting-edge concepts of critical importance in the field of education today, all of which have particular relevance to online learning experiences. These concepts, drawn from research, translate directly to practice, and become the *practical drivers* that instructors will infuse in their online teaching practice. As such, these key and distinct themes are highlighted and interwoven throughout the book's chapters.

Principles of Adult Learning (How People Learn)

The focus in this book is on how to facilitate and support deep and significant (as opposed to surface) learning within the **online learning context**. As we undertake the complex and compelling challenge of building capacity for instructors to meet the needs of all learners, we know that supporting adult learning has a direct and positive influence on increasing engagement, motivation, and achievement. Recognizing and understanding how adults learn informs us of best practices to ensure ways to facilitate and support their learning, right from the beginning phases of course design and development and continuing throughout one's teaching practice and pedagogical approach.

Engage Through Presence

Research consistently recognizes **engagement** as one of the most significant factors impacting academic performance and overall achievement; with clear evidence that the issue of isolation and disconnection is an essential consideration for learner satisfaction with online courses and that such isolation inhibits engagement and learning. Learner engagement and instructor engagement are two sides of the same coin and are essentially reciprocal in nature. Learner engagement ensures ongoing motivation and persistence. Instructor engagement implies the idea of being "present" for your learners, thereby establishing a sense of "teaching presence." This requires reimagining your role as "teacher," and moving toward becoming a proactive and responsive partner in the educational experience by intentionally and thoughtfully developing meaningful working relationships so as to best support all of your learners.

Create a Learning Community

As educators transition from traditional classrooms to virtual meeting spaces and online classrooms, it is important to be able to create a community among their learners through meaningful interactions and social technologies. Establishing an online teaching presence contributes to learning and perception of community, thereby cultivating a **learning community**. Online learning can be a lonely and isolating experience, and the creation of community is key to developing a conducive online learning environment. Social belonging and opportunities to relate to others are significant in terms of promoting engagement, facilitating collaborative learning, and encouraging ongoing communication among learners and instructors. Failure to consider the relational dynamics in the online setting may produce greater feelings of isolation among distance learners, reduced levels of satisfaction, poor academic performance, and increased attrition. The notion of the learning community has been at the heart of distance education since its inception, and the challenge of fostering community remains a focal issue.

Ensure and Support Learner Empowerment

This book takes the dual concept of engagement one step further to focus on the key concept of learner **empowerment**, and developing the competencies needed by instructors as facilitators of learning and empowerment. This book is grounded in the idea that we need to move beyond engagement to empowerment, and this requires a significant paradigm shift: The learning experience is a shared space, but the primary owners are our learners. We achieve learner empowerment by offering—and ensuring—*control and choice*. We empower learners to claim their rightful space by relinquishing some of our power, building authentic relationships with them, and offering opportunities to interact and engage in open discourse and collaborative learning. The goal of education is to meet the needs of all learners, offering them the ownership, agency, and autonomy to actively engage in the learning experience, so that they are *empowered* to implement changes in their own personal and professional lives, and ultimately in the lives of others. As such, there is a strong focus throughout the book both on how to engage learners through empowerment, and reciprocally, how to empower them through engagement.

Respect Diversity and Ensure Inclusion

With the rapid increase in online education offerings, learner populations have become increasingly diverse. However, access to education does not necessarily mean inclusion; nor will access always necessarily ensure or engender justice and inclusion. The shift to emergency remote instruction starting in the spring of 2020 exposed how too many learners are on the wrong side of the digital divide, exacerbating this concern. Now, more than ever before, it is imperative that we implement **teaching strategies** and learning solutions that promote access, inclusivity, and a sense of belonging. An underlying tenet of this book is that every learning experience should be intentional in ensuring full equity and inclusion for all learners, including those of diverse cultural backgrounds and minority or underrepresented groups. The implication of **inclusive pedagogy** is that curriculum and teaching approaches will provide a sense of belongingness through course materials that represent a variety of perspectives that can be meaningfully applied in a diverse set of real-world scenarios; and teachers meeting learners where they are and helping them to meet course learning outcomes, and eventually being able to contribute to their field of study. The steady growth of online enrollments illustrates the value and importance of ensuring impactful online learning experiences. As we continue to grapple with the challenges and opportunities offered by emerging online learning spaces, we must continue to meet and support the needs of all learners by fostering an inclusive climate that will ensure equitable outcomes for all. This mission is paramount, given the diverse learners who are being served by the vast and globalized online learning context.

ADDITIONAL DEFINING FEATURES OF THIS BOOK

At the same time as writing this book, the author conducted her own research with online instructors in various contexts and fields, capturing verbatim quotes regarding what works best based on their experiences in the field. These "voices" have been appropriately integrated at specific points throughout the book.

With the rapidly transitioning online environment that was revolutionized in the spring of 2020 and which continues to evolve, instructors no longer have the benefit of a "runway" to prepare for online delivery. To address this need, the book includes a number of checklists, summaries, and other supportive aides that are designed to jumpstart educators. Designed to be particularly useful are the comprehensive action checklists that are included in the concluding synthesis section of Parts I and II. Both of these charts provide an at-a-glance overview of key action items and associated steps involved in course design, development, and delivery so that learner engagement remains at the forefront at all times. The penultimate chapter itself is based on a set of checklists that draw on key concepts that have been emphasized throughout the book to address multimodal engagement strategies; serving in effect as a broad checklist for the entire book. An extensive Glossary serves to clarify all terminology that is used throughout the book. For ease of reference, terms that appear in the Glossary are bolded on first mention.

The Appendix, which can be accessed through the Teachers College Press website, is comprised of a substantial collection of curated resources including samples, templates, guidelines, and access to relevant research, information, and services related to online teaching and learning. For your convenience, throughout this book, reference is made to multiple current resources that enhance online learning experiences, most of which are available free of charge. However, it is important to note that technology is continually and swiftly being updated and new **learning management systems (LMSs)** and **online tools** are being produced annually. To ensure that a book such as this does not fall into the trap of time, and to maintain relevance and currency, readers should be aware that because both research and technology are developing and evolving at a rapid pace, some of the technologies that are currently in use may become outdated or need to be updated. As such, be aware that many of the applications referred to in this book may typically need updating or replacing over time. So, as you proceed in your practice of designing and teaching online courses, be on the lookout for and embrace new and innovative developments in the field that will best suit your purposes. In this way, you will ensure that you remain current in providing the most cutting-edge and relevant learning experiences.

INTRODUCTION

Going the Distance
An Overview of Online Learning

When teaching in person, one does not expect learners to proceed without regular support and guidance. The same need for continuous instructor involvement holds true in the online environment, and this requires added thoughtfulness, planning, and care. Knowing about the online learning context and the online learning experience, and being aware of inherent barriers and challenges, will foster a greater appreciation of the factors that contribute to effective teaching and learning, including learner skills and the kinds of learner supports that are needed. Understandably, some readers may choose to bypass this introduction or just skim it in order to get to the core of the book; the "how-to" of designing, developing, and delivering high-quality online education. However, to get you started, we will briefly review some contextual information to familiarize you with the online environment and the critical role of the online instructor. You will be introduced to the current landscape of online learning, including challenges inherent in online learning, methods of online instruction, demographics and attributes of online learners, and the role of the online instructor. The main focus of this introduction is on the key concepts that were introduced in the Preface, which become the practical drivers that instructors will infuse in their online teaching practice. These drivers are incorporated throughout all of the book's chapters.

THE LANDSCAPE OF ONLINE LEARNING

Let us begin by defining online learning. As we have seen in recent times, the context and structure of the educational environment continues to change radically, and distance education is an integral part of this ongoing change. Distance education is the broad term of reference that encompasses all forms of learning and teaching in which those who learn and those who teach are for all, or at least most of, the time in different locations. The terms distance education and distance learning are used interchangeably in the literature; a usage that needs to be treated with caution, however, since institutions and instructors, as the agents of change, control educational delivery, while **learning** is ultimately the responsibility of the learner. In addition, the use of the term **online learning** is frequently interchanged with terms such as e-learning (electronic learning), remote learning, virtual learning, distributed learning, and web-based learning. Each of these terms essentially refers to a wide set of applications and educational processes that are characterized by the separation of teachers and learners in both space and time, and the utilization of information and communication technologies to mediate asynchronous as well as synchronous learning and teaching activities. These definitions will no doubt continue to evolve as the technology undergoes rapid and ongoing transformation.

Giant strides have indeed been made in what constitutes distance education; an evolutionary phenomenon starting in the late 19th century and progressing throughout the 20th and into the 21st century. Distance education can be traced back to as early as the 18th century, and its evolution and progression over the last 300 years runs parallel with innovations in communications technology (Kentnor, 2015). Prior to the widespread use of electronic communications, educators had begun to make use of print technology and the postal service, which became known as correspondence education. Oriented toward the adult learners, especially those who were unable to join institutions of higher education, correspondence learning helped thousands of Americans to learn new skills for specific jobs, and access a wealth of courses and learning materials. The Chautauqua Correspondence College was founded in 1881, and in 1883, this institution was authorized by the State of New York as the Chautauqua College of Liberal Arts to offer collegiate instruction by correspondence and to award diplomas and degrees (Kentnor, 2015; Moore et al., 2003). The founder of this college, William Rainey Harper, established a similar program at the University of Chicago, where he became the president in 1891. In the same year, the University of Wisconsin created three new extension programs with one of them offering the correspondence courses taught by the existing university faculty (Moore et al., 2003).

While beginning in the late 1800s, the rapid growth of distance education occurred in the late 1990s with the advance of the online technical revolution, and the field continues to reach new heights as the developments in technology advance and diversify. Online education essentially grew out of distance education, and has become entrenched in business and in higher education worldwide. With the development of the Internet and the World Wide Web, online education has come to include diverse learning programs in multiple academic areas, and can now reach learners globally, and through multiple platforms. This outreach capability became clearly apparent on a large scale with the COVID-19 pandemic, when the U.S. educational landscape was significantly and rapidly transformed during the spring of 2020 and into 2021, with instructors being forced to teach their classes in several formats, from fully face-to-face to hybrid/blended to fully online, with the charge to be mindful in shifting the modality of their classes with minimal interruption to their learners.

Methods of Online Instruction

As technology has improved and evolved, so have the means of delivering online education, and recent years have seen a massive proliferation of online experiences being offered by numerous prominent educational institutions and corporations. Present-day online education can provide high-quality educational resources in various forms of media, supporting both synchronous (real-time) and asynchronous communication between learners and instructors and between diverse learners. Currently, a variety of delivery mechanisms, platforms, and learning management systems (LMSs) are in place to meet the demands of the rapidly evolving online landscape.

The lines between online and traditional learning are blurring (Morris & Clark, 2018; Song, Rice, & Oh, 2019). In addition to fully online courses and degree or certificate programs offered by online educational institutions, some traditional universities now offer online curriculum components, thereby allowing the traditional course to be augmented or supplemented with online courses. These are commonly known as blended or hybrid programs. What is also rapidly occurring is the increasing size of online courses with the advent of the **Massive Open Online Course (MOOC)** movement, an important turn in the history of online learning, and which caters to thousands of participants at any one given time. In addition to the at-scale degree programs that have evolved out of the MOOC movement, learners can also choose to take non–credit-hour courses offered free of charge without being enrolled in the university. Some higher institutions in the United States have started offering MOOC courses for credit with stipulations that include enrolling in the university, attending meetings with the instructor, and taking additional required coursework. In addition to academia, many organizations have discovered online MOOC training as a cost-efficient and time-saving way to provide their employees or volunteers with consistent and effective staff development offerings. By the end of 2018, 101 million learners had registered in one or more of the 11,400 MOOCs offered by over 900 institutes worldwide (Shah, 2018), indicating that MOOCs continue to capture the attention of many universities and the public worldwide.

Who Are Our Online Learners?

Online learning is undoubtedly one of the most rapidly growing subsections of education, offering access and opportunities to diverse learners worldwide. Technological developments over recent years have increasingly enabled learners from rural areas with Internet connectivity to have the option to attend colleges and universities outside of their local communities. Moreover, diverse learners from countries outside the United States have been able to enroll, access, and complete degrees offered in Western culture, from their home countries. The emergence of online learning has also changed the profile of learners, particularly within higher education. Scholars agree that it is important to understand the makeup, attributes, and expectations of online learners, since this understanding will drive the design, development, and delivery of online learning experiences. Indeed, educators at all levels will increasingly need to understand and appreciate diversity, cultivate a critical mind to recognize and acknowledge the role of sociocultural factors, and develop the knowledge and skills that would allow them to be inclusive in their approach and teach ethically and responsibly in a diverse world.

Up until the beginning of 2020, research pointed to a very distinct online learner population; a relatively homogenous population that displayed very clear and specific characteristics and demographics. The majority of online college students at the undergraduate (51%) and graduate (70%) levels were shown to be employed full time (Learninghouse, 2019). The research of Fry and Parker (2018) indicated that the complex online learner population included multiple generations and segments. About half of online college students were millennials (ages 28 to 38), about one-third were from Generation X (ages 39 to 54), and the remainder was split between baby boomers (ages 55 to 73), and the current generation of learners, Generation Z (ages 18 to 22). Schwieger and Ladwig (2018) explain that Generation Z have unique characteristics and expectations because technology is an inherent part of their everyday life activities. Online learners were typically seeking educational opportunities for various reasons, including greater access, flexibility, and convenience (Sanford et al. 2017). Some chose an online course or degree program because of the physical distance from a university or traditional classroom, and some local university may not have offered the discipline that the learner was seeking, and so an online course may have been the only viable option. Additionally, many traditional course settings were beginning to augment or supplement their traditional education with online course components. As we have seen with the COVID-19 pandemic, more and more programs and courses at every level have rapidly transformed to online platforms, making online learning a necessary and indeed essential choice. In these cases, there was simply no option but to study online; nor was this necessarily a familiar or preferred method of learning and teaching. With this transition, learners and instructors had to move online very swiftly to address an urgent need: maintaining enrollment in their courses and programs of study.

Online learners, in the recent past, were categorized as **nontraditional learners**; defined as an adult at 24 years of age who was not attending college right out of high school, or who had a family and/or a full-time work schedule. Recent studies indicated that the attributes of the online learner were changing, and that learners were choosing to attend online universities to obtain a higher education degree directly out of high school or following undergraduate study in order to complete a postgraduate degree (Bettinger et al., 2017; Bialowas & Steimel, 2019). The online learning environment had evolved to encompass both traditional learners as well as nontraditional learners (Black, 2020; Ellis, 2019). With the rapid changes taking place in the world of education, as a result of the pandemic, the demographics of the online learner population shifted suddenly and dramatically. As a matter of necessity, almost everybody started learning online, making this population somewhat "intergenerational," and no longer as distinctive as it had been in previous years. No matter what the demographics or characteristics of this learner population, it is important to recognize that the expectations of today's online learner mirror the expectations of traditional classroom learners. Adult learners seek content that is relevant and applicable to their discipline, job, and real-world interests. It is important, therefore, that instructors understand online learners' expectations in order to adequately meet and address their needs and requirements.

Challenges of Online Learning

The flexibility and mobility of online learning make this an attractive way to study, and learners can access online programs—even across borders—without having to completely interrupt their already active lives. Yet despite these benefits, lack of persistence and attrition remain an ongoing challenge in online programs, and research indicates that higher education enrollment in online courses is consistently characterized by lower retention and degree completion rates than traditional courses (Berry, 2019; Muljana & Luo, 2019; Zeglen & Rosendale, 2018). Online classes, by their very nature as "distance learning experiences," present barriers to engagement and learning. Even more so now in the current environment with the rapid move to online contexts, with greater unfamiliarity on the part of many instructors and learners, as well as the lack of time needed for careful planning and preparation, retention rates are likely to decrease dramatically.

With the plethora of endorsements for distance education comes the concern that something of educational value might be missing in the virtual environment that uses technology as a way of linking learners with peers and instructors. Transactional distance (Moore, 1997) explains the "psychological and communication space" felt between instructors and learners. With the infrastructure of distance education being characterized by a clear separation in space and time of the majority of teaching and learning activities, distance education in the early years of its evolution was referred to as "disembodied learning" (Beckett, 1998), and as a "pedagogy of (dis)location" (Edwards & Usher, 2000). These terms can still apply to the current online environment, if not intentionally and proactively addressed. While holding the promise of expanding the time and location boundaries of traditional education offerings, online learning thus gives rise to new constraints for both learners and instructors, the critique being that in this environment, the sense of isolation and detachment are potential barriers to learning, and that online classes are wearisome and even trying at times.

Lack of engagement undermines skill development, human connection, and joy of education. The very nature of online learning indeed places additional demands on both learners and instructors. In face-to-face traditional courses, learners and instructors have no option but to interact synchronously with each other, beginning on the first day of class, and these first day "in-person" interactions may well set communication expectations for the entire course. In online courses, learners are likely to "attend" the first class meeting asynchronously with the instructor only. Further, online course structures with limited or no peer-to-peer interaction further complicate traditional notions of class meetings, attendance, and communication. Not only does the online course structure pose a challenge for many learners, but many instructors find this course structure challenging as well.

Research shows that in order to be successful in online classes, learners need to be autonomous and able to manage their time, motivate themselves to work on schedule, and seek help when needed, among other executive functioning skills. One major online learning challenge occurs because many online learners are still developing these life skills. Additionally, because of the flexibility it offers, online learning can also run the risk of simply becoming another appointment or engagement in their daily calendar, along with a range of other work and personal commitments in an environment without traditional boundaries, set hours, routines, and the regular types of interaction with instructors and peers as would occur in a traditional educational environment. In addition to feeling disconnected, many online learners are juggling work and family demands. Increasing numbers of learners also struggle with language needs and disabilities, as well as lack of familiarity with technological requirements, thus requiring additional and flexible time to grasp the scope of assignments, read and gather information, and process concepts in order to produce the required written and multimedia products and deliverables.

There is a perception that the world is now connected through a global electronic environment where learners may access the Internet and online courses from any location, and at any time. This perception becomes a challenge, especially for diverse, geographically separated learners who may be without electricity, Internet access, or limited and inconsistent bandwidth availability. Moreover, many lower-income learners and those from marginalized or disenfranchised groups simply do not have the necessary equipment, materials, resources, support, and access, and so risk of withdrawal becomes increasingly problematic. Difficulties in adjusting to online learning norms, requirements, and expectations, coupled with multiple external factors, have resulted in consistently high rates of attrition. Especially as institutions increase online course offerings and as enrollments rise, withdrawals are increasingly costly to both the learner and the institution. Those who withdraw from online courses and retake courses do so at a financial cost of repeating courses or the overall cost of failing to continue and complete a degree. A university's reputation, rigor, and enrollment numbers make retention of learners a critical factor, and institutions incur a financial loss associated with a course or program withdrawal when learners fail to complete programs and discontinue their educational pursuits.

THE ROLE OF THE ONLINE INSTRUCTOR

According to the research of Martin et al. (2019), online instructors assume five different, yet somewhat interrelated, roles: facilitator, course designer, content manager, subject matter expert, and mentor. Moreover, the common tasks of an online instructor course can fall into either or both of the following two areas: course design and teaching. In addition to the challenges that online learners confront, the online environment brings with it a unique set of issues facing instructors. Challenges facing instructors include not being able to regularly speak with learners, and separation from colleagues and peers, which can lead to a general sense of anonymity. Even when appropriately designed, online learning alters the roles of instructors, and can create challenges in promoting social integration, including barriers to both instructor–learner as well as learner–learner interactions. To recognize and appropriately address these barriers requires understanding and appreciation of both the limitations and the possibilities brought about by new modes of communication and technology. The key concepts that were introduced in the Preface of this book have particular relevance to the online learning experience. These concepts translate directly to practice, and are highlighted and interwoven throughout the chapters of this book, becoming the *practical drivers of online teaching* that instructors can take into consideration and infuse in their teaching practice.

To begin, it is critically important to recognize and understand the principles of adults learning in order to provide the most optimal learning experience that will engage and motivate all learners. Research shows that in order to be successful in online classes, adult learners seek to be autonomous and self-directed. Adults also seek material that is relevant and applicable to their lives and their experiences. Recognizing and understanding how adults learn informs us of ensuring ways to facilitate and support their learning by adopting a distinctly learner-centered approach. We strive for deep and significant (as opposed to surface) learning; that is, how learners will engage meaningfully with the learning materials that are presented to them. Instructors should provide personalized instruction that offers support and guidance throughout the course to achieve prescribed learning outcomes; remain available and responsive throughout the learning experience; ensure that dialogue and communication is established right from the start and sustained throughout; encourage critical thinking, reflection, and dialogue; and use language and grading practices that focus on encouraging growth and development. Instructors are also encouraged to build strong teaching relationships by regularly communicating with learners; offering opportunities for ongoing interaction; and making accommodations to address learning preferences by personalizing teaching and using appropriate tools and multimodal means of instruction. This is indeed a tall order!

The introduction of online learning technologies has indeed created a unique set of promises for equity and outreach for members of marginalized or **underrepresented groups**. However, while learners are offered unprecedented access to a global knowledge base, the pro-Western bias inherent in the technological foundations of distance learning can present an obstacle both to access and understanding. Achieving equity and inclusion in the online environment depends on a sincere willingness on the part of instructors to confront the all-pervasive, pro-Western, cultural bias within education, and adopt a culturally responsive pedagogical approach. Remember, access does not necessarily mean inclusion; nor will access necessarily engender inclusion. Throughout their teaching practice, instructors must intentionally and thoughtfully respect diversity and strive for an inclusive learning experience. Given the diversity represented among learners in a globalized online learning context, every learning experience should—and indeed must—offer full equity and inclusion for all learners.

In working with a vast diversity of learners in the globalized online learning environment, it is critical to foster collaborative learning opportunities where learners of different cultures, backgrounds, and ethnicities can work and learn together. When learners find their school environment to be supportive and caring, they are more likely to develop a sense of "connectedness," "belongingness," or "community." Online learning can certainly be a lonely and isolating experience. However, learners should never feel alone on their learning journey, and so the task of facilitating collaboration and building community among geographically diverse learners becomes an important component of successful online instruction. Interaction contributes significantly to **active learning**, ongoing motivation, and engagement, and so a key component of online learning is to provide space for the development of a learning community, thereby instilling a strong and pervasive culture of learning.

Research consistently recognizes engagement as one of the most significant factors impacting academic performance, supporting a clear link between instructor engagement, learner engagement, and *actual learning*; in this way, breaking the wall and isolation that is inherent in studying online.

Learner engagement and instructor engagement are two sides of the same coin and are essentially reciprocal in nature. Learner engagement ensures ongoing motivation and persistence. Instructor engagement implies the idea of being "present" for your learners, thereby establishing a sense of **teaching presence** (Garrison et al., 1999). The implication is that you are sensed by your learners as a "real person," who is offering their time and attention. To achieve this means that you are fully tuned to the needs of each learner, and making each of your learners aware that you are available, accessible, and committed to supporting and guiding them. As such, the focus of the instructor's role should be squarely on how to facilitate engagement to help all learners learn, develop, and ultimately succeed. A common complaint of online learners is that they feel alone and unable to manage the online course or class on their own because they do not have a "real" teacher beside them. What online learners really want is a "visible" instructor—one who is present and actively engaged. It therefore becomes imperative to strike the right balance between making your online classroom run with machine-like precision and infusing it with a strong, involved personal teaching presence, and this idea becomes a key focus throughout this book.

As Schroeder-Moreno (2010) pointed out, engaged online learning is essentially "instructor facilitated and student owned." There are two critical components at play here. First, is the idea of the instructor as facilitator. Second, is the idea of learner empowerment.

Instructor as Facilitator

By definition, adult learners have a self-concept of being in charge of their own lives and have a need to be seen and treated as being capable of taking responsibility for their own learning. As such, learners need to be given the freedom and autonomy to assume responsibility for their own choices and to be proactive in making decisions that contribute to their educational experiences. Rather than perform the role of the "sage on the stage," in working with adult learners, the instructor's role should be the "guide on the side"—a facilitator of learning, and a coach or mentor who works alongside their learners to promote achievement and academic success. The facilitator role extends beyond course delivery, and includes the broader pedagogical tasks that will support learners on their growth trajectories such as helping them effectively manage their time; fostering engagement; assigning meaningful and relevant learning activities; remaining responsive to learners' needs; communicating and checking in regularly; and providing timely, actionable, and substantive instruction that aids with ongoing improvement and success. The role of facilitator also means that the instructor promotes active dialogue, interaction, and collaborative learning. Increasingly, the expectation is that we prepare learners to interpret, critically analyze, and assess the world around them. The question to ask is how we can expect our learners to develop those skills without inviting and encouraging them to think deeply and share their own experiences, perspectives, and understanding by actively participating in conversations and discussions about the complex issues inherent in the content we teach.

Empowering Your Learners

This book takes the concept of engagement one step further to focus on the key concept of learner empowerment, with a focus on developing the competencies needed by instructors as facilitators of learning and empowerment. The learning experience is a shared space, but the primary owners are our learners. Autonomy, mastery, meaning, and purpose are key drivers of performance, satisfaction, and empowerment. We empower learners by building authentic relationships with them, and offering opportunities to interact and engage with us in open discourse (dialogue). We achieve learner empowerment by offering—and ensuring—*control and choice*. Relinquishing some control allows learners to be autonomous and take greater responsibility for their own learning. This also creates a space for learners to master tasks and apply their knowledge and understanding in a meaningful way, thereby supporting and deepening their learning. Empowered learners display self-efficacy by taking ownership of their work because it is meaningful and relevant to them, both personally and professionally. They have a choice regarding what they are learning and how they can prepare and present their work; they are developing the skills to pursue their passions and they see the need to develop these skills further; and they are provided the ability to build their own educational journeys and pathways. We want to foster the deepest approach to learning possible, by helping all of our learners engage with the material at the level that is most meaningful to them. The question to ask is how and in what ways our learners will be able to *understand and actually apply* their new knowledge and what skills are necessary for success in their everyday lives.

The bottom line for online education is fundamentally the same as for all education; that is, meeting the needs of all learners and *empowering them* to implement changes in their own personal and professional lives, and ultimately in the lives of others. It is important that educators, as active "reflective practitioners," think deeply about their teaching practice and consider the factors that can help to foster and promote learner engagement and empowerment, which will, in turn, have the potential to enhance satisfaction and performance outcomes. However, online education must go one stride further. To mitigate the effects of transactional distance, it is incumbent upon instructors to intentionally and thoughtfully incorporate and implement strategies that will keep learners motivated and actively engaged. Regardless of course format, be committed to ensuring a meaningful learning experience by building collaborative working relationships to support your learners on their growth trajectories, and encouraging an "I can do this" attitude. The task becomes how we craft the experience for our diverse body of learners, and engage with them in meaningful interactions and experiences within a virtual environment. However, the instructor and the relationships that instructors build with their learners *should not be virtual*, and herein lies the challenge! Between designing and developing rich and appropriate course content, welcoming, onboarding, and supporting your learners, establishing a sense of teaching presence and building working relationships with each of your learners, and actively teaching through those relationships, you can provide an engaging and empowering online learning experience. If you are knowledgeable and well-prepared, teaching online can be rewarding for you and your learners alike. Fast-forward your online pedagogical know-how and skills, and teach with confidence! This is the objective of this book!

The chapters of Part I and Part II address in detail all of the components that make up the online learning experience, including design, development, and delivery. Part I is devoted to course design and development, and includes all elements related to planning, preparation, and implementation. Part II focuses on the delivery of educational experiences; the *actual teaching*. Each chapter of the book concludes with a set of reflective questions to allow you to think more deeply about the impact of your teaching, thereby opening the way for new insights regarding improved practice. The reflection checkpoints that you will encounter throughout the book are designed to prompt you to *purposefully pause and reflect*. This book is focused on learning to teach online, and providing you with the knowledge and skill sets to do so. Because of the strong focus on learning and the *practical application of learning*, this book is thus predicated on the notion of developing instructors as "reflective practitioners." The implication is that learning and growth occur through self-reflection or self-reflexivity; that is, the ongoing process of reflecting on our teaching practice, and what we can do to become more engaging and responsive to our learners through new insights and awareness by asking ourselves questions such as: *What new insights have I developed?* and *What am I willing to try out to make a difference and therefore enhance my current practice?* When we continue to ask ourselves these kinds of questions, we ensure that self-reflection or self-reflexivity is not just a once-off occurrence, but remains an ongoing best-practice.

Part I

THE ART OF THE START: DESIGN AND DEVELOP ONLINE INSTRUCTION

THE SETUP CYCLE

A positive **culture** for online learning begins with excellence in preparation of instructional design and development. Instructors want and need practical online teaching strategies, access to and ease in using the technology, and the ability to customize instructional materials. The success of any course is determined by how well the course is planned and built prior to its delivery. To effectively design and develop online courses that address **diversity** and **inclusion**, and that engage and empower all learners, careful planning is essential. Your vision for the learning experience and the approach that you use to design and develop the course, as well as your expectations for learner success, will shape the course and determine its outcomes. Planning that uses relevant content, aligned **navigation** and technology tools, and educational **best practices** will avoid confusion or **disengagement** for learners, resulting in higher achievement and deep learning.

The common tasks of an online course instructor can fall into either or both of the following two areas: **course design** and teaching. Remember that you may not always be building your own courses. Oftentimes, you will be teaching courses that you did not author; you will be assigned a course to teach, and you may have no hand in choosing the course design and implementation. At other times, you may be offered the opportunity to tweak or enhance an already established course, or to make some added adjustments and enhancements. In any event, it is useful to understand the design process so that you are familiar with all of the necessary components and can therefore provide the necessary support to address your learners' needs most appropriately. Most institutions hire support personnel to help instructors with the process of designing and developing online courses. These individuals often have a working title such as instructional designer, instructional technologist, educational technologist, e-learning specialist, media specialist, or learning strategist and are many times housed in an educational technology unit or a teaching and learning center. The help provided could be related to writing effective

learning outcomes, designing course assessments, creating **course content,** infusing technology into online courses, and so on. It is important that institutions make sure that instructors are aware that such support personnel exist and are willing to help, whether that be through providing individual consultations, leading workshops, or even facilitating comprehensive online instructor training courses.

Whether this is your first time working with online instruction or whether you have previous experience, be aware that a course is considered a work in progress even after it is launched for delivery. As such, view your course as flexible and always remain open to revisions and ongoing improvement. A simple approach is to focus your work on defined learning outcomes, keeping in mind that one size does not fit all, and remaining open to the idea that course revision is inevitable. As you provide direction and management of the course, adjustments can (and will) be made as needed along the way. As you start out, a good idea is to request from your institution a review of some exemplary courses, if possible, in order to obtain some ideas regarding how best to structure courses and incorporate and use online course tools. There is no specific formula or method for online instruction. Just as any journey, there are many successful paths to each destination. The approach that you use should provide meaningful guidance and direction, ensuring measurable results when the journey ends. Additionally, if instruction is planned and designed strategically and thoughtfully, your future work will be more efficient when the course is offered again.

The approach to design and development is divided into three interconnected parts:

- **Course learning outcomes (CLOs):** The outcomes are essentially what learners should know and/or be able to do. Determining and selecting the learning outcomes is the starting point for course design.
- **Assessment of learning:** This is the evaluation portion of designing and developing course material. Assessments are derived directly from the CLOs (what the learner should know and/or be able to do). Once you have established your CLOs, you will need to begin planning for assessment in order to create appropriate ways to measure the learning that has occurred throughout the course.
- **Course content:** The content is the course material, including all types of media content as well as tasks, activities, and assignments that learners are required to complete throughout the course. The content that you develop and deliver will be based directly on and address the learning outcomes and will be framed by the principles of adult learning.

Figure I.1 that follows is a graphic depiction of the design and development process.

Figure I.1. The Setup Cycle: Designing, Developing, Delivering Online Instruction

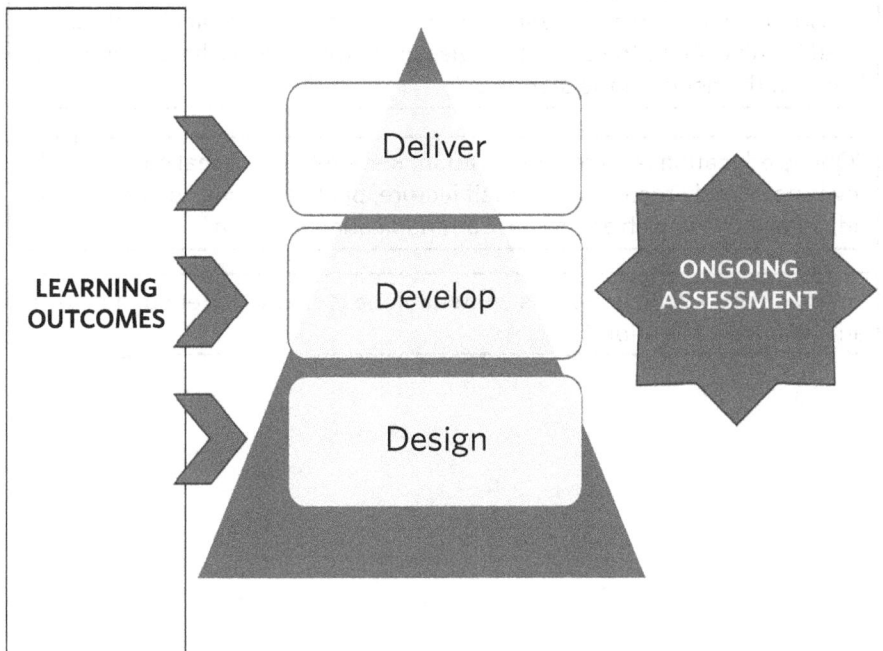

Table I.1, *Designing and Developing Instructional Materials: A Comprehensive Action Checklist*, which is included at the end of Part I, summarizes all elements involved in the setup and course preparation process, and is a further opportunity to be alert and remind yourself to address these elements.

INSTRUCTOR VOICES

"If you are new to online teaching, take this opportunity to learn more about how real online courses are created and consider how your lectures might be converted into rich, educational online content."

"To embrace one of the most effective practices in education, start with the end in mind. In the case of transferring instruction to the online environment, this would mean to reflect on what we want the students to learn. Once we are clear on that, we can then think about how to move them towards mastering those objectives."

"We don't need to do the same thing that we have done in the face-to-face classroom. In fact, in most cases we won't want to do that at all. Rather, we need to think about the best strategies given the tools we have, our expertise, and the needs of the students."

"Online education requires preparation. Remember that real online teaching is not simply recording yourself lecture, because doing so doesn't take advantage of the web as its own communication medium."

"Interactivity will be critical as content alone is rarely rich enough to keep an audience's attention."

CHAPTER 1

Develop Course Learning Outcomes

Designing an online course does not just begin with selecting the very best in technology and technical details. Front and center in your mind should be the importance and applicability of what your learners will *actually know and learn, and how you are going to get them there*. The power of design thus comes from leading all learners toward a meaningful destination. This end shapes the instructional goals, objectives, and outcomes, and this ultimately generates a more effective means. Determining your objectives and outcomes is therefore a necessary step before you develop the instruction. If you develop instruction for each objective and the learner accomplishes each objective, then the goal will have been met. This may sound like a basic tenet of teaching; however, when prepping new courses, instructors often start by thinking about what topics need to be covered, and developing content without giving much thought to what it is they want their learners to learn, know, and be able to demonstrate when the course is complete.

Understanding by Design (UbD), developed by instructional designers and educators Wiggins and McTighe (1998), is a curriculum planning approach that employs a "backward design"; that is, the practice of beginning with the end in mind by using the learning outcomes to design curriculum units, performance assessments, and instruction. This approach focuses essentially on *teaching to achieve understanding*. As McTighe and Wiggins (2014) state, "What should students know, understand, and be able to do . . . and what enduring understandings are desired?" (p. 2). Selecting appropriate and relevant learning outcomes (what the learner should know and/or be able to do) is the starting point for course design, because, through your course activities, you want to facilitate understanding and deep learning. The learning outcomes that you create, therefore, shape and drive the overall course design. You will then determine how learners will demonstrate that learning (e.g., create assessments) and then develop teaching materials and course activities to achieve that. This can be a significant paradigm shift for many instructors, and consultation with an instructional designer or other learning specialist can be beneficial.

Today, more than ever before, we are compelled to focus on deeper and richer experiences of teaching and learning in order to engage and empower all of our diverse learners. Courses should be established on functional and purposeful relevance and **significant learning**, not just on content alone. Backward design works well because we first determine our end goal and then think carefully through the steps we will take to get there. As Moore (2015) points out, one key benefit of backward design is that it promotes higher-order thinking for educators during the curriculum design process, thereby challenging us to think more critically. Moore also explains that instructors should be willing to move our learners beyond the lower levels of thinking (like basic understanding), and make a shift in the direction of transformative thinking. Learners must be able to learn something over and beyond what they can simply search for on the web. Remember that learners want to, and indeed have the right to, know "so what?" and "how will this be of benefit to me?" In providing meaningful learning experiences, we strive for learners to be able to master and apply new concepts, and derive new knowledge that will address or resolve real-world issues or problems. The "so what?" questions come from thinking about what you expect your learners to be able to do in terms of integrating new knowledge in the future, beyond the actual course itself, so that what they learn is personally and professionally meaningful. Mostly, in striving to engage your learners, the goal is to ensure that they will remain intellectually curious, self-directed, and motivated toward academic success so that they are *empowered* to implement changes in their own personal and professional lives, and ultimately in the lives of others. Therefore, CLOs, *the objectives of the learning experience*, represent the top-priority abilities for your learners to accomplish and master.

Learning outcomes are clear and direct statements that identify what learners will achieve or be able to do after various stages of their learning; these learning outcomes drive course design. As you create these learning outcomes, remember that these essentially establish the *tone* for the rest of the course. Following are some guidelines to keep in mind as you go about developing your CLOs, and maintaining alignment throughout the design process:

1. Outcomes are aligned with your vision for the course.
2. Outcomes are sequenced.
3. Outcomes are specific and measurable.
4. Course content is aligned with outcomes.

OUTCOMES ARE ALIGNED WITH YOUR VISION FOR THE COURSE

Once you develop a clear *vision* for your course, learners will experience better teaching, because the vision clarifies the purpose and goals, teaching strategies, and learning activities. In turn, you will be in a better position to help your learners understand how and to what extent they are moving forward in the course, and what is needed for ongoing progress and success. The learning outcomes that you select should directly and clearly state what learners should be able to do, perform, or demonstrate significant or deep learning. Outcomes must therefore essentially be learner-centered, because when you develop a course, you have the learner front and center in your mind. You want to make sure that they are learning the material in an effective way, in order to retain the information, and that they are able to use each course as a base to build upon as they progress not just in their education, but in their careers.

To make sure that you are aligning your vision with the CLOs, you can utilize **Bloom's Taxonomy**. In 1956, Benjamin Bloom led a group of educational psychologists in defining the levels of intellectual behavior important to the learning process, and stressed the importance of problem solving as a higher-order skill. **Problem-based learning** has long been regarded as an effective technique to develop higher-level thinking skills. Presented with a specific problem, learning becomes more meaningful by applying new knowledge to evaluate, analyze, and eventually solve the problem. The pyramid, known as Bloom's Taxonomy, includes a series of levels, with each level representing an incremental "step" in understanding. This taxonomy is a way to organize learning objectives, and given that a well-written learning objective should be measurable, each objective would begin with a single, measurable verb reflecting the level of thinking power or *cognitive effort*. Following Bloom's Taxonomy meant that educators would strive to cover all levels of the pyramid, thereby creating a well-rounded educational experience. Classifying instructional objectives using this taxonomy helps to determine the levels of learning included in an instructional unit or lesson. Bloom conceived of the taxonomy as more than a measurement tool, believing that it could serve as a common language about learning goals to facilitate communication across persons, subject matter, and **grade** levels. Moreover, he viewed the taxonomy as the basis for determining for a particular course or curriculum the specific meaning of broad educational goals such as those found in the currently prevalent national, state, and local standards. Bloom's (1956) *Taxonomy of Educational Objectives Handbook: Cognitive Domains* remains a foundational text and essential reading within the global educational community. Anderson and Krathwohl (2001) and Krathwohl (2002) made changes in an effort at helping Bloom's Taxonomy retain its relevancy. The nouns associated with each of Bloom's Taxonomy levels were replaced with verbs to more accurately produce evidence that would demonstrate actual learning. A higher-order thinking skill, which you can see toward the top of the pyramid in Figure 1.1, *Adapted Levels of Bloom's Taxonomy*, is one that requires more thinking power—or *cognitive effort*—than lower-order thinking skills. Typically, tasks require incrementally more cognitive effort as you move up the pyramid, beginning with "knowledge" and finally achieving "evaluation."

Figure 1.1. Adapted Levels of Bloom's Taxonomy

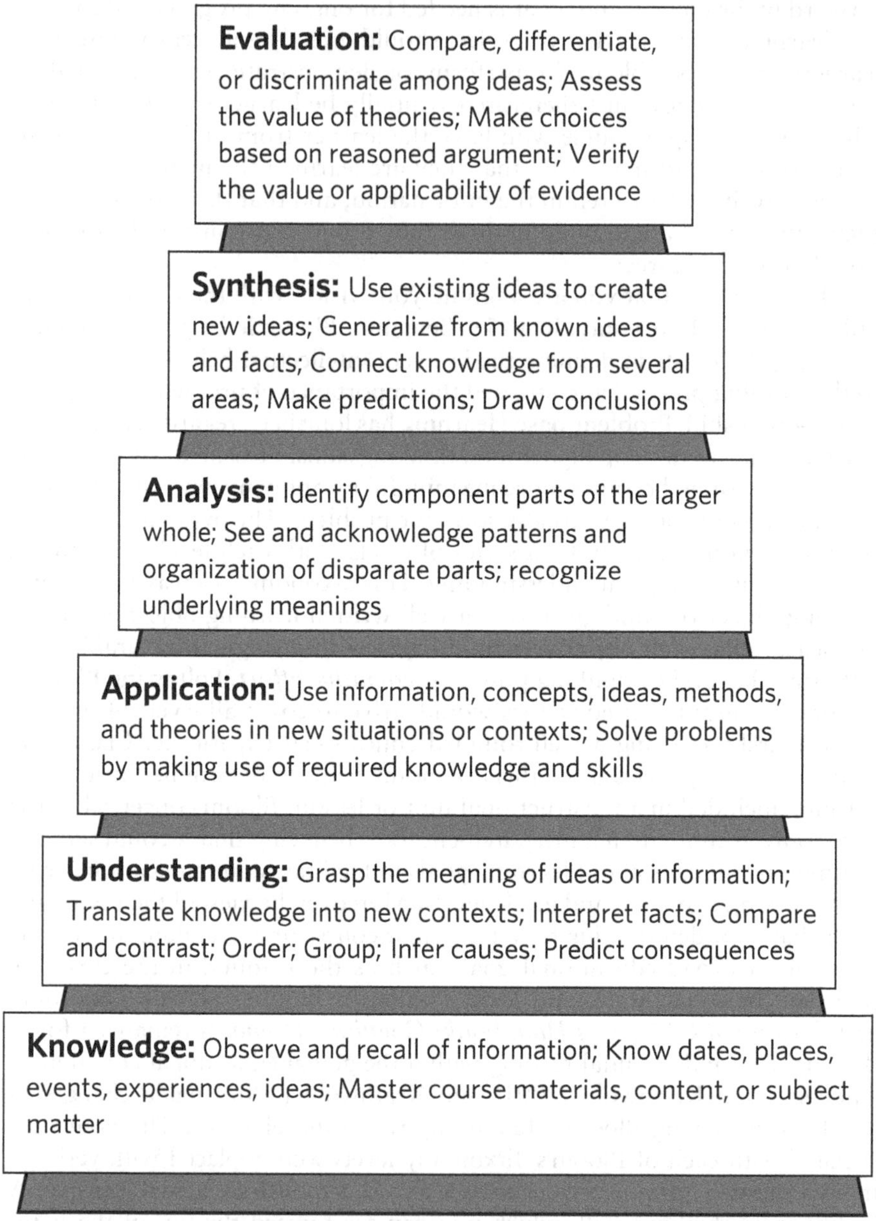

Evaluation: Compare, differentiate, or discriminate among ideas; Assess the value of theories; Make choices based on reasoned argument; Verify the value or applicability of evidence

Synthesis: Use existing ideas to create new ideas; Generalize from known ideas and facts; Connect knowledge from several areas; Make predictions; Draw conclusions

Analysis: Identify component parts of the larger whole; See and acknowledge patterns and organization of disparate parts; recognize underlying meanings

Application: Use information, concepts, ideas, methods, and theories in new situations or contexts; Solve problems by making use of required knowledge and skills

Understanding: Grasp the meaning of ideas or information; Translate knowledge into new contexts; Interpret facts; Compare and contrast; Order; Group; Infer causes; Predict consequences

Knowledge: Observe and recall of information; Know dates, places, events, experiences, ideas; Master course materials, content, or subject matter

Source: Adapted from Benjamin S. Bloom, *Taxonomy of Educational Objectives.* Published by Allyn and Bacon, Boston, MA. Copyright 1984 by Pearson Education.

More recently, Cope and Kalantzis (2015) focused on the concept of a *pedagogy of multiliteracies* (originally developed in 1996 by the New London Group, a consortium of international literacy researchers, as a way to approach literacy in the face of the emergence of new technologies, social and cultural diversity, and increased globalization). This group developed the term *multiliteracies* to represent the existence of multiple communication channels. Cope and Kalantzis (2015) approach the pedagogy of multiliteracies as an extension of Bloom's Taxonomy. These authors recommend that educators should design instruction that encompasses four processes or dimensions that reflect the ways that knowledge is constructed: experiencing, conceptualizing, analyzing, and applying. *Experiencing* includes the production of new ideas and the extension of prior knowledge. Learning activities that support this dimension will require learners to describe, differentiate, explore, predict, and examine content. *Conceptualizing* involves making mental and theoretical connections among concepts. Here, learners may be required to propose, synthesize, estimate, and classify content. *Analyzing* refers to drawing on prior content and experiences to think critically and reflectively. Learners may draw conclusions, critique resources, and make judgments regarding the relevance and applicability of information as they engage in their learning activities. *Applying* involves the transfer of knowledge to relevant real-life contexts. This may be accomplished through composing, compiling, constructing, depicting, planning, illustrating, and portraying representations of their learning.

Appendix A, provided for your convenience, is a chart based on Bloom's Taxonomy, and adapted according to later developments of the original taxonomy. The chart is centered on the different levels of cognitive abilities and associated action verbs that are arranged in ascending order of increasing complexity. First, learners need to simply *remember information* provided to them. However, simply reciting something does not necessarily demonstrate having learned it, only memorization. With *understanding* comes the ability to explain the ideas and concepts to others. Learners are then challenged to *apply the information* and use it in new ways, helping to gain a deeper understanding of previously covered material and demonstrating that understanding as they move forward. Questioning information is a vital part of learning, and both analysis and **evaluation** do just this. *Analyzing* asks a learner to examine the information in a new way, and *evaluation* requires that the learner appraise the material in a way that allows them to defend or argue against it as they determine. The final step in the revised taxonomy is *creating*, which entails developing a new point of view. In other words, how does this new knowledge impact the learner's world? Furthermore, how can the knowledge be used to impact not just the learner's education but the way that they use and apply that knowledge as they interact with their surroundings? Bloom's Taxonomy has therefore become a powerful teaching and learning tool that places the focus on learners' understanding and observable outcomes. As such, this can be useful in formal learning contexts to address levels of learner mastery by creating clear learning objectives that are interwoven throughout a course.

OUTCOMES ARE SEQUENCED

When writing your CLOs, these must be sequenced. The implication is that outcomes are not viewed in isolation, but rather that they are connected to program competencies, general education outcomes, and also professional accreditation standards. To make course design a seamless and integrated process, outcomes later in the program of study should of necessity build on earlier outcomes. To do this means that you should be knowledgeable of the broader program track; that is, where your course fits within the program, including courses that both precede and succeed your course. Thoughtfully creating and structuring learning outcomes in this way ensures that your course is indeed contributing to a true *learning trajectory*.

Outcome mapping is a methodology for designing courses or programs, and is a valuable way of planning, monitoring, and evaluating a course or program. Instructional designers will often make use of an *Outcomes Planning Map* in developing the instructional task analysis for any learning program, and this is a key element of the design process, making sure that **course learning outcomes (CLOs)** are aligned with **institutional learning outcomes (ILOs)** and **program learning outcomes (PLOs)**. Let us pause for a moment to define each of these types of outcomes:

Course Learning Outcomes (CLOs). A description of what a learner must be able to do at the conclusion of a course. This is one sentence that clearly states or signifies the intended learning by using concrete, measurable action verbs.

Program Learning Outcomes (PLOs). These relate to the knowledge, skills, abilities, and attitudes that learners will acquire as they progress through the program. A well-formulated set of PLOs will describe the competencies to be attained by graduates of the program. The PLOs must link to the ILOs.

Institutional Learning Outcomes (ILOs). These are the competencies (knowledge, skills, abilities, and attitudes) that learners are expected to develop as a result of their overall experiences throughout all of their courses and programs. These outcomes are developed at the institutional level.

Table 1.1. is a template for an *Outcomes Planning Map*. By completing this map, you begin to build successive program learning outcomes, and ensure that the outcomes of prior and succeeding courses are sequential and

Develop Course Learning Outcomes

Table 1.1. Outcomes Planning Map

ILOs	• [Insert ILO].
	• [Insert ILO].
	• [Insert ILO].
	[Add as needed]
PLOs	• [Insert PLO].
	• [Insert PLO].
	• [Insert PLO].
	[Add as needed]

Add CLOs for current and previous course/s

COURSE A: Outcomes	COURSE B: Outcomes	COURSE C: Outcomes
Indicate multiple outcomes if applicable	Indicate multiple outcomes if applicable	Indicate multiple outcomes if applicable (if these are already known)
• [Insert CLO].	• [Insert CLO].	• [Insert CLO].
• [Insert CLO].	• [Insert CLO].	• [Insert CLO].
• [Insert CLO].	• [Insert CLO].	• [Insert CLO].
[Add as needed].	[Add as needed].	[Add as needed].

well-aligned with each other and also with the broader ILOs and PLOs. This map also enables outcomes mapping from one course to another, aligning CLOs with ILOs and PLOs. Remember that you will not be required to develop PLOs or ILOs, because these will typically be set by your institution.

OUTCOMES ARE SPECIFIC AND MEASURABLE

Once you have ensured that your CLOs are (1) aligned with your vision for the course, and (2) appropriately sequenced, you need to make sure that the outcomes are specific and measurable, rather than broad and intangible. In developing your CLOs, it is essential to keep in mind that the outcomes (what the learner should know and/or be able to do) *must be able to be measured*. If the outcomes cannot be measured, there would be no way to tell whether and to what extent the learner has achieved the learning outcome. In fact, you will start taking into consideration outcomes assessments prior to designing your content and activities. Therefore, after identifying the CLOs, it is a good idea to create some tentative appropriate assessments that will measure the learning outcomes. We will be circling back to outcomes in Chapters 2 and 3 when discussing details about how to plan for assessment of learning, and, following that, how to design and create course content.

COURSE CONTENT IS ALIGNED WITH OUTCOMES

Alignment and coherence are two critical features of successful course design and development. Ensuring alignment and coherence means that all elements of a course—the content, learning activities, and assessments—are in line with and reflect the CLOs. As you begin to think about creating learning activities for your course, you will be asking yourself two questions: What types of assignments (activities or tasks) would measure the knowledge, skills, and attitudes associated with the relevant learning outcome? What types of assignments would allow learners to practice the specified knowledge, skills, and attitudes and thereby have an opportunity to develop proficiency before the assessment?

The *Outcomes Planning Map* in Table 1.1 was designed to enable you to carefully and appropriately map outcomes from one course to another, making sure to align CLOs with ILOs and PLOs. The *Course Outcomes Map* in Table 1.2 is a template that can then be used in conjunction with Table 1.1 to ensure the course activities or assignments will align with and support the stated CLOs. This table is a "heads up," illustrating how you will need to ensure that the course activities or assignments will be in alignment with and support the CLOs. A tool such as this helps you to identify which CLOs each **assignment** will align with. Your task will be to create

Develop Course Learning Outcomes

Table 1.2. Course Outcomes Map

Module or Week	Assignment (activity or task)	CLOs (Indicate multiple outcomes if applicable)
1		• [Insert CLO]. • [Insert CLO]. • [Insert CLO]. [Add as needed].
2		• [Insert CLO].
3		• [Insert CLO].
4		• [Insert CLO].
5		• [Insert CLO].
6		• [Insert CLO].
7		• [Insert CLO].
8		• [Insert CLO].

assignments that will support and assess learning outcomes. Establishing thoughtful and relevant CLOs is therefore critical so that each assignment will clearly align with at least one CLO. You will learn much more about developing course content in Chapter 3.

The Integrative Instructional Model in Figure 1.2 illustrates two essential components that are related to learning outcomes when designing a quality online course content: course content and navigation. Because engagement and learning are enhanced with the use of more than plain text, content will include both print and technology-based resources and activities (audio and video). Navigation provides strategic direction for learners in the form of tools, such as a **syllabus**, learning schedule, and general course and technology guidelines and instructions. Thoughtful design, including course content and navigational tools, all aligned with the learning outcomes, will serve to support learning, achievement, and success. All of these elements work together, as illustrated in this model.

Figure 1.2. The Integrative Instructional Model

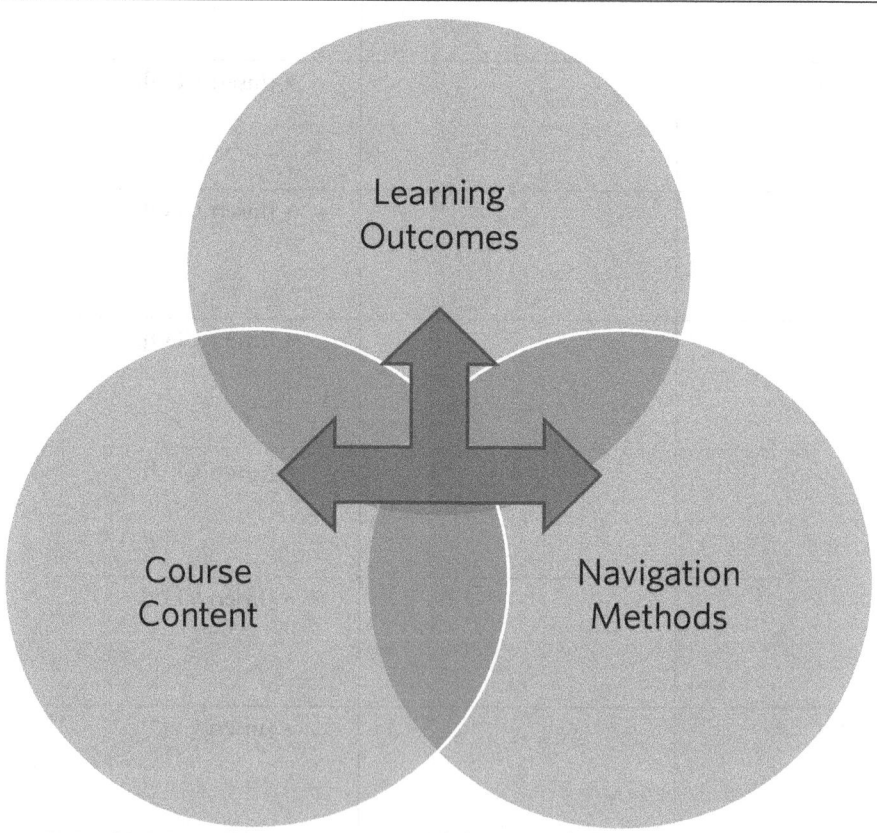

CHAPTER SUMMARY AND SYNTHESIS

Designing and developing an online course that addresses diversity and inclusion, and that engages and empowers all learners, does not just begin with selecting the very best in technology and technical details. Front and center should be the importance and applicability of what learners will *actually know and learn,* and *how you are going to get them there.* The success of any course is determined by how well it is planned and built prior to its delivery by determining and establishing strong and viable CLOs that will shape and drive the overall course design. As you proceed to Chapter 2, you will learn more about planning for assessment in order to create appropriate ways to measure the learning that has occurred throughout the course.

To foster reflection about what counts as a meaningful learning experience and significant (deep) learning, ask yourself the following essential questions that are related to the expectations for designing and developing CLOs as discussed. Remember that as a reflective practitioner, you want to make sure that you are carefully considering all of the factors, strategies, and practices that can help to foster and promote learner engagement and empowerment, and thereby enhance performance. By examining your practice, you will be in a better position to make any needed changes or revisions.

CHAPTER 1: REFLECTION CHECKPOINT

Develop Course Learning Outcomes

- How can I start to think about developing the CLOs?

    TIP: A course should be based on clearly stated and measurable learner-centered outcomes. These must be included in the syllabus, as well as presented for each unit and module.

- What is my overall vision for this course?

    TIP: What deep and significant learning do you want your learners to come away with? Your vision will clarify the purpose and goals, teaching strategies, and learning activities.

- What is the significant learning potential of my course?

    TIP: Remember that your goal is to engage and empower your learners to implement changes in their own personal and professional lives, and ultimately in the lives of others.

- What are the most important concepts that I want my learners to learn, and why do these concepts matter?

    TIP: What do you want your learners to understand and know? How can their knowledge and understanding be applied practically in the real world?

- What is the overall purpose of the course?

    TIP: The goal is to ensure that all learners remain intellectually curious, self-directed, and motivated toward academic success and self-discovery.

- How do the CLOs fit with the program competencies, general education outcomes, and professional accreditation standards?

    TIP: A key element of the design process is making sure that CLOs are aligned with ILOs and PLOs.

- Are the outcomes that I create actually measurable? In other words, will I be able to assess or evaluate that the learning objectives have been met?

    TIP: Consider what assessment will look like while you are still developing your CLOs. This is important because if your CLOs are not measurable, there will be no way to tell whether and to what extent the learner has achieved what the course sets out to accomplish.

CHAPTER 2

Plan for Assessment of Learning

Once you have determined your CLOs, you will be in a position to move to planning for assessment. Assessment mirrors the CLOs and in turn will help ensure the integrity of the course content. The terms *assessment* and *evaluation* are also used interchangeably; therefore, it is important to ensure that you and your colleagues are using the terms in the same way. Typically, the term *assessment* is used to refer to learner assessment, while the term *evaluation* refers to program and product evaluation; in other words, you assess learners and you evaluate products and processes. In its simplest form, assessment is a cyclical process of defining what you want learners to know or be able to do, providing learning opportunities for them to gain these skills or knowledge, collecting and analyzing evidence of that learning, and making changes to educational processes so that learners can continue to make progress. Outcomes assessment is an ongoing process aimed at understanding and improving learning.

By making our expectations for learning explicit, clearly articulating course and program outcomes, identifying success criteria, and providing purposeful opportunities for learners to achieve, we create opportunities to gather, analyze, and interpret assessments of their learning. The results of those assessments are used to make informed decisions regarding the improvement of learning, teaching, and for planning ahead. Monitoring learning and tracking progress through regular assessments is therefore an integral element of an instructor's role. The CLOs are what you want your learners to *understand and know*. Assessments are derived directly from the CLOs, and so right at the beginning of developing your learning outcomes it is a good idea to begin thinking and planning for assessment.

Remember that while many LMSs provide tools for assessment and analysis, it is the instructor's responsibility to determine whether the assessment is appropriate and relevant, and to adjust or revise as needed. In addition, it is important to ensure that assessment and **grading** are culture fair and unbiased to favor any one culture more than another. Planning carefully for **assessment of learning** serves to create a climate of trust and academic integrity. Explaining to learners and providing them a rationale for how completing assessments will help them achieve the learning outcomes is key. Clear expectations and detailed guidelines for assessment and

Table 2.1. Properties of Effective Assessment

Valid	Directly reflects the learning outcome being assessed.
Reliable	Offers inter-rater reliability when subjective judgments are made.
Actionable	Results help identify what has been learned and what still requires further improvement.
Engaging	Learners have the opportunity to apply and demonstrate the extent of their learning.
Triangulation	Including multiple assessments will serve to build a more holistic picture of the learning that has occurred.
Culture fair	Assessment is unbiased so as not to favor any one culture more than another.
Transparent	Clear expectations and detailed guidelines for assessment and grading policies are provided so that the process is understood.

grading policies ensures that the process is understood and fully transparent. Assessment and grading must have meaning for learners, and they should learn through assessment. Table 2.1 is a useful and brief overview of those factors that characterize effective assessment, and what would constitute a viable assessment procedure.

ASSESSMENT INSTRUMENTS AND METHODS

Assessment of learning can be conducted using a variety of available instruments and methods. You may in some cases be required to design your own methods, but mostly the LMS will have a built-in rubric tool, which offers time-saving features. Performance **rubrics** are commonly used as a way of classifying and categorizing identified criteria for successfully completing an assignment or task and to establish levels for meeting these criteria. A rubric is a tool that explicitly represents the performance expectations for an assignment by listing criteria, and for each criterion, describing levels of quality. Rubrics contain three essential features: (1) performance criteria that learners are to attend to in completing the assignment, (2) markers of quality (typically these are rating scales), and (3) scores or indicators of success. Markers of quality provide learners with a clear idea about what must be done to demonstrate a certain level of mastery, understanding, competency, or proficiency. Clear performance or criteria—whether in the form of a rubric or a narrative—is key to learners' success. In order to think more deeply about how we are grading, we also have to ask ourselves what assumptions we make about our learners. What does it mean to have learned something? What do we think our learners already know? What do we prioritize in an

Plan for Assessment of Learning

assignment or activity, and more importantly, why is that the priority? And finally, of course, do our priorities align with the CLOs?

Rubrics can be used for any assignment in a course, or for any way in which you ask your learners to demonstrate what they have learned. These can also be used as a checklist to facilitate self-reviews. For both you and your learners, the rubric indicates how they will evaluate according to specified criteria, making grading and ranking simpler, more transparent, and fairer. Additionally, they can be used as a teaching tool to help learners understand the level of learning expected, shed light on their current level of learning, and self-evaluate their progress by identifying areas for improvement. A rubric therefore becomes a working guide for both learners and instructors, and is usually available before an assignment is due in order to allow learners to think about the criteria on which their work will be judged. Making the rubric available also provides the **scaffolding** that is necessary to prepare accordingly and improve the quality of their work.

Common Features of Rubrics

Rubrics can be created in a variety of forms and levels of complexity; however, they all contain three common components that will establish the levels for meeting the criteria of an assignment or task:

- Focus on measuring a stated learning outcome (performance, behavior, or quality)
- Use a range to rate learners' performance (a rating scale)
- Contain specific performance characteristics arranged in levels indicating the degree to which a standard or "level of performance" has been met

As you can see in Table 2.2, the criteria listed on the left describe the key elements of a learner's work. Along the top of the rubric, the rating scale identifies levels of performance. Under each section of the rating scale, the

Table 2.2. Basic Rubric Template

	1	2	3	4
Criterion 1				
Criterion 2				
Criterion 3				
Criterion 4				
Criterion 5				

indicators will provide examples or concrete descriptors for each level of performance.

Advantages of Using Rubrics for Assessment

Rubrics offer several advantages in supporting both instructors and learners:

Rubrics support instructors in the following ways:
- Improve performance and achievement by clearly and directly showing learners how their work will be evaluated and what is expected.
- Communicate to learners the specific requirements and acceptable performance standards of an assignment. This serves to create an understanding of expectations and demystifies assignment expectations so learners can focus on the work instead of guessing "what the instructor wants."
- Develop consistency in how you evaluate learning throughout a course, ensuring that your assessment and scoring is accurate, unbiased, and consistent, and hence more transparent to your learners.
- Accommodate diversity and inclusion by offering your learners a range of quality levels.
- Provide you with useful **feedback** regarding the effectiveness of your instruction.
- Reduce your time spent on evaluating and grading, and increase time spent on teaching.

Rubrics support learners in the following ways:
- Promote awareness about the criteria used to assess performance, in order to focus efforts on completing assignments in line with clearly set expectations.
- Provide a clear understanding of the evaluation criteria before they even begin the assignment. When instructors evaluate a task or assignment, they know implicitly what makes a good final product and why. When learners receive rubrics beforehand, they understand how they will be evaluated and can prepare accordingly.
- Help learners become better judges of the quality of their own work. They are more easily able to recognize the strengths of their work and areas in need of improvement, and thereby direct their efforts accordingly.
- Encourage self-reflection regarding their learning, and making informed changes and revisions to achieve the desired learning levels.

Tables 2.3 and 2.4 illustrate some types of assessment rubrics that may be used:

Table 2.3. Sequential Developmental Rubric

	Beginning 1	Developing 2	Accomplished 3	Exemplary 4	Score
Stated Objective or Performance. These are your CLOs.	Description of identifiable performance characteristics reflecting a beginning level of performance.	Description of identifiable performance characteristics reflecting development and movement toward mastery of performance.	Description of identifiable performance characteristics reflecting mastery of performance.	Description of identifiable performance characteristics reflecting the highest level of performance.	
[State CLO 1]			X		
[State CLO 2]				X	
[State CLO 2]			X		
[State additional PLOs as needed]			X		

Table 2.4. Rubric Based on Bloom's Taxonomy

CLO	Inadequate 0	Remember 1	Understand 2	Apply 3	Analyze 4	Evaluate 5	Create 6
	This item represents lower academic achievement than expected and is inadequate for foundational knowledge.	Information cited by the learner is clearly defined or accurate but any solutions or analysis are merely re-stated from others' work.	Goes beyond repetition to display a personal understanding of the material. Facts are stated with some elaboration. There is little or no original thought.	One or more solutions and their potential benefits are provided. These are appropriate for the situation, but are obvious and based upon commonly accepted practices or procedures.	The learner dissects information to deliver a composite picture supported by theory and/or research. Conclusions result from the learner's own reasoning and analysis.	The learner is able to critically appraise and assess the implication of relevant theories and/or principles. Incorporates evidence from multiple sources to support all assertions.	The learner is able to synthesize relevant theories and/or principles. Novel or new strategies are offered. Synthesis is evidence based.
[State CLO 1]							X
[State CLO 2]						X	
[State CLO 3]			X				
[State additional PLOs as needed]							

FORMATIVE AND SUMMATIVE ASSESSMENT

Assessment is essentially an ongoing process aimed at understanding learners' progress and their grasp of the **course material**. Assessment is based on the CLOs because these specify what the learners will be able to do and/or understand throughout the course and after the successful completion of the course. Therefore, there are two types of assessment that work together but have different purposes. **Formative assessments** are "knowledge checks" that occur during the course and are used to monitor progress. Formative assessments also serve to inform the learner of their progress and update and alert the instructor about providing opportunities for learners to improve their knowledge or skills. **Summative assessment** occurs at the end of a learning experience or set of learning experiences and is used to evaluate the achievement of the learning outcomes at the end of a course. Assessments can include direct measures that focus on the review and evaluation of a learner's work including examinations, quizzes, research papers, essays, projects, and presentations. It is equally common to see assessment processes include a variety of indirect measures including surveys, focus groups, self-evaluation, reflections, and exit interviews. Direct and indirect measures can occur as either formative or summative assessments.

Remember that every course typically has a **signature assignment**—an integrative, representative, or summative course assignment, project, or activity in which multiple key course outcomes are embedded. This assignment usually counts for a significant portion of the final course grade, and is a form of summative assessment. In addition to a final summative assessment, it is recommended that shorter formative assessments of different types are administered periodically throughout the course to enable learners to be able to evaluate their ongoing progress and have opportunities to develop retrieval practice. Formative assessment is critical to success by providing ample opportunities for learners to practice new skills or demonstrate knowledge and receive information on how to improve. Moreover, research has shown that frequent short assessments improve learning, course satisfaction, and retention.

One basic idea is that assessments can be used *for* learning, *of* learning, and *as* learning. Simply put, assessments can be used by instructors and learners to improve learning during the educational experience itself through feedback (e.g., assessments *for* learning). Learners can also reflect on their own learning journey as they participate in various assessment tasks and activities (e.g., assessment *as* learning). Finally, assessments can be used to describe the overall learning of an individual or a group of learners at critical points in the learning experience (e.g., assessments *of* learning). A theme across the field of assessment is the push/pull that exists between engaging in assessments to improve learning (assessment *for* learning or assessment *as* learning) and engaging in assessment for accountability purposes (assessment *of* learning).

Table 2.5. Assessment Point Markers

Program										
Course										
		Program Learning Outcomes					Institutional Learning Outcomes			
CLOs		PLO #1	PLO #2	PLO #3	PLO #4	PLO #5	ILO #1	ILO #2	ILO #3	ILO #4
		Bloom's	Bloom's	Bloom's	Bloom's	Bloom's	Written Communication	Research skills	Critical Thinking and Problem Solving	Self-Directed Learning
Week	Assignment Name									
1	Assignment Name									
2	Assignment Name									
3	Assignment Name		I	I			I		I	
4	Assignment Name									
5	Assignment Name				D			D	D	D
6	Assignment Name									
7	Assignment Name									
8	Assignment Name	M	M	M	M	M		M	M	M

Plan for Assessment of Learning

Online educators may use formative assessments, summative assessments, or a combination of assessments in online course design. Often, the discipline will drive the assessment. For example, the disciplines in math or science may find weekly formative assessments more suited to assess the topic addressed that week. The use of weekly or more frequent assessments allows the online educator to assess the progress of the learner and change, modify, or alter the direction of the course based on the success in achieving the prescribed learning outcomes. Alternatively, in an art or social science discipline, weekly assessments may not be required to provide learners additional time to work on assignments. Utilizing a thoughtful combination of assessments and conveying the purpose of the assessments allow the adult learner to feel as though they are a part of the learning process and to take ownership of their learning.

Remember that ILOs and PLOs are typically set by the institution. And, you may or may not have had a hand in developing the CLOs or even creating the assessments. In any event, it is important to realize that assessment points are staggered throughout a course to incrementally and most appropriately assess learners' progress. Table 2.5 is an example of marker points where assessments will occur incrementally throughout a course, and once you have developed the course content, you can create appropriate assignments to address these assessment points. Table 2.5 includes three levels of achievement:

I = "Introducing" (the learner is at the beginning stages of grasping a concept/idea)
D = "Developing" (the learner has progressed to a more complete understanding of the concept/idea)
M = "Mastery" (the learner has fully mastered a concept or idea)

GUIDELINES FOR EFFECTIVE ASSESSMENT

Following are some important strategies and guidelines pertaining to assessment:

Test Your Assessments!
- While you may have started thinking about what assessments to use while determining your CLOs, by now your assessment strategies will have become clearer, more specific, and more focused.
- A good idea is that prior to administering any of your assessments, take these for a "test drive" by running these by a colleague for feedback so that you can tweak or do some final polishing. Be sure to make any changes as needed.

Use a Mix of Assessment Measures
- Assessment can include a variety of direct measures focusing on the examination of learner's work including exam questions, research papers, essays, and presentations.
- Assessment can also include a variety of indirect measures including surveys, focus groups, self-evaluation, reflections, and exit interviews.
- **Direct and indirect assessments** can occur at the end of a learning experience (summative assessment) or at points during the learning experience itself (formative assessment).
- Thoughtfully applied **multimodal assessments** offer learners the opportunity to engage with the course content in meaningful ways.

Teach for the Test
- Assessment should never be a mystery to learners regarding what is expected.
- Ensure that learning outcomes are identified throughout the instruction and prepare the relevant and appropriate assessments around those outcomes.
- Proctored assessments can be used as necessary, and this will require coordination with your institution's or organization's protocol.
- It is essential that all learners are provided with clear directions, requirements, and procedures.

Consistency and Frequency
- Plan to consistently and frequently monitor progress and development throughout the course.
- Do this by using different types of assessments that include **preassessments, progress assessments**, and final evaluations.
- Learners should always be aware of assessment points.

Equitable Assessment Is Essential!
- Make sure that all the assessment criteria are thoughtful, equitable, manageable, and clear to all learners.
- A learner should never have to wonder why they received a particular grade or score, and so your rationale must be explicitly stated or explained! Grading will be further discussed in Chapter 6, *Multimodal Teaching Strategies to Engage and Empower Learners*.

CHAPTER SUMMARY AND SYNTHESIS

Monitoring learning through regular assessments is an integral element of an instructor's role. By making your expectations for learning explicit, clearly articulating course and program outcomes, and providing purposeful opportunities for learners to achieve, you create opportunities to gather, analyze, and interpret assessments of their learning. The results of those assessments are used to make informed decisions about learning, and also implement the necessary improvements with regard to teaching and instruction. Once you have determined your assessment measures, you will be in a position to think about content development and at the same time ensure that the learning outcomes will establish the foundation of a course. As you proceed to Chapter 3, you will be able to think more deeply about addressing learners' needs and develop rich and relevant learning experiences to address these needs. You will learn that online course content development requires thoughtful preparation and planning.

To foster reflection about assessment of learning, ask yourself the following essential questions that are related to the expectations discussed in this chapter. Remember that as a reflective practitioner, you want to make sure that you are carefully considering all of the factors, strategies, and practices that can help to foster and promote learner engagement and empowerment, and thereby enhance performance outcomes. By examining your practice, you will be in a better position to make any needed changes or revisions.

CHAPTER 2: REFLECTION CHECKPOINT

Assessment of Learning

- How do I start planning for assessments?

    TIP: Assessments are derived directly from the learning outcomes, and include periodic as well as final assessment. Therefore, start by examining the CLOs!

- How do I envision learners' progression through learning activities from week to week (such as simple-to-complex, cause-effect, or other types of progression)?

    TIP: Learning is ongoing, and each week's learning builds on the weeks preceding it.

- What tools or rubrics will I use to apply formative and summative assessments?

TIP: Use assessment tools or rubrics in accordance with CLOs. Formative assessment occurs during the course and is used to monitor progress. Summative assessment occurs at the end of a lesson, unit, or course and is used to evaluate the achievement of the learning outcomes at the end of a course.

- How often will assessment occur throughout my course?

    TIP: Offer learners ample summative and formative assessments. Be careful not to overload learners with too many assessments because that would be overwhelming and also unnecessary.

- Am I considering all CLOs when I plan my assessments?

    TIP: Assessment must of necessity be directly linked to CLOs. Therefore, it is imperative that the CLOs are front and foremost in your mind when planning assessments.

- Will my assessments align with course content?

    TIP: Think back to when you were creating CLOs and what you had in mind regarding what you wanted learners to know and understand.

CHAPTER 3

Create Course Content

In developing course content, strive to foster deep (as opposed to surface) learning by helping your learners engage with the material at the level that is most meaningful to them. When learners can identify with the learning activities and relate the assignments to their real-world career paths and experiences, and when interactions with their instructors raise the level of **critical thinking** about the material, we create an environment for deep learning to occur. There are some important strategies to consider as you go about developing and structuring your course content in order to facilitate and support learning and achievement. These strategies are based on theory and research-based literature that support learner engagement, thereby opening up the possibility for deep learning. Learning is not a solitary activity; it is largely derived from the interactions between learners, instructors and learners, and also the ways in which instructors and learners interact with learning spaces and tools. Although online models may support some of those interactions, they only scratch the surface when it comes to offering diverse, rich, and multimodal educational experiences. This responsibility is ultimately that of the instructor. Therefore, to achieve deep learning, instruction must be oriented essentially to constructing meaning by providing your learners with relevant and meaningful activities and experiences. Additionally, as will become clear to you in reading this chapter, in many ways and on multiple levels, online course design has some unique capabilities and applications; it is not simply a matter of directly translating face-to-face instruction into a digital delivery model.

Schwieger and Ladwig (2018) discuss the current generation of young adult learners, Generation Z, who have unique characteristics and expectations. Individuals from this generation were born between 1996 and 2012, and like millennials, they were raised with technology. However, for Generation Z, technology is an inherent part of their everyday life activities. Understanding Generation Z's unique characteristics will help instructors re-think what they are doing in their classrooms, and become more conscious about their learners' needs and implement new ideas, including ways of assessment and tools for how we present material and content. As such, it is necessary to become more familiar with different types of programs and applications that can be integrated into your courses so that you can develop relevant and meaningful activities for your learners.

ADULT LEARNING PRINCIPLES

In preparing to develop course content, let us begin by exploring some important **adult learning principles** that will shed light on how adults learn best, under what conditions they learn, and what contributes to their learning. Developing an understanding of adult learning principles and being able to apply these principles in practice will be of great benefit to instructors in promoting success across diverse adult learners, right from the beginning phases of course design and development and continuing throughout their teaching practice and pedagogical approach. Two theories of adult learning that are particularly relevant are **andragogy** and **transformative learning**.

Andragogy

Defined by Knowles (1984, 1986) and Knowles et. al. (2015) as "the art and science of helping adults learn," andragogy builds upon the theory of **constructivism** that suggests that learning is an active process, whereby adult learners typically construct meaning based on their own experiences. Adults have a self-concept of being responsible for their own decisions and of being able to direct their own learning. Adults seek guidance and consideration as equal partners in the process. They do not want to be told what to do, and they want to choose options based on their individual needs. Adults enter the learning experience with a great wealth of life experience, and that experience is a resource that can be drawn upon to provide meaning to new ideas and skills. Experience is also a source of an adult's self-identify. As opposed to children who are subject-centered, adults are life-centered, and so they seek to draw on their own knowledge and life experiences. The richest resource for learning lies within the learners themselves, and therefore the learning content must of necessity tap into learners' experience to ensure a "readiness to learn."

Moving beyond textbooks and traditional classroom lectures and encouraging learners to draw from their own work and life experiences is one way to create contextually and culturally authentic learning experiences (Bloomberg, 2014). Research increasingly points to the effectiveness of contextually and culturally authentic learning activities that provide adult learners with opportunities for problem solving and group interaction and to develop and apply critical-thinking skills. Active engagement, problem solving, and solution exploration place learners as the focal point, allowing them to construct personal knowledge rather than passively absorb it. Instructional materials that target these strategies promote higher mental-order skills, such as evaluation, synthesis, and analysis, and transform learning tasks and information into engaging and meaningful learning experiences.

Andragogy provides a framework for assessing the needs of adult learners so that academic programs can be tailored to serve this growing demographic within online education. Knowles' insights are especially important for higher education, where online technology is used extensively for adult learners in traditional and continuing education programs, competency-based learning, and career/professional development. Applying the learning principles of andragogy to online course design promotes engagement and success across diverse adult learners. Course material must of necessity demonstrate the relevance to real-world application so that learners can connect what they are learning with their current and past experiences, and be able to see possible future implications. In order to be relevant, useful, and goal-oriented, learning activities should therefore be presented within the context of real-life situations, and should include tasks that will help adults address issues that they confront in their daily lives. When learners "see themselves" in the readings, they can identify more readily with the learning activities and relate the assignments to their real-world career paths and experiences. This has implications for the concept of **usable knowledge**; that is, knowledge that is directly relevant and useful regarding application to real-life experiences.

Transformative Learning

Also referred to as transformational **learning theory** (Cranton, 2016; Kegan, 2000; Mezirow, 1991, 1994, 2000), transformative learning encompasses four phases: (1) an enhanced level of awareness of the context of one's beliefs; (2) a **critique** of the assumptions underlying these; (3) a decision to negate an old perspective in favor of a new one or to make a synthesis of the old and the new; and (4) an ability to act based on the new perspective. Perspective transformation involves an empowered sense of self, a more critical understanding of how assumptions and experiences shape and influence one's beliefs and knowledge, and more functional strategies and resources for moving forward. In sum, learning is essentially about *making meaning of our experiences,* transforming what we know, which in turn influences the way that we think and behave.

One feature that makes transformative learning theory applicable to teaching adults is the sharp focus on the idea that the most significant learning arises from critical reflection, and to achieve deep learning, ongoing critical thinking is key. Therefore, it is essential to build critical-thinking opportunities into your course content by asking questions and posing content that prompts deeper thinking. Critical thinking occurs through reflection and dialogue, commonly referred to as discourse. The implication is to provide opportunities for learners to fully participate in dialogue and reflection. Activities and tasks that require learners to reflect on what they have learned and share their reflections with their instructors and peers extend and enrich their reflection. For instance, blogs and journaling, whether used as group exercises or as individual activities, have evolved into appropriate tools for learners to engage in critical reflection, dialogue, and ongoing learning. Encouraging learners to explain and describe their progress helps them to stay focused on their goals. Helping them think about what they have accomplished and learned also ensures that they are aware of their own progress and what they have yet to complete. The concept of *active learning*, where learners interact and participate, contribute to discussion, and engage in critical thinking, places the learner at the center of the learning experience, and has significant applicability to engagement and empowerment in the context of online learning.

THE MULTIMEDIA PRINCIPLE

Research has shown that learners generally grasp and understand new material better and can remember it longer when the presentation is multimodal. Based on the **multimedia principle** (Clark & Mayer, 2011), the role of an online instructor can and should extend beyond verbal and written communication to include audio and video modes of communication and teaching. The technology that is currently available allows you to increasingly diversify your **instructional strategies** by creating alternative ways of communicating information, thereby broadening engagement opportunities, and expanding the ways in which learners can express and present their learning. Diversifying your content helps to adjust for differences in **learning preferences**, abilities, and skills. In addition to multimodal assignments, using multiple modes of assessments offers learners the opportunity to engage with emerging forms of media, express their creativity, and complete work in areas in which they are interested and feel confident. By providing choices for learners in terms of the input of information and their own output, you provide entry points for learners from a multitude of backgrounds. Therefore, be sure to include both print- and technology-based content in your course, and include both auditory and visual media whenever possible. Remember to remain flexible throughout the process of developing your course content and be aware and cautious of what ways *you* like to communicate and present information since you may tend to overuse those techniques or activities. This relates to our own implicit biases regarding *how people learn* and what we believe others *need to learn*.

Working in the online environment means that you will have access to a variety of tools and resources that may not be available or applicable in traditional classrooms. Different technologies can be used to effectively create and deliver content, enhance instructor presence, communicate, and facilitate learner-to-learner interaction. Today's online platforms or LMSs are equipped with so many engagement tools, and instructors often assume that if a course is offered online, they need to use a wide variety of technologies to successfully teach the class. That is not necessarily true, because using too much technology can indeed be overwhelming and stressful for both learners and instructors. What is critically important is not to confuse technology with teaching; the technology is essentially a means to an end. Know that technology's tools of engagement are just that—tools—not the actual engagement itself.

Offer multiple ways for your learners to engage in the course, and commit to ensuring a learning experience that promotes deep learning. As an instructor, you have a responsibility to recognize which tools and formats (document and media) support accessibility and which do not. Be aware of using content and materials thoughtfully and inclusively, including both synchronous and asynchronous. As you go about developing your course content, also remember to not become too wedded to specific tools, because technology is constantly in flux, and therefore many of the currently used tools may soon become outdated or need to be updated. Essentially, learning should drive instructional design; not the other way around. Thoughtful facilitation methods and combinations of options will ensure inclusivity, leading to greater engagement and persistence. In Chapter 6, you will be provided with details regarding the use of technology, and specific strategies to effectively incorporate audio and visual materials into your teaching practice.

Asynchronous and Synchronous Tools

Instructors may choose to engage their learners either synchronously or asynchronously, or make use of a combination of modes, depending on the course content or material. There are advantages and disadvantages to both teaching options.

Asynchronous Tools

What Are These? In the online environment, learners studying the same material are situated at different locations and time zones. Asynchronous means that learners do not come together at a unified time, but instead, they complete tasks in a self-paced manner within a given time frame. Tools include communication and teaching methods that do not occur in real time, such as **discussion boards**, Prezi or PowerPoint presentations, YouTube, WeVideo, Screencast-O-Matic video, and podcasts. Social media options can also be used to creatively and meaningfully to deliver learning educational content, including Facebook, Twitter, Instagram, Snapchat, Kahoot!, Padlet, MindMeister, and Quizlet. The online classroom requires instructors to develop and implement a comprehensive asynchronous communication strategy—something separate from the actual course content. The announcement feature is one tool that is integrated in most LMSs, allowing instructors to operationalize for this purpose. The announcements that you post form an essential first point of contact, and a touchstone for your learners every time they log into the classroom. You can also leverage your online platform by using announcements to deliver just-in-time logistical broadcasts, or concentrated bursts of instructional content. Making use of an *"Ask the Instructor"* discussion board is also a place where learners can post ongoing questions to you.

How and When to Use? With the advent of the COVID-19 pandemic, asynchronous learning has emerged as a predominant model because of its flexibility in allowing learners to learn anytime and anywhere. Use discussion boards and the announcement tool wisely and often so that learners feel your presence. Effectively incorporate audio and visual materials by rethinking face-to-face teaching materials and transforming these into content that makes best use of the online medium. Rather than simply creating audio and video materials by transcribing and posting face-to-face lectures, amplify the learning experience with images. This makes abstract concepts easier to understand and remember. To ensure that video materials are accessible, captions will need to be included, allowing learners to read the text together with viewing the images. Rather than to be employed as the sole method, asynchronous learning can be used wisely to "bracket" live synchronous sessions, both before and after.

Advantages and Disadvantages of Asynchronous Teaching. Asynchronous tools add value by accounting for time zones and learners' work and family commitments by allowing them to access, listen to, or view content at the time, pace, and place of their choosing. This can potentially lead to greater engagement since they will have more time to explore the course material. This option also creates an accessible archive of past materials. One disadvantage is that learners may feel dissatisfied without the social interaction between their peers and instructors. Additionally, course material may be misunderstood or misconstrued without real-time interaction and without the opportunity to ask questions and receive the needed explanations or clarification "in the moment." Although convenient, asynchronous tools require learners to exercise a high degree of self-regulated learning (Zimmerman, 2008), calling for a high degree of motivation and self-direction. For those who lack self-regulated learning skills, asynchronous learning can be extremely challenging and overwhelming, which in turn can hinder their motivation to succeed.

Synchronous Tools

What Are These? Synchronous class sessions are when participants gather in real time, and complete lessons and activities in sync with one another. Synchronous classes can meet with the use of video, audio, and chat features. Tools include real-time communication methods such as instant messaging, group chats, video or web conferencing, and phone communication.

Applications such as Google Hangouts, Google Docs, Google Sheets and Slides, Google Meet, VSee, Zoom, Skype, GoToMeeting, and Microsoft Teams allow instructors to participate in and monitor synchronous chat sessions, instant messaging, and video and audio interactions with a single learner, a select group of learners, or with the entire online class. Some video and web conferencing tools such as Flipgrid offer combinations of communication mechanisms, affording learners opportunities to simultaneously text, chat, share material, and video conference. There are several other strategies as well that can be used to ensure the work is collaborative such as think/pair/share, jigsaw, and flexible grouping, which can be set up by way of Zoom breakout rooms, or shared Google documents. Appendix O, which is provided for your convenience, includes a variety of applications and tools to support and enhance teaching and collaborative learning.

How and When to Use? The use of synchronous tools requires instructors to coordinate with learners and set times and dates to meet so that all learners have equal access. Especially as learners in online courses are typically geographically dispersed, one technique to overcome this challenge is to schedule multiple synchronous opportunities on different dates and at different times to offer options to learners. As an additional consideration, instructors may choose to offer multiple synchronous activities in order to provide opportunities at different times within a course, thereby allowing for greater access and participation. It is worth exploring what options are available and which will fit with your course design, and as explained in greater detail in Chapter 6, in setting up synchronous activities it is essential to ensure inclusivity and equitable access. In addition to all of the synchronous tools described here, instructors should also always be sure to provide online office hours for in-person meeting with learners via multiple synchronous tools so that your presence and availability is constant and ongoing.

Advantages and Disadvantages of Synchronous Teaching. Incorporating synchronous techniques allows learners and instructors to sync with one another, thereby creating interaction and fostering connectedness and community. Immediate personal engagement increases enthusiasm for learning because it occurs in "real time" and can therefore lessen feelings of isolation. Responsive exchanges between learners and instructors may also prevent miscommunication or misunderstanding. While synchronous experiences can be more responsive and can create more engagement, synchronous learning is, in general, more resource-demanding, and can present technical and logistical barriers. Active learning activities are challenging to implement when learners are "going to class" at different times and are not located in proximity to one another, and so instructors will need to coordinate availability so that all learners have equal access. Additionally, many learners face technical difficulties because they may not have a reliable Internet connection accessible to them. Many learners may also not have access to a quiet learning environment and so synchronous activities may be to their disadvantage.

Table 3.1 is a way to consider which online tools you may decide to incorporate to ensure the optimal conditions for engagement and learning. Remember that you want to avoid overwhelming your learners (and yourself!) with too many tools, so be sure to select these judiciously.

The Asynchronous–Synchronous Balancing Act

Because both online learning structures have advantages and disadvantages, instructors often grapple with determining the optimal combination of tools to ensure learning. Each educational provider has had to determine what works best for their population of learners and instructors. While distance education alters what this learning environment looks like, it should not change the value of establishing a **rapport** with learners through direct interaction. Many instructors have reported that despite alterations to their teaching beginning in the spring of 2020, the one aspect that remained intact was their ability to speak with their learners, and that it was important to maintain a sense of personable engagement and connection through the deliberate action of live dialogue. Over the last two decades, teaching has moved away from the traditional teacher-centered format, and we must be mindful that online learning, specifically an overreliance on asynchronous features, does not undo years of progressive, learner-centered pedagogy. Yes, the classroom itself has certainly changed dramatically. But let us not forget the power in human connection!

Dialogue Leads to Positive Rapport. Engaging in conversation is a natural way that we create relationships. Through dialogue, we interpret nonverbal cues, which contributes to a sense of trust, and enhances our openness to build connections. In an online course, dialogue provides an opportunity to humanize teachers and learners, allowing individuals to display their interests, inquiries, and concerns. Essentially, the synchronous classroom conveys the message that "showing up" matters.

Synchronicity Provides a Normalizing Structure. In traditional teaching, class schedules serve as a structure that holds learners accountable. Learners show-up in person because it is expected. They know that if they miss class, they will miss vital information. In self-regulating asynchronous classes, learners are not mandated to log in for a specific class session but only for self-paced learning and assignment deadlines. With no clear set times to attend live sessions, there is no expectation to "show-up," and it is easy for learners to lose track of time, forget about their work, lose interest, and not submit critical assignments.

As educators have prepared for teaching courses online, especially since the onset of the COVID-19 pandemic, many have faced adjusted schedules

Create Course Content

Table 3.1. Tips for Selecting and Evaluating Online Learning Tools

What are the key features and functions of the tool?

- Clear directions and instructions for use
- Way/s to prerecord directions and instructions
- A means for learners to submit work
- Way/s for instructors to perform teaching functions
- Ways for learners to interact and work collaboratively
- Way/s to provide feedback to learners about their work
- Way/s for learners to provide feedback to one another
- Way/s for learners to interact regarding course content
- Assessment tools that allow for formative and summative evaluations
- Grading tools or rubrics are included
- Way/s to share work and learning
- Way/s to communicate on multiple levels
- Way/s to host meetings (individual meeting platform or group meeting platform)

How and in what ways does the tool support learning and engagement?

- Ability to seek and find knowledge and information
- Ability to use (engage with) knowledge and information
- Ability to create knowledge and information
- Ability to share knowledge and information
- Promotes reflection
- Promotes problem solving

Can the tool be easily accessed?

- How will learners with limited Internet access engage with this tool?
- Are there alternative tools that will support the same outcomes?
- Does the tool have adequate accessibility features that are aligned with digital compliance requirements (e.g., closed captions, screen-reading software)?
- What necessary accessibility features are offered?

Can the tool be easily used?

- Can the tool be used with minimal assistance?
- Are there available support resources (e.g., library, instructional technology services)?
- Are the navigation features of this tool clear?
- Are the individual components of the tool intuitive?
- What challenges are associated with the tool that may hinder engagement and learning?

Additional useful information and recommendations

- How and in what ways could this tool be used in the future?
- What other tools could be used in conjunction with this tool? For what purpose?
- How could this tool be improved and/or enhanced? What purpose would this serve?

that provide less live class time than they used to have when teaching in person. There are many ways to incorporate synchronous qualities and strike a balance with valuable asynchronous qualities. Over-reliance on heavily scored discussion threads intended to mirror live discussions is not the answer. Discussion boards can tend to appear arbitrary with complicated requirements and confusing visual navigation. Structured incorrectly, this task is typically met with frustration and stress. All of this implies that instructors will have to make decisions about what material to ask learners to engage with on their own time (asynchronously), what material to keep in the live sessions (synchronously), and what material to simply eliminate. To help steer your thinking regarding finding the optimal split between asynchronous and synchronous materials, there are two key questions to ask:

1. How should I split my course content into asynchronous and synchronous material?
2. How can I leverage asynchronous learning to help me conduct better synchronous sessions?

The answer to the first question depends on what you think is the comparative advantage of a live class session over activities that your learners can engage in asynchronously. In other words, for what learning activities does being together *make a difference*? This will vary based on your learning goals, the material that you teach, and your style of teaching. Following are some guiding principles.

Asynchronous learning is preferable when you think it is important to achieve the following objectives:

- Learners need to develop a common foundation before class (learning basic ideas or concepts).
- An assessment of your learner's perspectives or background on the subject, because this will affect how live classes would be conducted.
- Learners being able to engage with the material at their own pace. This is especially useful if prior knowledge of the material varies significantly across learners.
- Learners require time for reflection and deeper thinking.

Synchronous learning is preferable when you think it is important to achieve the following objectives:

- Exchanges of perspectives among your learners.
- Learners learning with and from each other.
- Interactions in which the instructor plays the role of facilitator or mediator.
- Opportunities to establish and build community.

Create Course Content

In sum, reserve your live synchronous sessions for those learning experiences that benefit learners from being together at the same time. Asynchronous learning is useful to "bracket" live sessions, both before and after. When you ask your learners to engage with asynchronous material before synchronous sessions, it could be beneficial to collect some feedback from them that will allow you to teach a more productive and engaging live session. Engaging with asynchronous tools following the live sessions can serve as a useful platform for a summary or synthesis of the learning that occurred synchronously.

TRANSFORMING TEACHING MATERIAL INTO AUDIO AND VIDEO CONTENT

Most LMSs have a way to create and integrate teaching tools and resources. Effectively incorporating audio and visual materials begins with understanding how to rethink or reimagine face-to-face teaching materials and transform these into content that makes best use of the online medium as its own unique communication forum, to make the learning experience both effective and engaging. There are four types of multimedia that you can use in your course: audio, video, voiceover presentations, and screencast. Screencast can be described as a way of using video that is accompanied by a voiceover. This approach is often considered more effective than a "talking head" video, especially when you are explaining a complex process, because learners are able to both see and hear your explanation in real time. Using video by way of sharing your screen allows you to focus on specific aspects of their work, and show learners how to *actually* make recommended improvements. To facilitate engagement, you would speak to your learner as though they are sitting next to you, acknowledging good work, and suggesting any necessary improvements.

While video is being integrated more and more into online courses, this can create barriers for learners with hearing problems. If a learner asks for an ADA (Americans with Disabilities Act) accommodation for a video, you will likely be scrambling at the last minute to create a text supplement. For this reason, it is good practice to create a text supplement at the same time that you create a video. Many instructors use separate transcripts to add text for hearing-impaired learners. However, this can make it challenging for a deaf or hard-of-hearing learner to absorb the visual and auditory information simultaneously, because they need to shift back and forth between the images and text. The better way to create accessible video is with captions that appear within the video itself, allowing learners to read the text with the images. While captioning takes time, the steps are not difficult to master, and there are a variety of options for adding captions to online videos. A common way to caption videos is to do it yourself, either in two steps, creating the transcript and then adding it to the video, or in one step with appropriate software that creates the captions automatically from the video. Refer to Appendix N, *Online Support Resources*. The resource *Engaging online students with synchronous and asynchronous learning tools* contains very useful information regarding creating accessible videos for online classrooms (pp. 8–9).

The essential purpose in developing video material is to create memorable content that learners will retain. Creating these materials is not simply a matter of transcribing your face-to-face lectures into a document that you then post in your LMS. Some instructors choose to create online videos by just adding narration to a PowerPoint presentation. Once again, they are thinking in terms of the face-to-face paradigm by reading pages of notes. In the online environment, audio and visual content should not be used for projecting your detailed notes; rather, the purpose is to skillfully convey the concepts to be learned, and amplify the learning experience with images

Table 3.2. Tips for Creating Video Material

Find a theme
Too often, instructors will go into the course development process with the "content coverage" mentality where the focus is on touching all the necessary topics. This approach conveys information to learners with little or no context. Remember that the human mind is built to remember significance, and so the first rule of teaching is that "only significance matters." Thus, the first task is to identify the significance in the information, and develop a single theme for each audio or video presentation.
Start with motivation
Whether delivered through an in-person presentation or a video, the content must grab the learner's attention immediately, or you will "lose your audience." The opening must pique their interest and make them want to hear and learn more. Let learners know right upfront why the material is important and how it will benefit them in the course and beyond. This will motivate them to engage in the material. Only after gaining their attention should you begin the actual lesson.
Include images that will resonate with your learners
Once you have developed a theme and stated the significance of each part of the lesson in terms of that theme, proceed to record the narration and add relevant images. Be cautious of cluttering your presentation with too many images, or alternatively trying to create something that looks like a slick and elaborate professional product. The point is to create material that is clearly and logically presented, and that learners will find interesting, relevant, and meaningful, so that they will engage in the content and learn from it.
Interactivity is key!
Make your online class interactive and discussion-oriented rather than simply resorting to lecture mode. Include spaces throughout the lesson where you invite and encourage active participation!

that provide an emotional emphasis and visual analogue to the concepts being taught. The imagery itself is what makes the abstract concepts easier to grasp, understand, and remember. Online instructors should thus be cognizant of reconceptualizing their face-to-face lecture materials to produce an effective audio or video-based format. In the process, it is essential not to get bogged down with the technology, but to really focus on *pedagogy* and *engagement*. Remember that technology is not a substitute for authentic interactions. Rather, it is a tool to facilitate interaction and engagement. Table 3.2 offers a few simple rules.

ORGANIZATION AND PRESENTATION OF MATERIAL

An online course that is well-organized and structured with clear and predictable navigation builds learners' confidence in their ability to succeed. Furthermore, when materials and activities are presented in a logical and coherent order, learners are better able to make connections among topics and effectively and meaningfully integrate their knowledge. Such connections contribute to learners' ability to think critically and to apply their knowledge to new situations.

Content Has Relevance and Value

The ways in which you organize and present your material provides you an important opportunity to connect with your learners and maintain their engagement. However, even if you engage learners at the start, you will not maintain ongoing engagement if they fail to see the relevance and value of the course material. Remember that by nature, adults typically have a need to know why they should learn, and are motivated to put time and energy into learning if they know the benefits and applicability thereof. Learners may wonder how a particular course or class can help them with completing their program of study process, and why this particular course or class is important. To be motivated to learn, they must of necessity understand and appreciate its relevance and value. By offering learners choices in how they can demonstrate their learning, we help them to tap into their natural creativity, curiosity, and intrinsic motivation. Because they are drawn to tasks that are personally relevant and challenging—creating multiple pathways to approach their own learning (process), demonstrate their learning (product), or customize their learning (content), will allow learners to deepen their understanding and increase their engagement and academic achievement. The more choice that we can offer learners through this type of **differentiation**, the more they can exercise control over their own learning and select options and tasks that are relevant for their own personal, academic, and career goals. Learners are more engaged with their work when they see the value of it and when they have some say in what they choose to do. Poor performance is inevitable when learners don't "buy in" to a required assignment, activity, or task.

There are a number of guidelines to be aware of in order to ensure the relevance and value of course content and materials in order to enhance motivation and **persistence**. In developing content, focus on making connections to link the subject matter to prior experiences and relevant content; helping learners identify and set meaningful and realistic goals; and adapting the course content to their interests and needs so that they can apply what they are learning to their own lives and goals. In this way, you will begin to develop "a need to know," thereby making a case for the value of the learning. Help learners see the relevance of the course content by pointing out how this can lead to achievement and success both in the current course and beyond. Demonstrating transparency will avoid assumptions that certain assignments are pointless or irrelevant. Additionally, wherever possible, offer choices with regard to assignment topic and format so that learners can be motivated to apply their own strengths and skills. What is relevant to one person may not be relevant to another. In developing relevant content, be aware of different aspects of finding relevance:

- Personal association (this occurs when a learner makes a connection to something outside of the classroom and wants to know or understand more)
- Personal usefulness (this is derived from a learner's belief that a task, activity, or text will help them reach a personal and/or professional goal)
- Personal identification (this stems from a deep understanding that the task, activity, or text aligns with their identity or sense of self). The learner sees the course content reflected and valued in terms of their own experiences.

Content Is Clear and Intuitive

Course organization means that your materials and content are clear and intuitive. Commonly, online learners become confused, frustrated, and disengaged simply because it is difficult to find and access the course content and activities. Discouraged learners are less likely to learn, and more likely to disengage. Remember that online learners cannot generally ask quick questions in real time. Therefore, be sure to avoid any confusion that might be inherent in the design and setup of the LMS by giving explicit, direct, and clear (unambiguous) direction throughout the syllabus, and making use of clarifying and explanatory pointers wherever you can.

The design and sequence of content throughout the course should be methodical, systematic, and purposeful. Help learners move through activities smoothly and seamlessly, so that they remain engaged. If they have to click out of a **module** and into another folder to watch a required video, that can be distracting and certainly frustrating if it is hard to locate. As such, try to order materials and activities so that the flow makes sense for someone new to the course. Think about how the use of menus, modules, folders, subfolders, and other organizing structures of the online platform can either help or hinder learners' progress throughout the course. Be conscious of striking a balance between scrolling and clicking. Learners should be able to easily and intuitively access content, assessments, and learning activities without constantly having to access more and more links. Equally important, use LMS tools such as folders and pages to keep the course activities and tasks systematically organized. An online course should not be one giant website of endless scrolling. Nor should it be a complex maze of nested and subnested folders. Aim for a good mix of navigational approaches so that your learners will experience neither scrolling nor clicking fatigue.

Instructor Participation Plan

It is critical to think about and actually create an instructor participation plan prior to teaching online courses. Doing so can help instructors ensure that they are routinely interacting and communicating with their learners, and can also help estimate the workload associated with a course. Items within an instructor participation plan could include posting regular course announcements, offering virtual office hours, providing feedback on assignments or other assessments, responding to learners' questions, participating in online discussion forums, and offering synchronous exam reviews. Having such a plan established prior to the start of the course can help you feel more organized, prepared, and confident once the course gets underway. Teaching online can be challenging, and instructors often underestimate the workload associated with teaching their online course. To better manage one's time, it is advisable therefore to think about and estimate the workload associated with various aspects of their course (communicating with learners, participating in discussion forums, grading and feedback, and so on) prior to a course starting. A common strategy to ease the workload burden while teaching is to reuse certain components—course announcements, discussion forum summaries, feedback on assessments—from one term or course module to another. While these will likely need to be revised and updated, this can be a considerable time saver.

Course Syllabus

To organize and prioritize all elements of the instruction, an essential step is to include a strong and very explicit course syllabus that has consistent structure, and that focuses directly on achieving the clearly stated learning outcomes. As mentioned in Chapter 1, you may not always be building your own course and often you will have no hand in creating the syllabus because this will already have been developed by an instructional design team. At other times, you may be offered the opportunity to tweak or enhance an already established course, or to make some added adjustments and enhancements to the syllabus. In the event that you are charged with developing your own syllabus, the guidelines provided here will assist you with approaching the development and creation of strong course content in a way that is streamlined, systematic, and structured.

The "syllabus," in effect, is the entire course outline that provides a structure for planning and success, laying out all the course requirements and expectations. As such, the syllabus is sometimes referred to as a **course guide**. It is important that your learners come to think of the syllabus as both a motivator and a source of vital information, serving as a "road map" of the course in its entirety. A well-designed syllabus includes a course title, course description, clearly laid out CLOs, lesson topics, activity schedules, due dates for all activities and assignments, required and supplemental resources, and clear assessment expectations. Courses should be divided into sections or modules based on logical topic areas. Within a section, there can be one or more weeks, and within each week, there are one or more logically related types of assignments. The use of weekly modules sets a structure for learners, allowing those who are self-directed to choose to access materials, and plan and prepare ahead. It is critical that content is logically created so that each task or activity builds off of those that precede it. Reflection opportunities must be thoughtfully built into the course design to support, facilitate, and enhance learning. In addition, be sure to plan a relevant conclusion for your course. This may take the form of a final signature assignment, or a reflection on what was learned in the course or module.

Signature Assignment. Typically, the final assignment of the course (sometimes referred to as the "signature assignment"), aligns with all or most of the CLOs and it therefore represents the application of learning gained throughout the course. As such, this assignment typically counts for a significant portion (at least 15–30%) of the final grade. The assignment usually requires considerably more work than the other assignments, so alerting learners to the signature assignment and providing an overview of this assignment's requirements early on in the course is a best practice as this can assist learners in preparing and planning ahead. Because of its importance within the course, this assignment should be composed first (with the possibility of some revision later in the process). The weekly activities are therefore composed after the signature assignment (and with the signature assignment in mind) and should support learners in demonstrating incremental proficiency toward the signature assignment.

Reflective Opportunities. The signature assignment does not necessarily have to occur in the final week of the course; it could occur in the penultimate week, saving the final week for sharing and an opportunity for reflection. Activities that incorporate a reflective component should be incorporated within any course, serving as a powerful pedagogical strategy, offering learners the space and time to think about their own learning. The concept of reflection as an "educative process" dates back to the work of John Dewey (1933), who pointed out that experience alone does not constitute learning; instead, a conscious realization must occur so that an experience can truly become a source of learning. More explicitly, helping your learners develop their intellectual, metacognitive, and (self-)reflective skills by way of reflective assignments provides an opportunity to engage in critical reflection and higher-order thinking, and also aids in the transfer of knowledge and skills. As such, using reflection as a pedagogical cornerstone is key.

The empowered learning environment provides learners with opportunities to assess their own learning and builds ways for learners to reflect on their learning and work, As such, this is a valuable way for learners to apply their knowledge to other experiences and to their workplace. Because reflection is a means of engaging critically and analytically with the course content, reflective exercises or tasks allow learners to demonstrate and question their understanding of the subject and explicitly think about their learning process as well as their progress, and to think more deeply about the impact or implications of a learning experience. Moreover, the opportunity to share one's reflections with others can also be additionally beneficial, because sharing leads to enhanced understanding and ongoing critical thinking and dialogue. Pedagogical activities that require learners to reflect on what they learn and to share their reflections with their instructors and fellow learners thus extend and enrich reflection, and can take many forms, including blogs and journaling.

To offer additional **metacognition** opportunities for learners at every writing level—where they can in effect *think about their own thinking*—you might consider adding audio reflection to your repertoire. When you want your learners to pause and consider their learning, either at the end of a project or before a new challenge, they can record their own voices in response to assigned prompts and submit the audio reflection as an assignment. Quick and accessible, routine audio reflection helps learners establish and reinforce metacognitive processing. The value of audio reflection also supports a broader range of learners. This type of activity can be more manageable for those who are insecure about their writing abilities, and the shift away from writing can help them elicit new insights that they may not be able to express on the page. Additionally, since audio reflections feature learners in their own voices, personalities come across more easily, the result often being a livelier and more detailed representation of cognitive processing. Moreover, from an instructor's standpoint, audio can be a welcome change from the ever-present stack of papers!

Up to this point, you have learned about how adults learn (adult learning principles) and also about the multimedia principle (incorporating multiple teaching methods, both asynchronous and synchronous). You have also been provided with guidelines regarding how to coherently organize and present the course material, including development of course syllabus, signature assignment, and building in reflection opportunities. There are a number of other underlying key factors to consider as you proceed to create course content, and we will proceed to examine each of these areas in greater detail:

- Collaborative Learning Opportunities: What are the activities that will foster collaboration among learners where they can learn *with and from each other*?
- Scaffolding: How can you design content to be incremental, thereby minimizing cognitive overload?
- Inclusion, Equity, and Accessibility: How can you present the content fairly so that all learners have opportunities to demonstrate their knowledge and skills?

COLLABORATIVE LEARNING OPPORTUNITIES

In the online environment, instructors are having to teach differently, which means new technology and new types of assignments are required to meet learning outcomes. Collaborative work can indeed be one of the effective strategies in this new learning environment. There are many opportunities to foster collaborative learning as a way for learners to work together on assignments or tasks, build knowledge collectively, think critically, and support each other's understanding. Interaction within online educational environments has long been advocated as conducive to learning. Recommendations for online learner engagement include building interactive opportunities between instructors and learners, learners and other learners (team work, collaborations), and learners and content. Interaction creates a more positive **sense of community** in online courses (Martin et al., 2019; Ouyang & Scharber, 2017). Creating community serves to combat isolation and build a sense of connectedness and ongoing engagement (McGahan, 2018). Let us turn for a moment to focus on how people learn, specifically through the lens of constructivism.

Constructivism

The essence of interaction among learners, teachers, and content is well understood and is referenced in many theories of education, most notably, constructivism (also referred to as constructivist learning). Adult education as a field has always valued learning from collaboration and experience, with Dewey, as early as 1916, making the claim that "the social environment . . . is truly educative in the effects in the degree in which an individual shares or participates in some conjoint activity" (1916, p. 26). Dewey (1916, 1938) viewed learning as a series of social experiences in which learners learn by doing, collaborating, and reflecting with others. While developed in the early part of the 20th century, Dewey's work is very much in evidence in a good deal of present-day social constructivist instructional design. Similarly, Vygotsky (1978) concluded that learning and knowledge is fostered through the social interaction of teachers and learners, and he called for an approach to learning and teaching that is exploratory and collaborative, with the teacher providing opportunities for learners to assemble with each other and learn together. Some years later, Lave and Wenger (1991) and Wenger (1998) drawing on the work of Vygotsky (1978) developed the concepts of "communities of practice" and situated learning, and their work is evident in many studies related to online education. This approach holds that learning is situated in, and derived from, participation in communities, and that real-world contexts are the most optimal learning environments. Learning is derived from the interactions between learners, instructors and learners, and learning spaces and tools. Although online models may support some of those interactions, they only scratch the surface when it comes to offering diverse, rich, and multimodal educational experiences. This responsibility is ultimately that of the instructor, and this can be accomplished through the skillful use and application of **collaboration tools**.

Use of Collaboration Tools

Foundations inherent in the constructivist learning philosophy can harness online collaborative learning tools such as blogs, online productivity suites, data visualization and modeling tools, and social media platforms. Remember that motivating online learners to remain engaged is a primary and ongoing task so that deep learning will actually occur. Successful collaborative efforts can be accomplished by way of thoughtful planning, and a balanced use of motivational strategies and resources to support our choices. Collaborative learning opportunities can involve either group discussions or shared tasks, activities, and projects. Online facilitation methods encourage participation, engagement, and interaction through synchronous and asynchronous tools, as well as a combination of tools, that can be incorporated for online **course delivery**. An online instructor may, for example, design a learning activity that begins with an asynchronous posting on a group discussion topic and culminates with a synchronous chat session discussing the posted topic. Thoughtful facilitation methods and combinations of methods and options will serve to build engagement and persistence. The choice and availability of educational technologies continue to improve and enhance the delivery of online course content.

Setting Up Group Activities

The development of innovative practices to facilitate collaboration, nurture relationships, and build community among geographically diverse instructors and learners becomes a key component of successful online course design and delivery (Schwartz et al., 2016). The skillful use of your LMS to create collaborative groups will ensure that your learners never feel alone on their learning journey, but rather a part of a thriving learning community. Create activities that require learners to work in small groups, share experiences, and actively communicate in order to solve problems or address learning issues. Employing content that allows and encourages learners to become facilitators' themselves will not only benefit every member of the group, but will also empower each individual within it. Your ability to use technology to build teaching relationships and develop a sense of community will depend greatly on the type of LMS available. Some platforms can lead to greater interaction and connectivity among users, and critical choices will need to be made regarding the ways in which different technologies can enhance (or limit) online learners' connections and interactivity. There are various ways to create effective collaborative learning experiences that will facilitate engagement and learning.

Discussion Forums. The online classroom typically includes some discussion board forums. This experience prompts engagement by allowing learners to demonstrate their knowledge of the learning activities from the week, and also build a sense of community with their peers. Discussions can be either synchronous or asynchronous. Asynchronous discussion, in particular, is increasingly becoming an important communication tool in online education because this allows learners to participate at times that work for them. Discussion forums are a significant part of online courses, because learners typically post and respond to other learners' posts weekly. However, as reported by Learninghouse (2019), only 66% of respondents stated that these forums are engaging, highlighting an opportunity for improvement. There are many ways to think about reimagining and redesigning discussion board forums, and to make sure that these are serving the function of encouraging dialogue and critical thinking. For example, in creating the traditional weekly discussions, you may choose to either randomly or purposefully assign learners to weekly breakout groups. Within the breakout groups, you may assign a team leader to facilitate the discussion on a topic that they find relevant and insightful. Additionally, different ways to enhance discussion forums include using them for small group activities, replacing research-based assignments with opinion pieces, and incorporating thought-provoking topics and issues. Remember that successful discussion isn't measured by the quantity of learners' responses; it is measured by the *quality* of those responses, and quality requires instructor engagement and thoughtful construction of discussion assignments that will generate dynamic interaction.

Some video and web-conferencing tools offer combinations of communication mechanisms affording learners opportunities to simultaneously text, chat, share material, and video conference, making the experience truly "multimodal," and opening up possibilities for ongoing engagement of diverse learners. For example, video-based discussion boards can be established through Flipgrid, where learners can post reflections for any asynchronous activities, including handwritten notes, imagery, and pictures. Edublog, Pear Deck add-on for Google Slides, and Nearpod are other ways to interact directly with content. This type of presentational flexibility conveys the message that you value their unique learning preferences as adult learners. Offering and considering choice also respects adult learners to establish a sense of autonomy regarding their learning experience, especially when they have been involuntarily shifted into online learning, as was the case with the COVID-19 pandemic. Appendix O includes a variety of collaborative applications to support and enhance teaching and learning.

Peer Review. One way to develop collaboration is to offer opportunities for learners to read and respond to one another's writing, and this is a common activity in online coursework. This is helpful to writers at all skill levels, in all classes, and at all stages of the writing process. Studies have shown that even strong writers benefit from the process of **peer review**, with learners reporting that they learn as much or more from identifying and articulating weaknesses in a peer's paper as from incorporating peers' feedback into their own work (van Popta et al., 2017). Most LMSs have embedded discussion boards that can be used to engage learners in peer review. Peer reviews can be useful for any assignment that you plan to have learners revise or build upon. Opportunities to engage in peer review, when well planned, can help your learners improve their reading and writing skills and learn how to collaborate effectively; thereby, learning with and from each other. More specifically, participating in the peer review process can help learners read carefully, with attention to the details of a piece of writing (whether their own or others'); clarify their own ideas as they explain them to classmates and as they formulate questions about their classmates' writing, learn how to strengthen their writing by taking into account the feedback that they receive; and learn how to gather and respond to feedback on their own work.

Preparing learners to provide substantive responses that constructively challenge the way that they think about the topic at hand is the most important aspect of this review activity. Developing an explicit peer review worksheet will provide learners with the guidance necessary to provide one another with helpful and substantive feedback. Appendix F: *Guidelines for Conducting Peer Review* will be useful in this regard. Designing activities that incorporate peer feedback will require careful planning and scaffolding.

Therefore, if you decide to incorporate peer review activities, you also will need to determine how, when, and where these will fit most appropriately within the course in order to be timely, productive, and relevant:

- **Decide which writing assignments will include a peer review session.** Given the time that is required to conduct peer review sessions successfully, instructors should incorporate peer review sessions for shorter assignments, so as not to overburden learners.
- **Decide when peer review sessions will occur.** Peer review can be helpful after learners have completed a first draft of an assignment, because this allows a more sophisticated engagement with the ideas, and deeper critique of their own work. You might also have learners review parts of an assignment at several points during the writing process. In this way, they can receive feedback from several classmates and work on revising their ideas as they work on a new draft.
- **Decide where peer reviews will occur.** One way is to set up discussion boards for peer reviews to occur in small groups. Another option is to make use of a collaborative tool such as Google Docs, Sheets, and Slides, or Microsoft Teams, which enable learners to share drafts and comment on each other's work. In this way, they each receive a set of detailed feedback from their peers.

Peer Dialogue Journals. Journal writing provides a risk-free venue to explore, think, and practice skills learned in class. It is a means for learners to reflect on new knowledge learned in class, solidify their learning experience by recording their evolving thought process as they progress further in their course, learn new material, and formulate new opinions and perspectives. Moreover, research shows that learners who reflect about their writing processes and decisions can essentially become more able and careful critics of their own work (Stevens & Cooper, 2009).

Used as a pedagogical strategy, the insights and awareness produced by **peer dialogue journals** take learning and critical thinking one step further by exploring learning experiences collaboratively, thereby fostering connection and community (Bloomberg, 2005). Appendix G: *Guidelines for Implementing Peer Dialogue Journals* offers some useful directions. In this type of journaling activity, two or more learners work collaboratively by sharing experiences via a common journal, examining and analyzing central questions and issues related to the course material, and offering each other insights and thoughts as the shared experience unfolds. Peers become "thought-partners in conversation" about issues related to the course material; and by "speaking through their writing," with the journal as medium. As they share and exchange ideas and thoughts that concern them, learners become engaged in a process of reflecting on their knowledge and experience as it unfolds. Through their dialogue, they build on each other's insights, reflections, and learning, and present each other with new ways of thinking and reasoning. The journal becomes an account of the learners' work in progress, but more essentially an opportunity for reflection on learning by providing *a shared experience* to critically and analytically engage with course content, and even to debate concepts and issues. In this way, peer dialogue journaling becomes a learning tool that encourages engagement and connectedness, by fostering reflection and dialogue, two of the conditions necessary for promoting transformative learning (Bloomberg, 2005).

SCAFFOLDING

While we expect our learners to grasp course content, not all learners will have the necessary knowledge or capability to perform as we assume or expect. Scaffolding is a design effort to provide support to learners as they familiarize themselves with the skills that are required to master and then go on to successfully complete tasks (Polly et al., 2018). By scaffolding, you break tasks into manageable subtasks, designing learning to be incremental, adding complexity in stages or layers. Just as a house needs to be framed as it is built, so in developing course content you can frame the content and guide learners as they build their understanding.

Minimize Cognitive Overload

Minimizing cognitive overload has its roots in cognitive psychology, where the focus is on facilitating deep learning and ongoing engagement. For example, Vygotsky (1978) promotes working within the "zone of proximal development" in order to support and guide learners toward success. Scaffolding not only helps learners to complete course-specific assignments; it also teaches them valuable skills regarding completing work independently on manageable sections without becoming overwhelmed. Scaffolded content enables the building of new information and skills on those that were previously acquired, as well as the integration of new information with what was previously learned, including making comparisons and connections with previously learned materials, and gaining practice in applying concepts in new and different ways. Through scaffolding, learning is designed to be incremental, adding complexity in stages or layers, thereby stimulating ongoing inquiry, motivation, and deeper learning. People tend to learn new material better and can remember it longer when they receive it in chunks or shorter segments rather than in one continuous long lesson. Commonly referred to as the segmentation principle, this is significant with regard to online learners who are removed from both instructors and classmates. Instructors' consideration of the role of scaffolding in course design can improve any learning experience, but is particularly important in the online context, which carries with it the high risk of isolation.

Guidelines for Effective Scaffolding

Following are guidelines to keep in mind as you go about developing scaffolded course content:

Avoid Dense Content.
- Dense content becomes a barrier to deep learning because it leaves too little time for learners to apply their knowledge.
- Continuous content, whether video or audio, should be divided into short segments rather than one long continuous lesson. Try to chunk information into smaller increments of information and provide optimally scheduled repetition to allow for knowledge construction, because in doing so, you are scaffolding your material to support and accommodate all learners.
- Finding natural breaking points in your course can result in better time management and course navigation. To be effectively received and learned, text should be segmented by the use of headings and subheadings, and assigning too much text at one time should be avoided.

Connect Current and Prior Knowledge.
- In creating content, be sure to attempt to connect learners' current knowledge with their prior knowledge.
- Be very explicit about how new topics and tasks link to concepts previously introduced in the course or prior courses. This will enable learners to understand the relevance and applicability of the course content.

Balance the Scaffolding.
- Types of scaffolding include indexes, glossaries, formula sheets, templates, scoring rubrics, samples of relevant projects and papers, as well as short videos to supplement background knowledge. Instructors can also scaffold individual assignments by asking for outlines or rough drafts.
- In an effort to support struggling learners, you may need to provide additional layers of scaffolding at different points in the course, and you will also have to determine the right balance of scaffolding.
- Higher levels of scaffolding are recommended for those who lack prior knowledge and have high anxiety or low motivation. For these learners, too little scaffolding often leads to frustration, anxiety, and loss of motivation.
- Finding the right balance for scaffolding is a shared responsibility and input from your learners will be welcomed. Therefore, be sure to ask them to help identify the level and type of scaffolding that

they may need or want so that you can work with them to set up the appropriate supports.

Content Must Be Interactive.
- Learners must be able to easily and intuitively interact with the content. Make use of a structure that provides instruction, practice, feedback, and remediation for the desired learning outcomes. A useful formula is Read it/See it/Study it/Do it/Discuss it.
- You want your learners to persist, and you want them to know that they have the skills to do so. It's essential that they feel motivated to learn and empowered because they can make sense of the way that they learn. When we invite learners to embrace active learning, we are also encouraging them to see themselves as strong, capable learners.
- Weekly discussions, which are often a core component of most online courses, can be optimally implemented in ways that contribute to learning and progress. To achieve a logical progression, online discussions should be structured in ways that generate meaningful dialogue and reflection so that learners can receive feedback on their ideas and build on these as they move forward.

INCLUSION, EQUITY, AND ACCESSIBILITY

Since the onset of the COVID-19 pandemic, there has been an increased interest for online courses and programs across the globe, enabling education to exist without time or place boundaries, providing learners with greater flexibility and an ability to self-pace their studies, thereby bridging a gap. At an institutional level, the shift in educational delivery has given instructors the ability to develop and deliver innovative methods of teaching and learner support. Some of these positive aspects are promising and, if strategically applied, these have a huge potential to meet the needs of learners. However, the pandemic and resulting digitalization of education has also redefined the discussion around accessibility and inclusion, highlighting the challenges confronting educational institutions in their efforts to provide equal teaching conditions and meet the specific needs of underrepresented communities (Beaunoyer et al., 2020; Chan et al., 2021). Essentially, the pandemic intensified and exacerbated a challenge that already existed, with the disadvantages that some learner populations have been facing now becoming more visible—and indeed glaringly obvious. Historically, underserved communities include people from low-income families, racial/ethnic minorities, learners of color, and indigenous peoples. When the emphasis on lifelong learning is taken into consideration, this definition is broadened in order to address the specific needs of elderly people as well as learners with different learning abilities. Thus, it becomes more important than ever to get a better understanding of the problems faced on a global level.

When creating content, remember that equal access to education is mandated by law, and is grounded in the hope that all people will indeed have equal access to course content. Therefore, offering and ensuring equal access is both an ethical and a legal responsibility. Online learning opens up access to education, but it does not necessarily provide more equitable access. With the numerous negative effects of the pandemic in terms of accessibility and inclusion, it has become increasingly challenging for educational institutions to provide equal teaching conditions for all learners. Unless we collect, create, and offer content that meets accessibility standards, learners do not all have equal access to content. In order to offer equitable instruction, it is therefore important to consider accessibility because of the unique needs of every learner. Accessibility refers to the features and attributes of a product (in this case, instruction) that communicate its ability to be used or understood. Essentially, web accessibility refers to a set of standards that guide the design of online websites, tools, and applications to ensure the ease of use for all users. In the technical sense, accessibility addresses auditory, visual, cognitive, and physical aspects of technology.

Learning Accommodations

In addition to concerns related to the **digital divide**, that is, the uneven distribution in the access to materials, and/or technology and connectivity issues (discussed in more detail in Chapter 6), there is a need to address access with regard to proper accommodations for those with **disabilities**, including learning disabilities, mobility impairments, ADD or ADHD, and health and medical-related impairments. Online education is a viable option for individuals with disabilities, and in addition to the convenience, online learning offers benefits in terms of flexibility that may not be as readily available in a face-to-face delivery format. As such, it is imperative to comply with the Rehabilitation Act of 1973, the Americans with Disabilities Act of 1990 (ADA), the Americans with Disabilities Act Amendments Act of 2008 (ADAAA), and Section 508 of the Rehabilitation Act, as amended in 1998, so that learners with disabilities have "equal access" to online course content. Invisible disabilities, also known as "hidden disabilities" or "nonvisible disabilities," are those that are not immediately apparent or obvious. Typically, these are chronic illnesses and conditions that can significantly impair the normal activities of daily living. Good practice means ensuring that a statement about accessibility is clearly included in all syllabi and also on institutional websites. Refer to Appendix B for a list of *Accessibility Resources*.

Each individual has preferred modes of receiving and processing information or demonstrating knowledge and abilities. It is therefore important to provide for flexibility in the ways that information is presented, in the ways that learners can become engaged, and respond or demonstrate their knowledge and skills. To achieve this, we need to proactively build learning experiences that recognize and acknowledge developmental diversity; that is, the different ways that individuals think and learn. Attending carefully to developmental diversity—like all forms of diversity—is one important way that we can create an environment of support and challenge that can reach and inspire learners with different needs, learning preferences, and ways of knowing; thereby, supporting learners' growth accordingly. It is critical, therefore, to minimize the barriers in instruction by providing appropriate accommodations, and *maintaining high achievement expectations for all learners*. When we provide content that allows for multiple means of representation, then our online courses will be accessible to a majority of learners with diverse abilities. Designing for accessibility means anticipating needs based on trends and institutional data, and creating a course where content is accessible to the greatest number of diverse learners.

When designing a course, be cognizant of building in accessibility right from the start. Make sure that all content is accessible; that it supports all learners; and that it provides multiple opportunities for engagement, interaction, and challenge. As an instructor, you are required to recognize which tools and formats (document and media) support accessibility and which do not. You will need to know how to make the course materials accessible by way of (1) making a clear path for success in the way you present materials; (2) integrating useful signposts and tips such as embedded hyperlinks; (3) presenting content in ways that do not require too much scrolling or user navigation; and (4) using media thoughtfully (synchronous and asynchronous). In addition, be sure to provide accessibility statements and contact information for online tools. Finally, always ask your learners if they have particular needs concerning access and accommodations. Because of the change in learning contexts, some learners may have accommodations that they had not previously requested, and some may need added modifications.

Universal Design for Learning Framework

Upon the creation of the ADA, there was an increased awareness of the challenges faced by those with disabilities, which resulted in a greater understanding of the need for accommodations. This increased awareness resulted in the concept of **Universal Design for Learning (UDL)**. The focus on designing architectural features of the physical world that could be accessible to all users, regardless of ability and without accommodation, embodied the UDL framework. A key idea inherent in the UDL framework is that variability in how learners emotionally engage with curriculum is a strength to be leveraged in course design and instruction. Beginning in the 1950s in the United States, UDL was considered as a means for removing barriers in the physical space, and it was only in the 1970s that a shift occurred from removing barriers for persons with disabilities to that of integration of all people in all environments. This shift aligned with legislation such as the Architectural Barriers Act of 1968, The Rehabilitation Act of 1973 and Section 504, and the Education of the Handicapped Act of 1975. The UDL framework indicates that supports will benefit all learners, not just those with disabilities (CAST, 2018). While the framework considers the variabilities of all learners, the COVID-19 pandemic exposed, and indeed highlighted, vast inequalities in higher education for both institutions and learners, with many learners from minority or underrepresented groups dropping classes during the online rush because they did not have reliable Internet or a personal computer or tablet. To leverage learner engagement, instructors and curriculum designers need to consider the variability of their learners (that is, culture, background knowledge, personal learning preferences, and so on) and how online environments can create both barriers and opportunities for engagement.

UDL incorporates three core guidelines: (1) provide multiple means of representation (the *what* of learning); (2) provide multiple means of action and expression (the *how* of learning); and (3) provide multiple means for engagement (the *why* of learning). The key phrase here is *multiple means*. UDL consists of seven principles to be used to develop products and environments in a manner that enable them to be used by all persons regardless of ability. These principles include equitable use, flexibility in use, simple and intuitive use, perceptible information, tolerance for error, low physical effort, and size and space for approach and use (Center for Excellence in Universal Design, 1997). Table 3.3, obtained from the Center for Excellence in Universal Design, provides the definitions of the seven principles that provide practitioners with guidance as they design learning environments that are accessible to all.

Online education can be a promising alternative for learners with physical and/or sensory disabilities, some of whom would struggle to navigate a traditional campus. Yet, even the most accessible online programs can still pose challenges for some learners, and you may need to work with your institution's instructional designer and disability-resources specialists to ensure accessibility. Table 3.4 includes tips for creating accessible courses and demonstrating due diligence with regard to accessibility and inclusivity. You will also be required to meet all ADA compliance regulations as you redesign any of your courses.

Guidelines for Ensuring Inclusivity

Following are some important points to keep in mind as you consider addressing and ensuring accessibility for all learners when developing course materials:

Create Course Content

Table 3.3. Principles of Universal Design

Principle	Definition
Equitable use	The design is useful and marketable to people with diverse abilities.
Flexibility in use	The design accommodates a wide range of individual preferences and abilities.
Simple and intuitive use	Use of the design is easy to understand, regardless of the user's experience, knowledge, language skills, or current concentration level.
Perceptible information	The design communicates necessary information effectively to the user, regardless of ambient conditions or the user's sensory abilities.
Tolerance for error	The design minimizes hazards and the adverse consequences of accidental or unintended actions.
Low physical effort	The design can be used efficiently, comfortably, and with a minimum of fatigue.
Size and space for approach and use	Appropriate size and space are provided for approach, reach, manipulation, and use regardless of the user's body size, posture, or mobility.

Table 3.4. Strategies for Ensuring Accessible Course Materials

Documents

- To begin, the course syllabus is a document that should include an accessibility statement that outlines ADA procedures.
- All text in a course should be searchable, which allows learners to search for words or phrases within a document.
- Ensure materials are accessible and mobile-friendly. PDFs are more accessible for those with disabilities who may rely on screen readers, and PDFs adapt to different devices and cellphones more readily than other formats.
- Test that all PDFs that you find online are tagged and searchable. If a PDF document is not searchable, an accompanying plain text version should be available.
- When linking documents within a course, the label of the link should have the file extension type at the end (.doc or .docx for a Word document, .ppt for PowerPoint, .xlsx or .xltx for Excel, etc.).
- Run the accessibility checker as you create Word Docs, PDFs, and/or PowerPoints and correct the errors and warnings as you work.
- Tables and charts need to have identifying headers and labels as well as summaries.

(continued)

Table 3.4. (continued)

Text Design

- When designing informational material, a sans serif font is easiest to read. Times New Roman and Palatino have additional strokes and should be avoided. Examples of acceptable sans serif fonts are Arial and Helvetica. Once a sans serif font is selected, use the same font throughout the course. Minimizing helps all learners stay focused.
- Improve visibility by making use of a dark-colored font on a light-colored background, known as "high contrast." The best option for readability is a black font with a white background.
- If you wish to use color, avoid using extremely bright background colors, such as red. Avoid red/green or yellow/blue combinations as contrasting colors because those with colorblindness are unable to differentiate the text from the background.
- Text formatting should follow the "less is more" rule. Use bolds and italics sparingly, only to emphasize extreme items.
- Avoid using underlining and bold to make a point.

Hyperlinks and URLs

- The only text to be underlined is text that is hyperlinked to meet ADA compliance.
- Ensure that all hyperlinks are text within a sentence to foster readability.

Images and Graphics

- Images and graphics can be a powerful addition to any course because these can exemplify content; however, these should be relevant to the content, visibly easy to view, and presented in high resolution.
- Avoid animated or blinking images.
- Use the formatting tools in your text editor, such as heads and subheads, to enable screen readers (a tool to help visually impaired learners).
- Pictures, graphs, and formulas need alternate text descriptions (for screen readers). Alt text is a word or phrase that describes the image or graphic. Most LMSs have an alt tag option when adding images or graphics.

Audio and Video

- Ensure clear audio and video content. Clear audio requires minimal background noises, clear word pronunciation, and consistent volume. Clear video means minimal movement to avoid blurred refocusing and high resolution in rendering.
- Both audio and video files require written transcription (subtitles), also known as closed captioning for videos.
- Provide transcriptions for all audio and video material. This benefits not only those who are deaf or hard-of-hearing, but also those who are participating in classes in noisy locations, those who do not have headphones, and those who might have English as their second language.
- Make sure that audio or video clips are 3–10 minutes in length. With longer content, create short, segmented videos, each ranging from 3–10 minutes in length.
- A final requirement regarding audio and video accessibility is to make use of a universal audio or video player (MP3 audio or MP4 video file formats).

Create Course Content

Accuracy and Relevance.
- Make sure that equity content is accurate and that it is also relevant with regard to the CLOs.
- Your pedagogy and teaching approach—not the convenience of technology—should drive all of your content choices!

First Impressions Count!
- Create a positive first impression with your home page by ensuring that it is easy to navigate and that it contains all the major course components.
- Learners benefit from a clear content focus, which includes appropriate titles for each week, module, or lesson.

Provide Easy Access to Resources.
- Establish clear academic, administrative, and communication policies for instruction. Include an accommodation statement in your syllabus or curriculum.
- Be sure to provide easy access links to libraries, learning resources, and appropriate social media, with both synchronous and asynchronous options. These options should be available and accessible on mobile devices as well.

Consider the Necessity of Video Material.
- Consider whether video is necessary in all cases, given how streaming videos require strong Internet connections (which is not always the case for all learners), and also how this can deplete data plans and memory on learners' (and your) devices.
- It is recommended that lessons are recorded so these can be downloaded and viewed by learners at their convenience.

Utilize Milestone Planning.
- Use a milestone plan or work schedule that clearly outlines what is going to happen and when.
- A visual flowchart can support the structure of your course design. This can include weekly previews and summaries to build bridges between chunks of content. These connections not only illustrate the course structure but also allow learners to see and understand the progression of the topic that they are studying.
- Make sure that the course flowchart includes the following sections: an overview to introduce the whole course, a preview for each unit and week, a summary of how a completed week or module relates to the upcoming week or module, a summary at the end of a unit, and its connection to the upcoming unit.

Simplify Navigation.
- Navigation processes and tools should be intuitive and consistent across courses.
- Explicit organization and clearly labeled segments clarify expectations and requirements, reduce learners' anxiety, and facilitate ongoing motivation and learning. Remember that clarity of structure is a hallmark of outstanding online course design.
- Intuitive navigation means using consistent design features and protocols. That is, instructions, materials, and assignments should be found in a consistent, predictable place in every course.

Make Changes as Needed!
- Finally, be sure to include a feedback or learner-review component throughout the course and/or at the end of the course. This important step allows you to make any needed changes or revisions accordingly. Being willing and able to obtain constructive feedback from your learners. Actually utilizing this feedback will enable you to continue to offer a worthy learning experience that is beneficial for all.
- Seeking feedback also ensures that your learners see themselves as partners in the learning process and that their perspectives and input are heard, valued, and respected.

CHAPTER SUMMARY AND SYNTHESIS

Following development of CLOs (Chapter 1), you moved to planning for assessment (Chapter 2). Chapter 3 focused on the creation of course content that will foster deep (as opposed to surface) learning by helping learners engage with the material at the level that is most meaningful to them. Designing and developing an online course can be a daunting task for instructors. However, thinking about some strategies on the front end can help make the **course development** process less overwhelming, more enjoyable, and more successful. As you develop your content and work toward sustained learner engagement, you were constantly reminded in this chapter of two key considerations: diverse content options and diverse communication options. When it comes to technology, take a gradual approach. Sometimes, when we learn about all the tools available, in our zeal to create the best possible learning experience, we run the risk of trying to do too much. Avoid jumping headfirst into all the bells and whistles, giving yourself time to grow incrementally. As you gain more experience, you will learn which tools best fit with your teaching style and pedagogical strategy. Finally, it is critical to ensure that all content is accessible; that it supports all learners and ensures equity and inclusion; and that it provides multiple opportunities for engagement, interaction, and deep learning. Accessibility is often a challenge in online courses, but a number of guidelines and tools have been developed to address this.

To foster reflection about what counts as a meaningful learning experience and significant (deep) learning, ask yourself the following essential questions that are related to the expectations for the design and development of course content and materials as discussed. Remember that as a reflective practitioner, you want to make sure that you are carefully considering all of the factors, strategies, and practices that can help to foster and promote learner engagement and empowerment, and thereby enhance performance outcomes. By examining your practice, you will be in a better position to make any needed changes or revisions.

CHAPTER 3: REFLECTION CHECKPOINT

Create Course Content

- How will I organize the course to maximize learning?

    TIP: The overall course structure and content should be clearly aligned with the needs of your learners. Think about what adult learners seek in the learning experience. What are their needs and interests?

- How and in what ways will I remain inclusive in order to meet the needs of all my learners?

    TIP: Materials should be multimodal, thoughtfully designed, and appropriately scaffolded.

- How can I be sure that I am ensuring relevance and value?

    TIP: Think about how you are presenting your material and the opportunity you are providing to connect with your learners and maintain their engagement and satisfaction. If learners do not see their work and activities as worthwhile, what could you do differently to change their viewpoint? Are you ensuring transparency?

- What can I do to create a strong sense of belonging and community through the course material?

    TIP: Think about all the resources and services that are available. Are you connecting learners to resources that will support them? Are you making an effort to connect learners to each other, pointing them in the appropriate direction? Are you explaining to learners the value and benefits of a learning community?

- How will I support and ensure accessibility for all of my learners?

    TIP: Entering and navigating the course should be easy and accessible to all learners. Navigational tools (syllabus, schedule, FAQs, LMS instruction, and general course guidelines) provide strategic direction for learners. Accommodations must be made for learners with disabilities to be able to appropriately respond or demonstrate their knowledge and skills.

- How will I support communication and interaction throughout my course?

    TIP: Choices regarding the incorporation of technology and multiple relevant forms of media should be guided by learning outcomes, assessments, teaching methodologies, technical considerations, LMS capabilities, and learner access.

- How can I ensure that my learners apply in the future what they learn from the course?

    TIP: You want to facilitate deep (as opposed to surface) learning to ensure transfer of learning to future tasks. Strive for learners' ongoing and sustained improvement, not just in the course you teach, but in their everyday lives. Deep understanding and the ability to actually apply knowledge is the ultimate objective.

Part I Synthesis

Up to this point, you undoubtedly realize that providing opportunities to develop and become self-directed and empowered goes a long way in terms of creating meaningful learning experiences. To maximize engagement, the course content must be multimodal, extending beyond just plain text to include audio and video components. As you develop content and work toward sustained engagement, remember the two key considerations: (1) diverse content options and (2) diverse communication options. Diverse content options are important because we want learners to be able to engage with content in ways that are meaningful to them. Diverse communication options are important because we want learners and instructors to be able to communicate in the modalities they prefer, and can best manage and use. Working to create engaging content for all learners will include thoughtful supports and resources.

Make sure that your online class will be an inviting and pleasant space! Ask yourself: Would you enjoy going into your online classroom? Does the space have good energy? Would you feel a sense of belonging there? Would you feel stimulated there? Will you look forward to communicating with your online learners in the same way that you look forward to interacting with learners in a physical classroom? Answering these questions will shed light on important design issues. The chart that follows, Table I.1, summarizes all of the key elements involved in developing rich learning content that will both engage and empower your learners. This extensive "cheat sheet" is an opportunity to be alert, check in, and remind yourself to make sure that all of these key elements are addressed.

Table I.1. Designing and Developing Instructional Materials: A Comprehensive Action Checklist

		DEVELOP COURSE LEARNING OUTCOMES	
	Action Task	Rationale	Action Steps!
1	Start with the end in mind: Establish CLOs (see Figure 1.1 and Appendix A).	The success of a course is determined by how well it is planned and built prior to its delivery. Determining strong and viable CLOs will shape and drive course design. CLOs, the objectives of the learning experience, represent the top-priority abilities for your learners to accomplish and master. Once you have developed CLOs, think about how learners will master those objectives.	• Align CLOs with your vision for the course and what you want your learners to accomplish and master. • Clearly identify what learners should be able to do or perform to demonstrate their learning. • Make use of the action verb categories of Bloom's Taxonomy to develop the CLO statements.
2	Ensure that CLOs are sequenced (see Tables 1.1 and 1.2).	To make course design an integrated process, outcomes later in the program should build on earlier outcomes. Thoughtfully creating CLOs ensures that the course content contributes to a true learning trajectory. CLOs are not viewed in isolation; they are connected to program competencies, general education outcomes, and professional accreditation standards.	• Be knowledgeable of the broader program track, including courses that both precede and succeed your course. • Make sure that CLOs are aligned with ILOs and PLOs. • Apply outcomes mapping to ensure that the activities or assignments will align with and support all of the CLOs.
3	Ensure that CLOs are specific and measurable.	What learners should know or be able to do must be measurable. If CLOs cannot be measured, there is no way to tell whether and to what extent learners have achieved what the course sets out to accomplish.	• Ensure that CLOs are realistic so that they can actually be measured. • State CLOs directly and clearly so that they are not confusing, vague, ambiguous, or irrelevant.

(continued)

Table I.1. (continued)

		PLAN FOR ASSESSMENT OF LEARNING	
	Action Task	Rationale	Action Steps!
1	Establish a detailed assessment plan (see Table 2.1).	Central to any assessment process is improving learning and the implementation of continuous improvement. The results of assessments are used to make informed decisions regarding the improvement of learning, teaching, and for planning ahead. Assessments are derived directly from the CLOs. Consider outcomes assessments prior to designing your content and activities.	• Create tentative assessments to measure the CLOs to determine appropriateness and relevance. • Plan to consistently and frequently monitor progress throughout the course by using different types of assessments (formative and summative). • Ensure that assessment is culture fair and unbiased so as not to favor any one culture more than another. • Be flexible as you refine your assessment plan and adjust as needed.
2	Use performance rubrics (see Tables 2.2–2.4).	Performance rubrics are commonly used as a way of classifying and categorizing identified criteria for successful completion of an assignment or task and establishing levels for meeting these criteria. Rubrics help learners understand the level of learning expected, make grading transparent and fair, and enable them to self-evaluate their progress and identify areas for revision and improvement. A rubric becomes a working guide for both learners and instructors. Ensuring that all assessment criteria are equitable and clear means that learners should never have to wonder why they received a particular grade.	• Use rubrics as a scoring or grading guide, to provide formative and summative feedback to support and guide ongoing learning efforts. • Provide access to rubrics before the assignment begins so learners can understand the criteria by which their work will be judged, and prepare accordingly in order to improve quality. • Advise learners to use the rubric in guiding their completion of assignments.

(*continued*)

Table I.1. (continued)

	Action Task	Rationale	Action Steps!
3	Ensure that all assessments are workable and meaningful.	Preparing workable and meaningful assessment tools will ensure that CLOs are being appropriately addressed. Assessments should not only occur at the end of a learning experience (summative assessment) but also during the learning experience itself (formative assessment). No assessment should be a mystery to learners regarding what is expected. Thoughtfully applied multimodal assessments will offer learners the opportunity to engage with the content in meaningful ways.	• Teach to the test or activity by providing the most appropriate and valid assessment for each activity. • Prior to administering any assessments, "test drive" these by seeking feedback. • Include a combination of formative and summative assessments. • Use a mix of assessment measures, including exams, research papers, essays, presentations, and surveys. • If you are making use of proctored assessments, coordinate with your institution's or organization's protocol. • All learners must be provided with clear directions and requirements.

DEVELOP COURSE CONTENT

	Action Task	Rationale	Action Steps!
1	Ensure alignment and coherence among CLOs and course content (see Table 2.5).	All elements of a course must be aligned with and reflect the CLOs. It is critical to take into consideration what types of assignments (activities or tasks) will measure the knowledge, skills and attitudes associated with the relevant learning outcome; and what types of assignments will allow learners to practice the specified knowledge or skills and thereby have an opportunity to develop proficiency prior to the assessment.	• Create assignments (tasks and activities) that will support and assess learning outcomes. • Check that each assignment clearly aligns with at least one CLO.

(continued)

Table I.1. (continued)

2	Foster deep (as opposed to surface) learning by helping your learners engage with the material at the level that is most meaningful to them.	When learners can identify with activities and relate to assignments in terms of their real-world experiences, we create an environment for deep learning to occur. Reflective exercises provide an opportunity for learners to demonstrate and question their understanding of the subject and think more deeply about the impact or implications of a learning experience. Moreover, the opportunity to share reflections with others leads to enhanced understanding and ongoing critical thinking and dialogue.	• Be aware of adult learning principles. • Avoid cognitive overload by scaffolding. • Make sure that learners are able to intuitively interact with content (Read it/See it/Study it/Do it/Discuss it). • Build in reflective opportunities as a means of engaging critically and analytically with the course content. • Build in collaborative learning opportunities for learners to work together, think critically, and support each other's understanding.
3	Source meaningful and appropriate content.	Content must have relevance and value since adults have a need to know why they should learn, and are motivated to put time and energy into learning if they know the benefits and applicability thereof. Poor performance is inevitable when learners don't "buy in" to a required assignment (activity, or task). Course content that addresses developmental diversity, and supports learners' growth, will be especially effective.	• Plan for signature assignment first (with the possibility of later revision). • Next, compose weekly activities to support learners in demonstrating incremental proficiency. • Remain flexible so you do not overlook individual differences. • Be aware of ways that you like to present information as you may overuse this.
4	Apply the multimedia principle (see Table 3.1).	Learners grasp and understand new material better and can remember it longer when the presentation is multimodal. According to the multimedia principle, to enhance learning and maximize engagement, online education should not be solely text-based. Most LMSs have ways to integrate	• Be prepared to move beyond written communication to include audio and video modes of teaching. • Incorporate audio and visual materials by rethinking or reimagining face-to-face teaching materials and transforming these into content that

(continued)

Table I.1. (continued)

		multiple teaching tools (asynchronous and synchronous), and these can be used singly and in combination.	makes the best use of the online medium as its own unique communication forum.
5	Keep the focus on learning and engagement.	It is critically important not to get bogged down with the technology itself, but to really think about pedagogy and engagement. These are the central tenets to effective online learning. Don't confuse technology with teaching. The technology is essentially a means to an end!	• Using too much technology or using technology inappropriately can be overwhelming and stressful for both learners and instructors. • Have a clear purpose for why you are using a given technology, with the goal of facilitating engagement and learning.
6	Ensure accessibility (see Tables 3.2–3.4 and Appendix B).	Online instructors take a great deal of time creating online courses that foster academic growth, but are often unaware of strategies to adapt their courses to meet ADA compliance, which states that all individuals should have equal access. ADA requires that all online courses be fully compliant. Employing the concept of UDL ensures accessibility right from the start.	• Ensure that a statement about accessibility is included in the syllabus and on institutional websites. • Build in accessibility right from the start, based on the principles of UDL. • Ensure that all content supports all learners and provides multiple opportunities for engagement. • Avoid confusion by giving explicit and clear direction throughout the syllabus. • Be aware of which tools and formats (document and media) support accessibility, and which do not. • If unsure, seek assistance regarding how to make materials accessible, including presentation, integration of signposts and tips, and thoughtful use of media.

Part II

TRAVELING THE EDUCATIONAL JOURNEY: DELIVER ENGAGING AND EMPOWERING LEARNING EXPERIENCES

THE ENGAGEMENT CYCLE

Instructors face many new and often unexpected challenges when delivering online instruction. Whether one is teaching in fully online or hybrid environments, instructors must master the tools of technology and serve as both a content specialist and facilitator of learning. Moreover, instructors will typically work with an increasingly diverse population of learners who live and work in a complex, global community. This second part of this book covers the ways in which instructors can offer learning experiences that support and enhance learner engagement in the online learning environment. This is important because research consistently supports a clear link between instructor engagement, learner engagement, and actual learning. The curated set of *Annotated Research Resources* included in Appendix M are provided as an additional resource to aid you with your practice. These studies shed light on the concept of engagement, explaining the key role that engagement plays in the online learning environment, and the ways in which different researchers have addressed this concept. Appendix N is a selection of curated *Online Support Resources* for those interested in accessing additional online support and services.

By welcoming, onboarding, and supporting your learners, building working relationships, and teaching through those relationships, you can provide an engaging online learning experience. In the upcoming chapters, you will explore effective practices for promoting engagement and learning by distilling key high-impact practices. These practices become the "how-to" guidelines and strategies for delivering engaging and empowering learning experiences, and multiple real-world examples are provided. Reflection checkpoints are built into each of the chapters that also serve as a summary of the knowledge gained in each chapter for purposes of facilitating practical application.

Figure II.1. The Multimodal Engagement Cycle

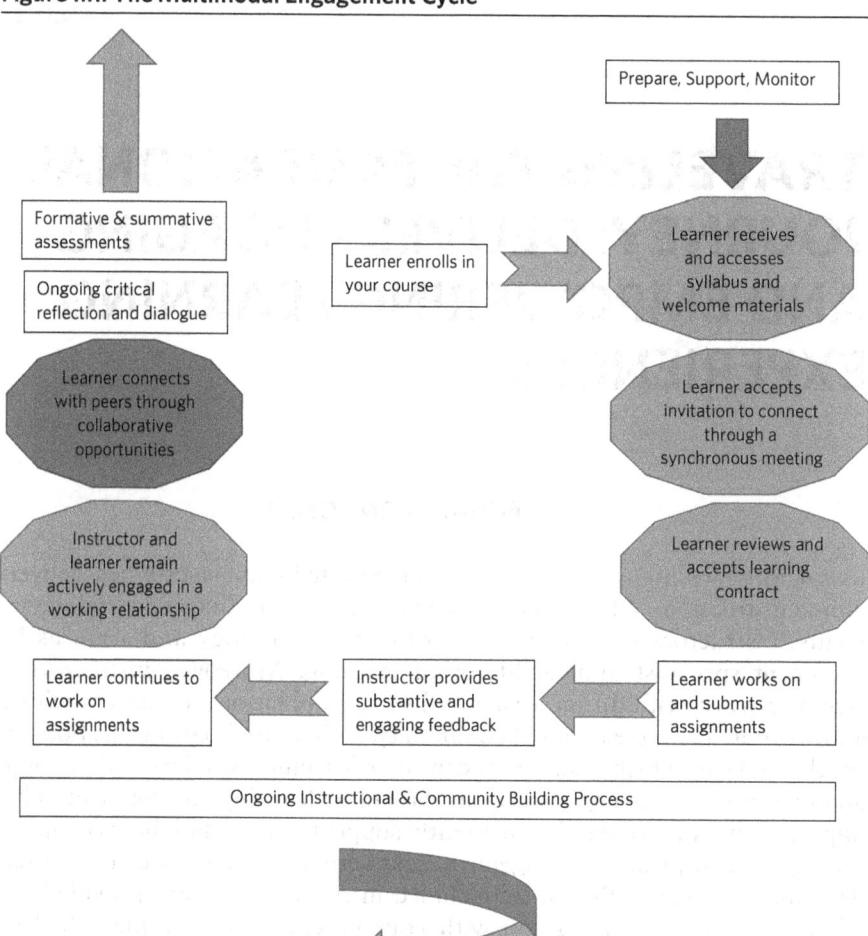

Figure II.1, *The Multimodal Engagement Cycle*, is based on the notion of teaching presence, a key component of the Community of Inquiry model developed by Garrison et al. (1999, 2001, 2003), related to instructors developing collaborative working relationships and interacting with learners to bridge transactional distance and generate greater engagement. As you work your way through this book, the broader ongoing instructional process in the online environment will become clearer to you, including the strategies that you can use to ensure ongoing engagement. Table II.1, *Engaging and Empowering Your Learners: A Comprehensive Action Checklist*, which is included at the end of Part II, summarizes the multiple touchpoints of learner engagement that you can strive for, and is a further opportunity to check in and remind yourself to address these touchpoints.

INSTRUCTOR VOICES

"Good online instructors go that extra distance to be "high touch" instructors. They truly "teach students" rather than 'teach content.' Get to know your students and allow them to get to know you, thereby establishing trusting relationships."

"We need to reach multiple modalities of our learners in the online environment . . . by providing content through a variety of modalities, the chances that your student will engage are much higher, and if we can match what types of content fit their modality of preference, we can increase retention and investment in the course."

"The foundational piece of it all is presence. It's really difficult to engage if we're not present. And while not everyone will want to meet with us weekly or even at all, if we're going to make any sort of positive impact we need to be present in our classrooms just like we would be if we were standing in front of a lecture hall full of students."

"I love to meet with learners where we can see each other, where questions are asked and answered in a conversation, where I can see if more explanation is needed, and where I can provide helpful tips and sources. The synchronous communication helps build relationships and increases engagement."

"Communication is crucial. I like to touch base as soon as possible so I can learn something about my student's goals and interests. It's so helpful when students share with me a little about their previous experiences so I can target my feedback to meet their needs."

"Provide appropriate feedback and additional resources, even when the assignment is well done. Students need to know when they are on target and when more work is needed to demonstrate an understanding of a concept, idea, or principle."

"Be flexible to the way students respond to assignments. It does not work to treat adult learners like traditional college students; adult learners have years of work experience, so they want to be respected for the knowledge and skill they have gained."

CHAPTER 4

Onboard and Welcome Learners

Educational institutions are charged with the responsibility of graduating all learners and making sure that they are equipped with the essential knowledge and skills necessary for success in their chosen fields. As an instructor, you are responsible to do your best to retain as many of your learners as possible. This is important for any institution that you represent. Your institution may have a specific expected retention rate, and there is often some pressure to make sure that you meet or exceed that expectation in order to remain a top performer. Whether you are an experienced instructor or new to online teaching, meeting this expectation may require developing or revising your strategies to ensure that all of your learners remain engaged. Research in the field of online education consistently supports a clear link between instructor engagement, learner engagement, and actual learning. Learner engagement ensures ongoing motivation and persistence. In essence, instructor engagement implies the idea of being "present" for your learners.

LEARNER ENGAGEMENT AND TEACHING PRESENCE

Transactional distance theory, developed by Moore (1997), explains the perceived "psychological and communication space" in the online learning environment, often causing learners to participate minimally, disengage, or completely withdraw. To mitigate the effects of transactional distance, it is incumbent upon instructors to intentionally and thoughtfully implement strategies that will keep learners motivated and actively engaged. As illustrated in Table 4.1, the notion of engagement can be broadly conceived as a metaconstruct that includes three interrelated concepts: behavioral, affective, and cognitive engagement (Fredricks, Blumenfeld, & Paris, 2004). *Behavioral engagement* refers to learner participation in a course, such as doing assignments. *Affective engagement* refers to learners' feelings toward the instructor, classmates, learning, and the course itself. *Cognitive engagement* refers to learners' thinking and understanding of the subject content. Engagement is driven essentially by motivation. One of the most frequently used theories

Table 4.1. Engagement Defined

Characteristics of an Engaged Learner	Characteristics of an Engaging Instructor
Pays attention	Gain learners' attention
	RATIONALE:
	Attention is a key ingredient of learning, but with so many distractions, it can be more difficult for learners to pay attention in an online environment.
Actively participates in learning	Make the course content relevant
	RATIONALE:
	Adult learners bring a wide range of knowledge and experiences that effects how they process new information and learn new skills. Building on their strengths will help connect learners with real-life examples, which improves their chances of retaining and successfully applying new information.
Interested and curious (rather than bored, anxious, or confused)	Foster inclusion and positive emotions
	RATIONALE:
	Reducing anxiety and negative emotions increases engagement through building positive teaching relationships, open dialogue, and ongoing clear communication.
Seeks understanding and useful knowledge	Provide cognitive and intellectual support
	RATIONALE:
	The goal of any learning experience is to promote deep learning by promoting learners' understanding throughout a course, repeating or restating information in new ways as needed, and encouraging learners to ask their own questions related to applying the information practically, in the real world.
Motivated to persist and succeed	Provide ongoing support and encouragement
	RATIONALE:
	Ongoing availability and support throughout a course helps keep learners engaged and stimulated, and ensures that they are encouraged to continue working toward their goals in order to achieve success.

to explain human motivation is self-determination theory (Niemiec et al., 2006), which posits that individuals possess three fundamental psychological needs that move them to act or not to act—the needs for autonomy (i.e., freedom to choose), relatedness (i.e., feeling of being connected to other people), and competence (i.e., sense of mastery) (Deci & Ryan, 1985).

Learner engagement is key to successful teaching and learning, irrespective of the content and format of the content delivery mechanism. However, engaging learners presents a particular challenge in online learning environments (Kahn et al., 2017). A central aspect to promoting learner engagement in the online environment, and in turn ongoing success, is the sense of presence. Presence is essentially a state of being or "nearness" in space or time; a state or condition of "now." Moreover, how online educators present themselves to their learners, or how they frame themselves, impacts positive behaviors on the course and opens the lines of communication even further. Many of us have experienced a teacher's presence; we have benefited from teachers who have attended to us, and given us what we need and when we have needed it. From a learner's point of view, this moment is one of recognition and of feeling seen and understood. As pointed out by Rodgers (2020), having a "presence" and being "present" are not the same thing. Having a presence means that your learner's attention is drawn to you. Being present means that you attend to and are attuned to the learner and their learning.

The concept of presence is a key component of the Community of Inquiry model (Garrison et al., 1999, 2001, 2003), which relates to instructors developing collaborative working relationships and interacting with their learners in order to bridge transactional distance and generate greater engagement and success. As described in this chapter and also illustrated in Figure 4.1, there are four elements of presence that pertain to online learning environments, all of which are interconnected and interactive. These four elements are defined as follows:

Social Presence

This relates to the activity of participants in establishing a personal connection to the group or learning community, thereby presenting themselves as "real" people (that is, their authentic personality or character), through the medium of communication being used. There are three forms of **social presence**: affective (which involves the expression of feelings, emotions, and mood); interactive (communicating, attending, understanding, and considering the responses of others); and cohesive (responses that serve to build and sustain a sense of connection to others, and an impetus to commit to shared goals and objectives). Social presence refers to collaboration between learners and instructors, as well as collaboration that takes place among learners. Providing opportunities for social interaction through group activities

Figure 4.1. Community of Inquiry Model

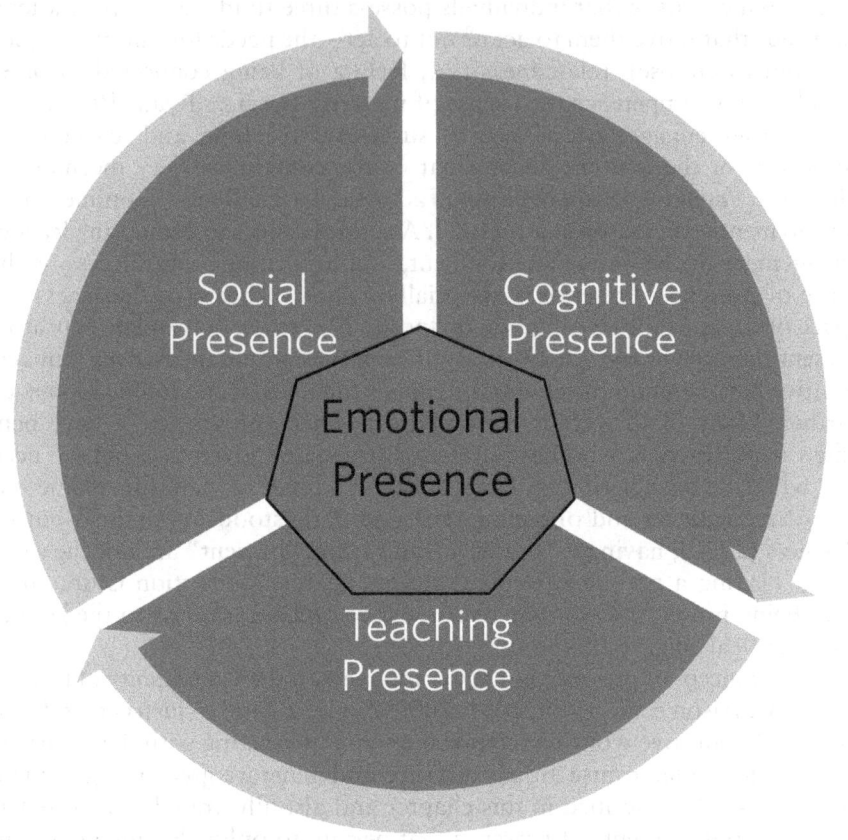

Adapted from Garrison et al. (1999)

and discussions may motivate learners, contribute to overcoming the sense of isolation, and increase the sense of community.

Cognitive Presence

This relates to instructors and learners being able to construct and confirm meaning through sustained discourse (dialogue and critical reflection) within a community of inquiry. **Cognitive presence** can be demonstrated by introducing and sharing new knowledge. The value of the discourse will depend upon the clarity, accuracy, relevance, and applicability of the knowledge being shared. Cognitive presence begins with the design of a course and includes providing choices of topics and options with regard to presentation so that adult learners may draw from their own personal and professional life experiences to complete the task, activity, or project.

Teaching Presence

This relates to instructors actively interacting with their learners, and establishing and maintaining collaborative and supportive working relationships. The implication is that instructors remain visible, approachable, and available to assist learners achieve their goals. As explained by Bloomberg and Grantham (2018), "teaching presence relates to the instructor actively interacting with learners, and establishing and maintaining a collaborative and supportive working relationship. Through shared interaction, the instructor serves as a model for the communication, and a learning facilitator" (p. 4). When learners enroll in online classes, they are often apprehensive. Research shows that presence in the online education context includes *learners' perceptions* of instructor involvement as a central factor, leading to greater satisfaction, higher levels of engagement, and a greater likelihood of course completion (Cole et al. 2017; Cole et al. 2019; Martin & Bollinger, 2018). Within the Community of Inquiry model, teaching presence overlaps with and encompasses both social presence and cognitive presence, and is a significant determinant of learner satisfaction and academic success. The clearer the communication, the more responsive the methods of interaction, and the frequency of feedback and communication serve to enhance teaching presence.

Emotional Presence

The Community of Inquiry model views "community" as something that emerges in support of online learning, which is based on the relationship between three elements: social presence, teaching presence, and cognitive presence. The central organizing element is teaching presence, that is, the design, facilitation, and, most importantly, the direction of cognitive and social processes for the realization of personally meaningful and educationally worthwhile learning outcomes. Cleveland-Innes and Campbell (2012) called for the possibility of an expanded role for emotional presence, as a key component of online learning, and which underpins the broader online experience. They defined emotional presence as "the outward expression of emotion, affect, and feeling by individuals and among individuals in a community of inquiry, as they relate to and interact with the learning technology, course content, students, and the instructor" (p. 283). Emotional presence is an addition to the original, well-researched Community of Inquiry framework, becoming a key driver to online learning; particularly because how learners actually feel has an impact on their motivation, self-regulation, and academic success. As Cleveland-Innes and Campbell put it, "To engage in education innovation with no reference to emotion, and continue to assume learners are little more than dispassionate thinkers, would be to miss a fundamental influence on education" (p. 270). Research regarding the impact of emotion and cognition provides compelling evidence of the relationship between emotion and learning, and there has been a growing interest in the role of emotions in academic settings, especially in how emotions shape engagement, motivation, and learning (Brookfield, 2006; Lehman, 2006). Moreover, Brookfield (2006) and Dirkx (2008) have suggested that emotion is often mistaken as a deterrent that impedes effective teaching and learning, and that it is likely that emotion plays a far more dynamic role in learning than merely inhibiting rational thought and reason. An understanding of the nature of emotions in the learning context thus enhances the learning experience, and as an instructor, it is crucial that you set up the learning experience in ways that arouse learners' feelings of security, well-being, and self-confidence.

As an instructor, you should be showing your learners—in multiple ways and throughout the course—that you are present by remaining visible, available, and accessible. Online instructors typically set office hours, posting availability for telephonic contact, an email address for contact at any time, as well as creating opportunities to connect synchronously via the many tools that are available. The LMS is also a venue to post messages in an announcement section, on bulletin boards, or through group emails. Being fully tuned to the needs of each learner in addition to making your learners aware that you are available and accessible will let them know that you are committed to helping them learn and succeed. Presence means interacting with your learners socially and cognitively, communicating and displaying interest, concern, care and mentoring, as well as sharing something about yourself that makes you "human." This implies being physically, emotionally, and intellectually available for your learners. Being physically present means that your learners can contact you and create opportunities to communicate synchronously. Being emotionally present means that they can discuss the hardships from completing their work successfully. Being intellectually present means that they can ask you questions about topics that are relevant to their course content. Engaging early and often is essential to creating and maintaining a sense of teaching presence and building relationships. Relationships develop through welcoming, preparing learners, supporting them, and monitoring their progress and development. As a start, you need to be well prepared to teach!

PREPARE FOR THE ONLINE LEARNING EXPERIENCE

An initial point in the process is your being prepared. Engaging with your learners is mostly going to occur within the LMS that is used to manage their work and provide feedback on assignments. The ability to use technology to build teaching relationships and community and promote meaningful and ongoing engagement will depend on your familiarity with the LMS to make connecting with learners both easier and more effective. Some best practices with regard to the LMS include the following:

- **Use the technology:** We all can get nervous using systems that we are not completely comfortable with. The best recommendation is to jump right in and familiarize yourself with the available technology and apply it.
- **Be consistent:** Learners become frustrated and are likely to disengage if they have to find information or communicate with their instructor in different ways depending on the day or week.
- **Be compliant:** This goes hand in hand with being consistent. Follow institutional guidelines when using technology. Learners should feel some sense of continuity when moving between instructors.

Following are three tips for increasing engagement through the use of email communication:

1. **Use it!**
2. **Check it!**—Get in the habit of checking your email and voicemail regularly so that you are timely in your responses to learners. The promptness of your response will determine your learner's progress (or lack thereof). Remember that as the instructor, you also serve as a model for timeliness so you will want to set a good example!
3. **Set it!**—Make sure to set your out of office reply when out of the office. Include when you will be out of the office and when you expect to be back. Also include whether you will be able to access email and/or phone or not and how often you plan on doing so. Finally, you need to provide a contact person in the event that the learner has an emergency and needs resolution to an issue before you are available get back to them.

STRATEGIES FOR ONBOARDING ENGAGEMENT

Once a course starts, learners will need to understand the course requirements, instructor expectations, ways to connect, submission deadlines, as well as determine the pace, schedule, and amount of effort required for each assignment. Often, a first-time learner is left to interpret for themselves the setup of the course, the expectations of the instructor, and the technological aspects of the LMS. Those who are unclear of the requirements or who have difficulty in accessing and obtaining information regarding the course will most likely feel isolated and unmotivated. As an instructor, you will therefore need to set clear and explicit expectations, and provide clear details regarding course objectives and goals, syllabus requirements, class schedule, and course calendar for your learners to access and reference. Remember that the more explicit your instructions, the greater the possibility that learners will understand all necessary requirements and protocol. There are several ways in which you can engage with your learners even before they begin their course with you, the focus being on orientating and welcoming them, and these tasks constitute your first set of engagement steps.

Classroom Management Plan

A class management plan is a document that you create that clearly and specifically outlines the norms, routines, procedures, and schedules that will be used. Experienced instructors may have internalized their classroom management plan, but an online learning environment requires some rethinking about what will potentially work best for you and your learners since new technologies invite the need for new rules. Your classroom management plan should include routines such as when and how to submit work, submitting revisions to work, and accessing necessary resources. Additionally, it is important to be very explicit about expectations and norms regarding classroom interaction and communication, including engaging in discussions and working collaboratively with peers. Norms govern how individuals with a group interact, and delineate what will be considered acceptable or not. During the first weeks of a course, you may have to revisit and apply these norms to specific learning tasks and/or collaborative tools.

Overall, your plan should emphasize the importance of maintaining a respectful learning environment and a collaborative spirit. The plan should also clearly let your learners know that your role is to foster learning. Committing to a thoughtful and well-constructed plan is a proactive approach and serves to clarify expectations early on. This also becomes a tool to maintain accountability and to respond to issues that may arise. Once constructed, the plan can be posted to the LMS and also shared through your initial communication with learners.

Formal Welcome Letter

Proactively welcoming learners into a teaching relationship with you is the basis for their learning. Sending a **welcome letter** shows that you are excited to meet your learners and that you will be working with them and supporting them throughout their journeys. It is so much easier to engage with your learners when they feel that you are dedicated to their success. A *Sample Welcome Letter* is included in Appendix C. To ensure that learners will actually receive and access your letter, this should be sent ahead of the course start date so that they can review it ahead of time and, if necessary, approach you with any questions or concerns that they may have. In addition to sending the welcome letter, the same information should be posted within the LMS, so that it is easily visible, accessible, and retrievable at all times. Often the "Bio" or "About Me" page is a good way to welcome your learners and introduce yourself as a real person, rather than an abstract instructor.

Remember that because many learners enrolled in online programs have little to no initial experience taking online classes, they sometimes assume that the elements for success are the same as those needed for a traditional class setting. Providing an explanation of the ways to meet the expectations and honing the unique skills needed to be successful in an online course is therefore imperative. An informative, warm, and engaging welcome letter should be customized for each course that you teach, by including a brief description of the course, where it fits in the program that the learner is pursuing, and the overall goals for the course. Your welcome letter establishes overall course expectations, includes vital information, and most importantly, welcomes learners into a teaching relationship that is the basis for their learning. Therefore, take care to compose your letter carefully and thoughtfully, by including the following components:

- As a start, your learners will want to know a little about who is teaching them. Therefore, include a brief introduction; where you live, where you studied, and your professional fields of interest. You may also include your teaching and learning philosophy; your beliefs about how teaching and learning should occur, and your views concerning community and diversity. This makes you a "real person," and also serves to reinforce your classroom management plan.
- You want to orient and familiarize new learners at the beginning of a course and help prepare them. To do this, make sure to specify the course expectations and all relevant departmental and institutional policies and procedures, including academic integrity policies and academic writing policies. Refer learners to your classroom management plan where you have outlined the norms, procedures, and schedules that will be used in the course. You might also consider providing information (or even a brief tutorial link) regarding how to access and navigate the LMS, and how to retrieve necessary materials and graded work. Remember that your goal is to be as supportive and transparent as possible!
- When working in the online environment, we are situated with a global context, and your learners are located in all parts of the country, and indeed perhaps throughout the world. It is therefore critically important to be aware of where your learners are, and their time zones, so that you can make yourself available at

mutually suitable times. Rather than listing when you are not available, provide details for when you *are available*, and make sure that you commit to the information you provide. Clearly state your own location time zone in your welcome letter, because you cannot assume that learners are necessarily in the same time zone as you. For example: *I am in Pennsylvania (Eastern Time). My regular office hours are Wednesday from 6:00–7:00 P.M. (ET) and Thursday from 9:00–10:00 A.M. (ET). I understand that these days/times may not be convenient for everyone. Please feel free to email me to set up another suitable time to talk.*

- Your letter should clearly explain the process for scheduling meeting times and appointments. State how learners can set a time to meet with you synchronously; that is, in real time. You can access free scheduling tools such as Calendly or Picktime. These types of tools allow appointments to be made in a way that seamlessly syncs with learners' and instructors' calendars. You can also make use of Google Docs for learners to easily book and reserve a time to meet with you. In this way, you would create an openly editable Google Doc or any document that includes a table of available time slots for learners to sign up for appointments.

Informal "This is Me" Welcome Video

The welcome letter that is posted on a welcoming website within the LMS should be accompanied by a brief **welcome video** that displays you as a committed and caring instructor. Posting both the letter and a video ensures that you are engaging with your learners on two levels: print and audiovisual. A brief video introduction not only introduces you to your learners but is also an impactful way to begin to build a relationship with them and ensure that your learners perceive that you are present and available. In the online learning environment, it is typical for learners to feel alone and isolated, and so this video is a powerful tool to help "put a face to a name," making your learners feel more comfortable, connected, and supported. The objective of the video is to give your learners an opportunity to see you, hear your voice, and get to know you a little better. The video is also typically brief, spontaneous, and somewhat less formal than the welcome letter and should show you in the light of being a "real person" in addition to an instructor. Furthermore, the welcome video is a viable way to meet the needs of **auditory learners** to help maintain their interest as they navigate through the online learning platform. This short video should be created in such a way that shows the instructor speaking directly into the camera, speaking to one learner at a time. The tone should be conversational, as though your learner is literally sitting across from you as you are sharing the information with them. You might also consider having your learners create their own introductory videos that represent who they are, their career goals, and even a fun fact. Sharing their introductions with you, and perhaps even with their group or cohort, reinforces the sense of connection and community, and allows for community-building and networking opportunities.

Synchronous Introductory Meeting

Arranging an initial synchronous meeting allows you to introduce yourself to each of your learners individually before they embark on their course. It is very important that this meeting takes place in "real time" in order to begin establishing *a real connection* with each of your learners right from the start! As such, the meeting can take place by phone or through another real-time platform such as Skype, Zoom, Google Meet, Microsoft Teams, GoToMeeting, or other **face-time technologies** that you and your learner have access to, and with which you and they are familiar and comfortable. The purpose of this first meeting is to have a conversation about educational goals, life circumstances, and specific needs or accommodations regarding learning. Encourage your learners to regularly access the course site. Discuss the importance of completing assignments as required by the syllabus, and submitting assignments on time. Sending your welcome letter to each learner ahead of the course start date allows the learner to review it ahead of time and, if necessary, come prepared with any questions or concerns that you can address for them in person at this meeting. Be aware that some learners will look forward to meeting with you during the first week, while others may not be interested, willing, or able to meet. Do your best to connect with all those who respond positively to your invitation and remind those that are not as responsive that you are here to help them throughout the course and will be available to connect when they need you. Following are some additional suggestions for making your first conversations with learners impactful and engaging.

__Focus on establishing a relationship.__ Welcome each learner to your course, and thank them for taking the time to meet with you. Get to know your learner's motivations and interests, concerns, and self-assessment of their strengths and weaknesses. Be goal oriented in your approach by asking questions about their educational and professional aspirations. Talk about how your course fits into their broader career picture, and explain how the course material will be of value to them as they move forward in achieving their goals. Use the conversation to help the learner envision being a member of an academic learning community; what they can contribute, and what value and rewards they will derive from being part of the community. If a learner has any specific needs, be sure to point them to the appropriate resources and assistance. Be approachable, professional, and respectful. ALWAYS!

Explain the value of personalized feedback. Because feedback on assignments is the way that you will most likely be teaching in the online environment, it is important that your learners understand how they are expected to use or address your feedback. You will be providing regular feedback as a method of instruction to build and enhance their skill set, and your feedback may take different forms including written, audio, and verbal. Encourage your learner to make use of and incorporate your feedback on each assignment as a guide to their ongoing improvement and success. Appendix D, *Learner Support Resource: How to Benefit from Feedback and Critique* is a document that you may choose to share with your learners to familiarize them with protocols and expectations regarding feedback on assignments.

SUPPORT LEARNERS TO BE SUCCESSFUL

Preparing your learners for the online learning experience by way of onboarding constituted the first set of engagement steps. The next set of engagement steps is to ensure ongoing and consistent support. For many learners, this may be the first time that they have participated in an online course, and learning online is significantly different in many ways from learning in a physical classroom. Because of the perceived sense of distance and isolation in an online course, you will need to encourage and support your learners to be committed and self-directed, manage their time very efficiently, and assume responsibility for their learning. You will also need to have a good understanding of what your learners need from you in order to be successful!

Learning Contract

To ensure ongoing engagement and success, you may at the very start propose using a **learning contract** with your learners that lays out an agreement to ensure that certain activities will be undertaken in order to achieve the learning goals (Knowles, 1986). This contract provides a formal way to structure learning goals and activities, which helps keep learners focused on course requirements and deliverables. The contract also serves to minimize misunderstandings and poorly communicated expectations. Importantly, this contract begins to establish a sense of empowerment, in that it offers your learners a sense of ownership, and establishes clear goals and timelines that they themselves have a hand in determining. A *Sample Learning Contract* is presented in Appendix E.

Time-Management Skills

Time-management skills are directly tied to learners' ability to manage their workload in order to successfully meet the unique demands of online learning. A common misconception among online learners is that not having to leave their home for class means that their studies will somehow be less time consuming. Indeed, this could not be farther from the truth. Because there is no physical commute to get to class, it is very easy to slip into the idea that one's studies can be "set aside for a while." Let your learners know how and when to participate and the extent to which they have choices. Encourage them to be proactive by accessing their course daily, completing assignments as required, and submitting work on time. A time management application, such as Todoist, will allow learners to remain efficient and plan ahead. Sharing time management tips will ensure that your learners stay on track by creating a realistic timeline or timetable, and setting aside suitable times that are specifically devoted to their studies.

Individualized "Just-in-Time" Guidance

Instructors should tailor their guidance to a learner's experience and provide support that targets learners of different backgrounds. This includes offering more intensive support for first-generation learners or learners for whom English is not their first language, as well as technical support for learners who may have limited online experience. Providing support structures right when these are needed will mean the difference between success and failure. Therefore, be mindful at all times of individual differences and needs, and set realistic expectations regarding appropriate timelines, availability for meetings, and provision of additional supports and resources as needed.

Formative Assessments

In Chapter 2, we discussed how vital formative assessment can be to learners during the learning process. This can also be a powerful tool to obtain an accurate read on how your learners are actually doing during the online learning experience. It is essential to evaluate learners on the academic aspects of their learning process; but it can also mean assessing the practical, physiological, and emotional aspects of that process. Especially if the move to online learning has been rapid and unexpected (as we saw with the pandemic), it is crucial that you take the time to get to reacquainted with your learners in this new environment. How are they handling having to learn online? What available supports and resources do they have? Do they know how to contact you? Do they know where to go to find their course materials? It is easy to pick up on social cues that alert you to how your learners are doing. In the online environment, those cues are no longer easily observed, and this is where formative assessments can come into play.

End-of-term evaluations help educators adjust and adapt their teaching for future semesters. But if you take the time midway to ask your learners how they're feeling about your course, you can gain some valuable insights and address their needs while there is still time for them to benefit from any adjustments you make. Seeking feedback opens up a dialogue around teaching and learning, and offers you some insights into the unique challenges experienced by your learners. If you explain that you welcome their feedback, process the feedback with an open mind, and commit to following up on the parts of the feedback that you can address, midterm feedback can help you grow as an instructor and reveal important course adjustments that will benefit your learners. Decide upfront what type of feedback you would like to receive based on key areas of the learning experience, including the following:

- The way the course is structured or organized
- The effectiveness of your teaching
- How the readings and assignments are understood and perceived
- The nature and quality of the course experience
- The workload and amount of effort that is required

With paper evaluation forms unlikely to be a viable option in online settings, you will need to choose an appropriate tool for surveying your learners. Some LMSs have a polling function. Other options include PollEverywhere, Learning Catalytics, Socractive, and Mentimeter. Features of these tools can be found in Appendix O. Remember that just as you owe it to your learners to provide feedback on their graded work, you also owe it to them to acknowledge their feedback regarding your teaching, and to let them know that you hear and appreciate their perspective. If you offer to change some aspect of your teaching or instructional approach in response to their feedback, make sure that you follow through and adjust!

Therefore, right from the beginning, your task is to create a safe, supportive, and secure learning environment for all learners. Supportive preparation builds rapport and is an indication of teaching presence, which must be ongoing throughout the course. Encourage your learners to view their online experience as a *collaborative learning experience*, with you as their instructor actively guiding and supporting and motivating them along the way. Motivation plays a significant role in determining how much effort learners will invest in their education, and the extent to which they will persist in completing the course. Numerous studies have illustrated that instructors can do much to enhance motivation, and those who perceive that their instructors genuinely care are much more likely to persist. You begin to build presence right from the time that you invite your learners to meet with you and express an interest in their learning and progress. Of course, establishing your presence goes beyond the initial introduction; communicating your accessibility and availability, and maintaining meaningful ongoing contact with your learners throughout a course serves to sustain engagement and, therefore, persistence. If you refer back to Figure II.1, *The Multimodal Engagement Cycle*, you will notice the numerous supports that are set in place for learners. These supports, together with the working relationship that you develop with each of your learners, will serve to enhance engagement. Chapters 5 and 6 provide you with additional detailed guidance regarding establishing and building strong working relationships as well as multimodal teaching strategies; all of which serve to further boost engagement and ongoing learning.

STRATEGIES FOR ONGOING SUPPORTIVE ENGAGEMENT

You are the live human face of your online course! Your learners will want to see you and connect with you. There are several supportive strategies in which you can establish, strengthen, and maintain engagement, right from the very beginning and throughout the course. Your focus should be on four themes: visibility and presence; availability and accessibility; trust and transparency; and flexibility.

Visibility and Presence
- Incorporating strategies into your teaching to be more visible directly relates to evidence of instructor engagement. Online learning should not be thought of as "alone learning." Between an engaging instructor and various support services and resources, your learners should never feel alone on their learning journey, but rather part of a thriving, learning community. Of course, also make sure that you are familiar with all available services and resources, so that you can better serve all of your learners and their diverse needs.
- Foster learners' active and constructive participation in the learning experience. This is accomplished by being approachable and frequently interacting with your learners. Interaction occurs through announcements, emails, and the feedback that is tied to submissions. Also, remain synchronously connected as needed.
- Have your learners re-orient you as you move from one meeting to the next. Make sure that you are well prepared for all phone calls, and that you are familiar with the learner's current work. Ask for updates regarding their progress, and begin your conversations with an idea of what you would like to accomplish with regard to specific issues or concerns.
- To demonstrate that you consider your learners as active partners in the learning experience, be sure to ask them for their feedback and

suggestions and make changes accordingly. This will reinforce your presence and will enable you to continue to offer a worthy and beneficial learning experience.
- Stay abreast of occurrences in your learner's lives to the extent possible, by remembering details and responding to any communication you receive from them, and also acknowledging that you understand or appreciate their circumstances. In this way, you display your presence and communicate your attention, thoughtfulness, or concern.

Availability and Accessibility
- Let your learners know that you are happy to speak with them not only in your welcome letter and welcome video, but also in your feedback on assignments. In this way, you keep reinforcing your presence and also your availability and accessibility.
- Set virtual office hours with details regarding availability and methods of contact. Whereas previously, instructors communicated solely via email and phone, online instructors are increasingly introducing the "virtual office" as a communication alternative within the online course.
- When you meet with your learners, be prepared to use your webcam and share your computer screen so that you are not just a "voice behind the screen."
- Learners should be reminded that questions are always welcome and that you are available for discussion as needed. Encourage them to keep you in the loop when life gets in the way. All adults have responsibilities, so encourage them to reach out and let you know when additional time or **learning accommodations** are needed.
- When learners contact you, be sure to respond as soon as you are able. Leaving learners "hanging" can be extremely discouraging, so it is important to regularly check email. If you are going to be away and unable to check email, let your learners know, and point them in the direction of someone who will be able to assist them during your absence. This is an important piece in ensuring ongoing engagement and should be set up with your institution in advance.

Trust and Transparency
- Gain and maintain the trust of your learners as their supporter and advocate. Convey that you are there for them and are concerned about their grasp of the course material and their ultimate success. Also convey that you are curious about and appreciate their experiences, viewpoints, ideas, and perspectives.

- Maintain open lines of communication with your learners throughout the course by indicating that you are available to discuss their work and your feedback. Being open with your learners while still maintaining professional boundaries can help them feel more comfortable in trusting your teaching and in approaching you for assistance or support when necessary.
- Although professional relationships entail boundaries, it is important to demonstrate empathy. Be aware of any stereotypes and generalizations on your part, as these undermine your credibility. Be aware of any assumptions you might be making, and seek additional information as needed. Encourage those who identify with a marginalized or underrepresented group to showcase, through their coursework, their own language, values, arts, beliefs, and traditions. This goes a long way toward ensuring equity-mindedness and inclusivity.
- If a learner requests a change in the schedule, or an accommodation, or if what is needed is a change of teaching modality, consider and honor their request.
- Building trust ensures that learning can occur in a place where it is safe to make mistakes. You can help learners overcome their view of errors as failures by conveying the message that not only are errors a natural part of learning, but we tend to remember what we learn through addressing and correcting our errors. In this way, you create valuable **teachable moments!**
- Make the path for success seem realistic, doable, and achievable by setting clear goals, clarifying instructions and requirements, and explaining learning outcomes, thereby minimizing potential barriers to learning such as anxiety and confusion.
- Be consistent and clear in what you say, and at the same time be aware of what your learners are saying to you. If you sense a double message, ask for clarification. Transparency is a critical component in the exchange of information, both in verbal and written forms.
- Find ways to communicate your expectations for assignments clearly and specifically. This type of transparency is essential to establish an **equity-minded** classroom. When you explicitly tell your learners what you're looking for, they are better able to produce an acceptable product. Weak performance is often less about the content and more about not having clarity or direction with regard to the processes in which you are asking learners to engage.
- Help learners understand the feedback and grading that you provide to them, and be sure to act on the feedback given to you. Using rubrics will make your grading more transparent to learners, and also less prone to bias because you can more logically "justify"

the grades that you assign. You want your learners to realize the meaning and relevance of the grade, rather than be confused or disappointed because the assigned grade is unclear or vague.
- In an endeavor to be fully transparent and gain the trust of your learners, remember that highly effective instructors will listen to their learners' feedback and will remain open to receiving and addressing this feedback so that they can enhance and improve their teaching practice.

Flexibility
- Offer multiple modes of communication so that learners can select what works best for them and suits their purposes. This is especially important when you are working with older learners who may have limited online experience and technical proficiency, or those for whom English is not their first language.
- When it comes to discussing delicate or complex issues with a learner, do so synchronously (in real time) rather than using email or a discussion forum. Based on your knowledge of your learners, select the most appropriate and suitable communication method for each situation.
- Through scaffolding, tasks are broken into manageable subtasks, designing learning to be incremental, adding complexity in stages. To support your learners, you may need to provide an additional layer of scaffolding. Finding the right balance for scaffolding is a shared responsibility and requires input from learners, so be sure to ask your learners to identify the level and type of scaffolding that they may need or want.
- Provide learners with opportunities to submit a series of drafts for instructor review or peer review so that they can address and build on constructive feedback. Allowing a progressive set of draft submissions is an opportunity to review and correct errors or omissions in preparation for developing the actual assignment.
- Disappointment over a bad grade can very likely fuel a feeling of futility. Allowing learners to resubmit an assignment extends the learning window to use specific, corrective feedback to improve their work and their grades. The goal is ongoing improvement! We want to offer opportunities for our learners to perform at their very best, thereby engaging and empowering them to do so.
- Finally, be willing to switch tactics if something is not working. There is no "one-size-fits-all" in education at any level, and thoughtfully and meaningfully addressing the needs of each individual learner is paramount. Above all, stay focused on making sure that your learners are informed and motivated, and keep a close eye on their being able to meet the stated CLOs!

MONITOR AND ADDRESS PROGRESS AND DEVELOPMENT

Because of the diversity that characterizes the learner population, you will encounter multiple different needs and academic skill sets. For example, you will notice that dependent learners generally tend to rely heavily on structure and receiving specific instructions; they tend to be limited in their ability to generate any ideas of their own. Independent learners generally prefer autonomy and tend to need less structure. You are encouraged to carefully and continually monitor your learners' needs and progress and identify and assist those who are struggling, failing, or otherwise disengaged as evidenced by nonparticipation in required activities.

STRATEGIES FOR EFFECTIVE MONITORING

Following are some suggestions to ensure that you are equitably and efficiently monitoring the progress and development of all of your learners.

Track Progress

Use available technology tools within the LMS to track learner progress in course activities, and to reach out to those who have not completed course requirements. Sustained interaction between learners and instructors ensures that instructors can recognize whether learners are experiencing technical difficulties or problems with course content, or whether they require additional support or specific resources to complete required activities.

The better you know each of your learners, the better you can serve them individually. Show your learners that you are paying attention to their progress early in the course. "High five" emails show learners you have taken notice of their hard work and want them to continue their efforts. When you notice that someone is struggling or lagging behind, reach out immediately. Contact those who have been missing, or who have not turned in assignments, letting them know they are not meeting expectations, and expressing your concern. Do not wait to address "at risk" learners at the midpoint or close to the end of a course but do so as early as possible to allow for more effective prevention and early intervention. Develop an early warning system to identify those who are at risk and have intervention strategies readily available to help them. This will help you have a better chance of retaining your learners and guiding them to success.

- Notify administration of all **at-risk learners** so that any challenges that impede their progress can be carefully monitored and addressed.

- Provide those who are struggling academically with additional resources and support, including referral to a learning resource or learning center.
- Make accommodations regarding technical competencies as needed. Those who cannot participate or who are having technical difficulties should be referred immediately to technical support so that they can receive the necessary assistance and resources.
- Refer learners with disabilities to Disability Services and ensure that they are provided with the appropriate accommodations and supports as needed.

Monitor Communication and Discussions

Much communication will take place via discussion forums within the LMS. These discussions may occur on an academic level (as required in coursework), as well as on a social level (informally through an institution's social media platform, if that is available). As an instructor, it is your responsibility to monitor trust levels and respectful interaction in all discussions and communications and intervene if necessary. Making sure that all communication and interaction is productive and will create a positive, trustworthy, and inclusive learning environment.

CHAPTER SUMMARY AND SYNTHESIS

This chapter provides strategies for onboarding, preparing, and supporting learners for the online learning experience, and planning ways to continually monitor their progress and development. The biggest takeaway for instructors working in the online learning environment is to connect with all learners, making them understand that they are present and engaged, rather than some "mystical entity." This connection needs to be intentional; person-to-person, one learner at a time. As you strive to connect with your learners, don't forget the power of encouragement in making meaningful and authentic connections and fostering a supportive learning community. Offer encouragement whenever you meet with your learners through the different modalities available, as well as through the feedback that you provide for assignments, tasks, and activities. In the spirit of collaborative learning and empowerment, always seek and be receptive to feedback from your learners regarding ways to make the course material more meaningful and relevant, and ask how you can assist. Remember that as a "reflective practitioner," you will want to listen to your learners' feedback so that you can improve your own teaching. You want to make sure that you are carefully considering all of the factors, strategies, and practices that can help to foster and promote learner engagement and empowerment, and thereby enhance performance outcomes.

As a reflective practitioner, you also want to make sure that you are carefully considering all of the strategies and practices that will support your learners. To foster reflection about what constitutes initial and ongoing support, ask yourself the following essential questions. Indeed, by continuing to examine the ways you support and monitor your learners' progress throughout their educational journeys, you will be in a better position to make any needed revisions.

CHAPTER 4: REFLECTION CHECKPOINT

Onboard and Welcome Learners

- What should I be looking to do at the start of the course in order to onboard my learners?

    TIP: Think of all the different ways of welcoming and establishing connections. What are the norms that you expect your learners to use as they interact with one another and with you?

- How am I "showing up" for my learners?

    TIP: A central aspect to promoting learner engagement, and in turn learner success, is the sense of teaching presence, the implication being that instructors are visible, approachable, and available.

- How does teaching presence impact the motivation of my learners?

    TIP: Communicating your accessibility and availability and maintaining ongoing contact and interaction serves to sustain engagement, and therefore persistence.

- How can I be sure that I am reaching all of my learners?

    TIP: Remember to address all needs, abilities, and interests.

- How will I know whether I have succeeded in supporting my learners to become successful?

    TIP: Think of all the ways that you can minimize isolation and enhance engagement. Think about ways to gauge your learners' progress through formative assessments and monitoring strategies.

- What type of instructor am I? What type of instructor would I like to be?

    TIP: Think about the ways in which your relationship with your learners is working or not working? How can you become a better and more engaged instructor?

- When should I check to see that my learners are doing well and achieving success?

    TIP: Consider when the most appropriate times are to monitor progress and address challenges or lack of progress. Consider what you might be looking for to inform you. Remember that your task is to equitably monitor the progress and development of all learners.

    What are YOU willing to try out to make a difference to your practice?

CHAPTER 5

Establish and Build Teaching Relationships

We begin to work toward a more inclusive educational experience when we take the time to understand our learners' contexts and unique needs through building meaningful and supportive relationships with them. To do this we must engage our learners by developing and nurturing working relationships in which they feel invested, and therefore share a commitment to the learning experience. Connecting with learners embodies a model of care, making them feel welcome and respected. When our learners know we care, they are more likely to reciprocate, and when they do, relationships are formed. The creation of strong teaching relationships significantly impacts motivation and persistence, and empowers learners to develop and thrive. Interactions among learners and instructors should be intentional, individually tailored, and continuous throughout a learner's academic journey (Bloomberg & Grantham, 2018). Research shows that strict content delivery, or what is often referred to as "sit-and-get" (Morrison, 2014; Murnane & Willett, 2011) does not have the same effect on learner achievement. As such, the instructor's role in this context becomes that of "guide on the side," or "learning partner," as opposed to the "sage on the stage" (a term first coined by Alison King [1993]). By serving as a coach or mentor, *working alongside your learners*, adopting a learner-centered approach, and relinquishing some control, you empower your learners to take ownership of their learning. This opens opportunities for deeper discourse and discussion, and creates space for learners to apply their understanding more deeply—all of which supports and enhances the overall learning experience.

Highly effective teachers are those who care about their learners and their learning goals. Caring about learners, and understanding their backgrounds and learning contexts, enables instructors to better accompany and guide them. International learners, for example, sometimes tend to have difficulty understanding an instructor's role as learner-centered; the instructor is perceived as a "guru" who transmits knowledge directly to the learner, and they are often not used to a more egalitarian model where instructors and learners are perceived as equals (Damary et al., 2017). It is therefore important to listen well and explain things well in order to help learners understand the expectations involved in the teaching relationship. Effective instructors show their learners how to learn and help them learn by offering support and assistance, and they use a variety of teaching strategies to help learners meet their expressed learning goals. Moreover, effective instructors will listen to their learners' feedback and will remain open to receiving and addressing it so that they can improve their teaching, thereby building and reinforcing the value of the teaching relationship.

BENEFITS OF POSITIVE WORKING RELATIONSHIPS

Positive relationships create a sense of safety, making it easier for learners to ask questions, challenge ideas, share experiences, and engage in thinking that helps them grow and develop. In turn, building positive relationships enables instructors to learn more about their learners' backgrounds, cultures, and personalities, and with that knowledge they can better advocate for their learners' needs. The relationship that an instructor creates opens avenues to honest conversations about their learners' needs, struggles, and successes, and makes it easier to have those difficult conversations with learners. These relationships therefore become shared collaborative experiences that allow both parties to value the other's perspectives, thoughts and ideas, thereby *learning with and from one another*. Moreover, at times, the working relationships that instructors develop with their learners can transcend the "classroom," and move toward a mentoring or coaching role that could potentially extend learning opportunities beyond course completion.

DEVELOP YOUR WORKING RELATIONSHIPS

Even if you have had previous face-to-face interactions with your learners, don't forget about reestablishing working relationships with them in a virtual space. When educators across the world rapidly shifted from face-to-face to online instruction in early 2020, we were reminded of the fragile and tenuous nature of working relationships, finding ourselves needing to understand and address our learners in new ways. Coupled with their regular challenges and stresses, online learners are far removed from both their instructors and their classmates. Being remote can make this a very lonely and isolated experience. With various barriers standing in the way of engaging with our learners, new types of support become increasingly necessary. As research consistently indicates, interaction is at the heart of the online learning experience, and so especially when online education is asynchronous, these barriers are compounded since we are not actually teaching in real time. One of the foundational theories in distance education is transactional distance theory. Transactional distance was conceived as a function of dialogue, structure, and learner autonomy. Moore (1997) explains transactional distance as the "psychological and communication space" felt between instructors and learners. Listening, perceiving, and communicating are key elements that can bridge this space, and serve as a foundation to build engagement and teaching relationships.

Listen!
- Focus on your learners by listening actively. Give your full attention to each learner. Seek an overall understanding of what learners are trying to communicate.
- Put yourself in the shoes of your learners in order to really understand their perspective and reality. Although professional relationships entail boundaries, it is important to demonstrate empathy.
- Use questions to clarify your understanding, to demonstrate your interest in what is being said, and also to promote critical thinking on the part of your learners. Questions indicate a willingness to understand the other person and engage in dialogue with them.

Perceive!
- In the online learning environment, your actions and nonverbal signals are exposed for everyone to see and hear. You are close up, and your behavior is noticeable to all!
- Be aware of any stereotypes and generalizations on your part, because these undermine your credibility. Check in with yourself as a means of increasing your own self-awareness. Be aware of any assumptions that you might be making, and seek additional information as needed.
- Be consistent and clear in what you say, and at the same time be aware of what your learners are saying to you. If you sense a double message, ask for clarification.
- Remain aware of any cultural biases embedded in your own teaching and presentation styles, and in your expectations. Ignorance of these biases can prevent you from seeing opportunities for more effective avenues of interaction with all of your learners.

Communicate!
- Respond to your learners in ways that acknowledge their experiences. Thank them for their input. Affirm their accomplishments and achievements, and provide positive feedback whenever you can.
- Allow for expression of all points of view, and be open to ways of thinking that may be different from your own. Using a "one-size-fits-all" approach to communication means that you will overlook

different personalities, needs, and expectations. In fact, your communication should address those differences as much as possible.
- Avoid abstract, overly formal language, colloquialisms, and jargon, which obscure your message. Don't make your learners have to guess or imagine what you mean. If they cannot relate to you and what you are saying, the relationship naturally suffers.
- Be honest with yourself, and focus on working well with your learners and acting with integrity. Ignoring, not responding, or responding inappropriately undermines effective communication.

ENGAGE THROUGH PRESENCE

Engagement starts with instructors developing a working relationship with each learner and sustaining these relationships throughout the course. The student body is widely diverse and includes learners with a vast array of different levels of ability, expertise, and personal and professional experiences and circumstances. As such, instructors are encouraged to be intentional about building their relationships, taking the time to proactively communicate with learners on an individual basis in order to demonstrate an interest in their courses, academic skills, and motivation to succeed. Presence, rapport, and ongoing communication are three factors that are crucial to building and sustaining ongoing relationships, thereby fostering engagement (Bloomberg & Grantham, 2018). Creating meaningful relationships in the online environment means *taking care to be present* by letting your learners know that you are "here for them," and that you are committed to helping them learn and succeed. With any online learning experience, technology is going to be a key part of maintaining relationships with your learners, and the ability to use technology to build teaching relationships and community will depend on the type of technology available. More important than just using technology to engage, however, is that you are aware of your online persona, and how you are "showing up."

Consider all of the ways you can connect with your learners to build and nurture productive and engaging teaching relationships.

"Humanize" the Learning Environment
- As a start, be sure to humanize the online learning environment in order to increase learner's investment in the educational experience. Learners are more apt to overcome whatever obstacles they are facing and have a greater sense of buy-in if they see their instructor as a human being. Your presence and visibility are therefore essential, since you serve as the primary link, supporting your learners throughout the course. When a learner first gains

access to their online course, they are searching for answers to a plethora of questions. Who is this instructor? Are they going to be approachable? Are they qualified? Providing answers to these types of questions will help instructors "humanize" themselves. To help ease this anxiety at the outset, you can strategically use your "Bio" or "About Me" pages to introduce yourself, add your welcome letter and video, and put learners at ease.
- Remain flexible and keep an open mind throughout each course so that you do not overlook individual differences regarding learning preferences and abilities. Each individual has a preferred way of learning, so be aware of what ways you like since we may tend to overuse those techniques. This relates to our own **implicit bias** regarding how people learn.

Be Proactive in Fostering Discussion
- Engage in ongoing and sustained communication. Transparency is a critical component in the exchange of information, both in verbal and written forms. Be sure to maintain open lines of communication with all your learners throughout the course by indicating that you are available to discuss their work and your feedback.
- Begin with conversations that are goal-oriented. Show a genuine interest in your learners' objectives and career aspirations. Once you begin learning more about each of your learners, you will be in a better position to begin cultivating a working relationship and providing individualized attention.
- Be respectful in all of your interactions with your learners, treating them as adults, responding on time, and not talking down to them. Responding late, inappropriately, or with a negative tone undermines effective communication, and limits the development of productive teaching relationships.
- Be consistent, clear, and direct in what you say and write. Take the time to communicate clearly so that your learners understand what you are saying and are able to actually use the information you are offering them. If a learner cannot understand what you are saying or they do not find what you are saying to them to be useful, the relationship naturally suffers.

Adopt a "Coaching-Based" Orientation
- Envisage moving away from a "grading-based" orientation of teaching to a "coaching-based" orientation. Teaching this way means viewing each learner as on a **growth trajectory**, with each assignment, activity, or task as a measure of their progress on that trajectory. Instead of just grading one activity after another,

focus on how you can help your learners grow and develop, becoming increasingly self-directed. The way in which we provide feedback determines to a large extent our relationships with our learners. This becomes the structure on which to model a solid working relationship in which each learner feels heard, valued, and respected.
- Let your learners know that you are learning with and from them. Even though as the instructor you are in a position of authority, focus on what you and your learners have to offer each other in contributing to the work at hand. In other words, make it clear that the learner's opinion is valued. Strive to instill in your learners a sense of autonomy, whereby they feel as though they are active participants in a dynamic working relationship. You do this by avoiding the "sage on the stage" or "sit and get" approach to teaching, and in doing so you empower your learners. Presenting yourself as a co-learner goes a long way to building trust, respect, collaboration, and motivation.
- Gain and maintain the trust of your learners as their supporter and advocate. Convey that you are there for them and are committed to their ultimate success. Also convey that you are curious about their experiences, viewpoints, ideas, and perspectives. Being open with your learners while still maintaining professional boundaries can help them feel more comfortable in trusting your teaching and in approaching you for assistance or support when necessary.

Engagement is the foundation of the teaching–learning relationship. An effective relationship is reciprocal and creates shared learning goals: Instructors engage their learners so they can learn and improve and meet learning outcomes. By developing collaborative working relationships and interacting meaningfully with learners, you bridge "transactional distance" and generate greater engagement. When learners recognize that their instructors have something useful to contribute to their success, they are motivated to learn and succeed. As such, productive teaching relationships provide the foundation for a successful online learning experience. The challenge becomes how we develop working relationships with our learners within a virtual environment, while remembering that these relationships should be real, and not virtual!

FOSTER A GROWTH ACADEMIC MINDSET

Equally important to actively engaging with your learners through your teaching presence is that you also develop, right from the start, an empowered sense of self-motivation, and an "I can do this attitude"; in essence, a **growth academic mindset**. According to Dweck (2007), as opposed to a "fixed mindset," a "growth academic mindset" involves the attitude that intelligence can be developed, leading to the motivation to learn and the tendency to embrace challenges and value constructive feedback. By nature, adults do not want to be viewed as passive receptors of knowledge, but rather as active participants in their educational experiences. Being intentional in encouraging a growth mindset in your learners will ensure that you focus your teaching on how they can improve, and that you provide the necessary support and motivation to ensure ongoing learning and development. Dweck's research indicates that an understanding of mindset allows instructors to challenge themselves and their learners, thereby fostering growth for both themselves and their learners.

Learner Mindset

Dweck (2007) explains that learners with a "growth mindset" believe that intelligence can be developed through experience and effort, and also from the encouragement and support of others. Because they feel autonomous, they will view a learning task as doable within the scope of their knowledge, abilities, and resources, and will value achievement, thereby challenging themselves, expecting success, and striving to achieve their goals. These learners are confident in their ability to learn and have a greater sense of **self-efficacy** and have the tendency to embrace challenges and persist in the face of setbacks. They also typically appreciate and apply constructive feedback. A "fixed mindset," on the other hand, refers to the belief that one's intelligence, talents, and abilities are innate, changing very little, if at all, over time (Dweck, 2007). Those learners with a **fixed mindset** will feel less inclined to set goals or view learning tasks as doable, and will also not expect to be successful. They tend not to try to learn what may seem overly difficult or impossible, and they also feel that they have limited control over their academic fate. Some may even sabotage their own success in order to protect their self-esteem so they can blame their lack of studying rather than their perceived lack of ability. Because learners with a fixed mindset hold this belief, they will likely avoid challenges or give up easily, and will tend to ignore or reject instructor feedback.

Instructor Mindset

Instructors with a fixed mindset can create an atmosphere of judgment and typically give up on learners who are not performing well. Also, because they do not believe in improvement, they may not attempt to foster it. Alternatively, if you are an instructor with a "growth mindset," you will adopt an *asset-based approach to teaching*, focusing mostly on learners' strengths and not just on their deficits. As such, you would hold the view that extra time and effort are well worth it. You will understand that positive, supportive confidence-building experiences help learners believe in their potential to solve complex problems. Moreover, you will find it rewarding when you witness your learners' progress and achievement. As Dweck (2007) states, "Great teachers believe in the growth of the intellect and talent, and they are fascinated with the process of learning" (p. 194). This means that instructors with a growth mindset are more likely to look for new ways to foster learning, recognizing that not all strategies will work with all learners, and intentionally drawing learners' attention to progress (even small steps!). As an instructor, your role is a change agent, and you should believe that all learners can improve and succeed. By adopting a growth mindset, you are more likely to provide encouragement and motivation for your learners to keep working and persevering at all stages of the educational journey. In line with the concept of a growth academic mindset, it is important to have high expectations for all your learners, motivating them throughout their course and supporting them to work toward achieving the CLOs. Importantly, help your learners to see and realize their potential! If you pause for a moment and think back to some great teachers you have known throughout your life, you will likely be able to think of things they said or did that exemplified a growth academic mindset, thereby instilling and fostering motivation and persistence!

Strategies for Enhancing a Growth Academic Mindset

As you work toward fostering and encouraging in your learners a growth academic mindset, the following strategies can contribute to your learners' sense of self-efficacy and their positive expectations for success:

Set Your Learners Up for Success.
- Make the path for success seem realistic, doable, and achievable by setting clear goals, clarifying instructions and requirements, explaining learning outcomes, and offering opportunities for dialogue and reflection. Making a clear path minimizes potential barriers to learning, such as anxiety, frustration, and confusion.
- Provide multiple opportunities for success by conceiving learning as an ongoing process, pacing the course to accommodate diverse needs and abilities, and offering multiple chances to practice application of learning and knowledge.
- Share and promote strategies and tips for success regarding the most efficient and effective ways to manage time, stay organized, learn and retain the material, think critically, write clearly, and study effectively.
- To sustain ongoing achievement and success, provide referrals to support resources as necessary, including academic success centers, learning centers, library, tutors, peer reviewers, and editors.

Create an Environment of Trust and Support.
- Help learners understand feedback and grading that you provide to them regarding their work, and be sure to act on the feedback given to you. If a learner requests a change in the schedule, or an accommodation, or if what is needed is a change of teaching modality, consider and honor their request.
- Build trust so that learning can occur in a place where it feels safe to make mistakes. Help learners overcome their mistaken view of errors as failures by conveying the message that not only are errors a natural part of learning, but we tend to remember what we learn through addressing and correcting our errors. In this way, you create valuable teachable moments for your learners!

Ensure Ongoing Motivation.
- With your asset-based approach to teaching, and your intention to develop a growth mindset, you will always acknowledge your learners' strengths and provide praise and encouragement for their achievements. This ensures that the focus is mostly on what they are doing well and not only on what needs improvement or revision.
- Teaching online learners by way of establishing collaborative and respectful working relationships, valuing learner autonomy, and incorporating materials that invite active learning and participation *while at the same time* providing structured and supplemental support, goes a long way toward sustaining ongoing motivation. Autonomy, mastery, and purpose are key drivers of intrinsic motivation, impacting satisfaction and performance. Giving up the reigns and allowing learners a sense of autonomy requires not only knowing when to step in and when to let go, but in the end, creating an empowered learning environment, thereby fostering lifelong learning.
- Those who are successful will envision their educational and professional goals and maintain the motivation to reach them. Help learners articulate their goals and see how the skills and content that they acquire can lead to achieving these goals. Making connections between current learning and realizing dreams can be a powerful motivator! These are obvious connections, but those in the middle of several years of graduate studies may lose sight of what their hard work is for and how every course has a direct connection to later real-world success.
- Provide ongoing encouragement by asking targeted questions in your feedback on weekly assignments in order to stimulate critical thinking. To do this, consider using multiple avenues, including written, audio, and **video feedback**. Your learners will appreciate

that you are engaged and interested, and that you are supportive of their progress and development. Details pertaining to providing feedback for assignments, and the use of critical questions to promote deep learning are discussed in greater detail in Chapter 6.
- Incorporate motivational strategies and activities throughout your course, including use of encouraging language and ongoing acknowledgement of perseverance, achievement of milestones, and success. Encouragement can come in many forms, including check-ins through emails, phone calls, and video messages. Learners often need reminders to be able to see beyond the present. They also like to hear that their instructor believes in them. Be sure to remind them of this and that you are always there to help. This will create a welcoming and trusting learning environment where learners will feel valued and motivated to do their very best. One way to encourage motivation and persistence is to utilize a video technique called "Midweek Motivation," which consists of creating a set of short videos, used to ensure perseverance through the academic and/or personal challenges that your learners may be experiencing.

POWER AND POSITIONALITY

Engagement and presence take on significant meaning when we look at educational endeavors through the lens of inclusivity. As an instructor, it is important to consider the ways in which race, ethnicity, gender, sexual orientation, gender identity, socioeconomic class, disability status, or other cultural factors impact the instructor/learner dynamic, and how you as the instructor "show up" and relate to and communicate with your learners, a concept that is referred to as **positionality** (Cervero & Wilson, 2001). The idea of the instructor as a facilitator is a hallmark of adult education. Yet, it is clear that facilitation does not occur on a neutral stage, but in the real world of hierarchical power relations.

Because the broader social context is duplicated in the microcosm of the classroom, enacting the facilitation role will reproduce the inherent power structures that privilege some, silence some, and deny the existence of others. Those of us who are equity-minded are aware of the historical context of exclusionary practices in education and recognize the impact of this history. We also recognize the contradiction between the ideals of democratic education and the social, institutional, and individual practices that contribute to persistent inequities in the broad field of education. Being equity-minded does not mean lowering standards. In fact, it is quite the opposite. When you communicate to learners that we understand they have limitations and that you sympathize with those, you are displaying a fixed mindset by sending the message that learners should not expect more from themselves, which can lead to greater self-doubt and poorer performance as a result. Conversely, as an instructor with a growth academic mindset, you can work with your learners to support them and thereby enhance their academic and critical-thinking skills.

In order to be attentive to issues of diversity and inclusion, it is important to highlight the ways that learners who identify as part of minority or marginalized groups can feel as they engage with instructors in the learning environment. The online classroom environment can tend to feel safe for learners of such groups because the sense of anonymity the environment can provide. However, you should not assume that power and privilege are not impacting the online environment, particularly those who identify with underrepresented or marginalized groups. Research indicates that power and privilege are clearly manifested in the online environment, with marginalized learners facing challenges, including imposter syndrome, implicit bias, and **microaggressions**. The latter are indirect, subtle, or unintentional discriminations against members of marginalized groups that are not blatantly offensive, but are clearly intended to be hurtful or dismissive (Pierce, 1970; Trippany Simmons et al., 2016). Instances such as these can lead to a greater likelihood of learners feeling alienated or disconnected. An individual's ability to learn is indeed influenced by their sense of belonging, and, without an intentional focus on inclusive teaching practices, instructors can unknowingly alienate certain learners, causing them to withdraw mentally, emotionally, or physically.

Guidelines for Addressing Power and Positionality

Creating an inclusive climate means proactively addressing your own biases and assumptions, and ensuring that all your learners feel valued and respected. Following are some ways to ensure that you are sensitive to and address issues of power and positionality so that you are focused at all times on achieving equity and inclusion:

Address Learners Appropriately
- Make sure that you know how your learners would like to be addressed and how you can be attentive to their identities.
- Be proactive in reaching out to each learner and ask for their preference and choice. When meeting with a learner for the first time, be aware of which social identities they are most connected with.
- Perhaps the learner identifies with a marginalized or underrepresented population, and if so, how might you work to better understand how this affects their educational experience? As you think more about your learners' social or cultural identities, consider how they may have multiple intersecting identities that

impact their learning experiences. For example, how do race, socioeconomic class, ethnicity, gender, and sexual orientation coalesce in the educational setting? Does the learner come from a Western educational background? If not, what experiences and elements in their background and prior educational experiences might be different than what we might assume regarding their background, experience, and exposure?

Build Capacity
- Giving up the reigns and allowing learners a sense of autonomy and ownership requires knowing when to step in and when to let go, but in the end, creating an empowered learning environment and fostering lifelong learning for all.
- To maximize learner engagement and agency, we must appreciate the multiple intersecting identities that learners bring to the classroom and support them with a curriculum (and pedagogy) that affirms and embraces diversity. One curricular approach in helping learners feel valued is to offer them both a voice and a choice in their learning. This means that they can choose topics that are interesting and culturally or professionally relevant to them, can demonstrate their learning in different ways (e.g., a paper, video/visual presentation, or podcast), can choose their readings within a topic or theme, and can provide input regarding assessment criteria.
- Be proactive in determining the strengths or limitations of your learners to help provide instruction that can speak directly to those strengths, and build capacity as needed. For example, if a learner shares with you that they are an avid reader, you might consider creating a list of sources that can provide access to material that further deepens their understanding. If the learner shares that they struggle with academic writing, you can assist by connecting them with the appropriate and available resources and support services.

Ensure Safety
- Ensure that your learners feel safe and supported as they explore sensitive topics.
- Encourage those who identify with a marginalized or underrepresented culture to showcase, through their coursework, their own language, values, arts, beliefs, and traditions. This goes a long way toward a sense of ownership and empowerment! When learners see themselves in and identify with the readings, when they can relate the assignments and learning activities to their real-world career paths and experiences, and when interactions with their instructors raise the level of critical thinking about the material, we create a fertile environment for deep learning to occur.

Hold Yourself Accountable!
- Holding yourself accountable to ensure those high expectations are met (maybe even redefining for yourself what that high expectation is) and supporting your learners' educational journeys every step of the way ensures that you build your teaching practice on a strengths-based model rather than a deficit-model.
- Exemplary teachers are those who care about each individual learner and their expressed learning goals. Caring about each of your learners *as real people* and understanding and appreciating their backgrounds and learning contexts enables you to better accompany and guide them throughout the learning experience.
- We can work toward a more inclusive educational experience when we take time to understand our learners' contexts and unique needs through building authentic relationships with them and empowering them to take ownership of their learning, to think more critically and reflectively, and to develop as self-directed lifelong learners.

CHAPTER SUMMARY AND SYNTHESIS

The benefits of constructive working relationships are worth the time, and make a significant difference to the overall educational experience. Instructors should be facilitators of learning who connect with and meaningfully engage with their learners, nurturing a growth academic mindset in your learners, thereby inspiring them to continue to remain motivated and engage in ongoing learning. As you are aware from reading this chapter, there are multiple touchpoints involved! The key message is that the more engaged instructors are, the more engaged our learners will be. We begin to work toward a more inclusive educational experience when we take the time to understand our learners' contexts and unique needs through building meaningful and supportive relationships with them. The instructor's role is "guide on the side," or "learning partner." This chapter covered the benefits of positive working relationships, and how to go about developing working relationships that will facilitate and sustain learning. The implication is that instructors remain visible, approachable, and available through the collaborative and supportive working relationships that they establish with learners.

The ways in which power and privilege impact the online classroom cannot be overlooked. Integrating the principles of inclusion, equity, and accessibility into your teaching is essential to ensure learning, progress, and success for all learners. No matter how open and approachable we might profess to be, it is important to recognize that as instructors we do have both advanced education and power. For learners to thrive, instructors must be self-reflective and attuned to the ways in which their own biases, prejudices, assumptions, and lack of knowledge and exposure can impact their learners, thereby shifting thinking and behavior, and rooting out the ways your own beliefs and behaviors can undermine learners' success. Ongoing **reflective practice** is therefore strongly encouraged to critically examine the effectiveness of your instructional approaches and strategies as you work to build and nurture strong teaching relationships with your learners.

> ### CHAPTER 5: REFLECTION CHECKPOINT
>
> **Establish and Build Teaching Relationships**
>
> - How do I start to build a relationship with each of my learners to support and encourage them?
>
>   TIP: Think about what you can do to encourage a sense of engagement and connection right from the beginning? What are the multiple touchpoints to consider in building and maintaining engagement? What specific strategies might be helpful? What are you doing you meet your learners "where they are"?
>
> - How can I be sure that my teaching presence is making a difference in my course?
>
>   TIP: How are your learners responding to you? Do they appear engaged or disengaged? Remember that your learners' perception of teaching presence is a critical factor, resulting in greater engagement and higher levels of achievement.
>
> - How can I be sure that my learners are connecting with me and feel supported?
>
>   TIP: Consider the different ways that you establish connections with your learners and examine how they are (or are not) responding. Think carefully about how your teaching approach can impact learners in meaningful ways, so that they continually work toward meeting their educational goals. Are you presenting yourself as a "sage on the stage" or a "guide on the side" and "facilitator"? Are you creating a warm or a "chilly" classroom climate? What are you doing to foster and maintain good teacher-learner relationships?
>
> - How can I check to see that I am addressing any and all barriers as they arise?
>
>   TIP: Think of all the ways that you can work toward making the online learning experience less isolated and lonely. What are all the different barriers you should be attending to, including those on the part of you, the learner, the

Establish and Build Teaching Relationships

course material, or even the distance learning context itself? How are you reaching "hard-to-teach" or "hard-to-reach" learners?

- What should I be looking to do in order to instill and sustain motivation, thereby building a culture of ongoing learning?

    TIP: Think about the role that motivation plays in determining how much effort learners will invest in their learning, and whether they complete the course or program and achieve the learning outcomes. Consider all the factors that contribute to developing a culture of learning. What are you doing to increase your touchpoints with each of your learners?

- In what ways might my instructional approach exclude any of my learners, especially those from minority, marginalized, or underrepresented groups?

    TIP: How do you describe your own positionality within the learning context? What is your "position" in the hierarchies that order the real world, including those based on race, gender, class, sexual orientation, and ability? Who holds the power in the teaching relationship? Who has privilege in the learning experience? How do you define inclusive pedagogy? What role can you play in creating a more equitable and just environment? What can you do to enact positive change? How can you create spaces for participation of "marginalized voices" to promote and encourage knowledge sharing? Think about how you can remain aware of *and address* (that is, *actually act on!*) your own biases, assumptions, and preconceived ideas.

    What are YOU willing to try out to make a difference to your practice?

CHAPTER 6

Multimodal Teaching Strategies to Engage and Empower Learners

Throughout the book and also woven in this chapter is a strong focus both on how to engage your learners through empowerment and how to empower them through that engagement. This book's approach is to foster deep learning by helping learners engage with the course material at the level that is most meaningful to them, and it is ultimately the responsibility of the instructor to offer diverse, rich, and multimodal learning experiences. The multimedia principle introduced in Chapter 3 explains that to enhance learning and maximize engagement, online education should not be solely text-based but be extended to include multiple media. Considering the workload that you may encounter in working with multiple learners at any one time, which can become overwhelming, a key purpose of this chapter is to introduce you to some useful streamlining strategies so that your online teaching practice is as efficient as possible without diminishing the quality thereof. Leading up to these strategies are a number of key concepts that set the stage for online instruction: diversity and inclusion; **culturally responsive teaching**; access to technology; and community-building.

RESPECT DIVERSITY AND STRIVE FOR INCLUSION

By 2045, the United States will become a "majority-minority society," with less than 50% of the population being non-Hispanic Whites (Frey, 2018). Adult learners today are also more diverse than ever before in various ways (Schaeffer, 2019). Diversity refers to anything that sets one individual apart from another, including the full spectrum of human demographic differences and the different ideas, backgrounds, and opinions that people bring. This includes the spectrum of qualities and characteristics that differentiate individual people, and it is the combination of these qualities that makes each person unique. Online learners, like all learners, present a diverse set of learning needs and a range of cultural experiences and identities. Educators at all levels will increasingly need to understand and appreciate diversity, cultivate a critical mind to recognize and acknowledge the role of sociocultural factors, and develop the knowledge and skills that would allow them to be inclusive in their approach and teach ethically and responsibly in a world characterized by a complex diversity. It is important to realize that people from different cultures may learn the same things, but they may learn *in different ways*. As such, we need to proactively create learning experiences that recognize and acknowledge developmental diversity; that is, the different ways that individuals think and learn. Attending carefully to developmental diversity—like all forms of diversity—is one important way that we can create an environment of support and challenge that can reach and inspire learners with different needs and learning preferences.

Inclusion represents the extent to which individuals feel valued, respected, encouraged to participate fully, and able to be their authentic selves. Inclusive pedagogy describes curriculum and teaching approaches that encourage learners to have *a sense of belongingness*. This includes course materials that represent a variety of perspectives that can be meaningfully applied in a diverse set of real-world scenarios; and teachers meeting learners where they are and helping them to meet CLOs, and eventually be able to contribute their field of study. Pedagogy that prioritizes inclusion—whether the courses are online, in-person, or a combination of the two—asks us to consider how we can help *all learners* succeed. Addressing diversity and inclusion—to support the growth of all learners—is something that should be infused throughout your teaching practice right from design and development of a course, through implementation and assessment. We can work toward a more inclusive educational experience when we take the time to understand our learners' contexts and their unique needs through the relationships that we build with them. Inclusion is rooted deeply in the democratic principles of both justice and opportunity, and educators have a responsibility to ensure that all learners can fulfill their goals of completion. Toward this end, every learning experience should offer full equity and inclusion for all learners.

CULTURALLY RESPONSIVE TEACHING

As learning environments continue to become increasingly globalized, instructors must seek to reduce barriers to education in order to provide a high quality of education for *all learners*, regardless of their background, social and cultural contexts, or past educational and life experiences. No other time or place in history has brought together such a diverse array of cultures, backgrounds, and identities. However, with that diversity comes a great deal of responsibility for educators, who must be able to communicate effectively with learners of multiple cultural backgrounds, and also empower their learners to celebrate diversity. We begin building relationships by working on ourselves and reflecting on our role as a teacher by examining how our personal and cultural experiences inform our teaching practices and biases.

The Center for Advanced Research on Language Acquisition at the University of Minnesota defined culture as "shared patterns of behaviors and interactions, cognitive constructs, and affective understanding that are learned through a process of socialization. These shared patterns identify the members of a cultural group while also distinguishing those of another group" (CARLA, 2009, p. 1). It is important to recognize that cultural diversity is not only based on ethnic or national differences. Within any culture there are also regional differences; differences of upbringing; and differences of age, gender, ethnicity, sexual orientation, and ability. Individuals from different cultures engage in and expect different communication practices and behaviors during interactions in learning or work environments. Therefore, it is vital for instructors to be aware of how an individual's life experiences and social and cultural contexts may shape their relationship with learning and with their instructors. The growing multicultural nature of the learner population makes it critical that instructors working in online learning environments develop the necessary skills to deliver culturally sensitive and culturally adaptive instruction. Challenges can be overcome through increased awareness, culturally sensitive communication, modified instructional design processes, and efforts to accommodate the diversity of online learner populations by considering adjustments to our teaching strategies to include and support all learners.

The multicultural learning environment has a unique potential for bringing learners and teachers of different cultures together, thus bridging the gap in cross-cultural understanding (Damary et al., 2017). However, as pointed out by Smith and Ayers (2006), "Technologically mediated learning experiences may accommodate the singularities of a dominant Western culture at the expense of cultural responsiveness to the cultural backgrounds of all participants" (p. 1). While members of marginalized or underrepresented cultures are offered unprecedented access to a global knowledge base, the pro-Western bias inherent in the technological foundations of distance learning can indeed present an obstacle both to access and understanding. Increased awareness will help us teach in ways that better include and support our culturally diverse learners, facilitate their achievement, and create inclusive learning experiences.

ADDRESS UNEQUAL ACCESS TO TECHNOLOGY

Historically, there have been concerns related to economic inequality, the "digital divide"; that is, the uneven distribution in the access to or use of technology and the fact that the wealthy have access to better technological systems and larger and more private spaces to participate. The shift to emergency online instruction in the spring of 2020 exposed, and indeed highlighted, that a significant number of learners are situated on the wrong side of the digital divide, therefore exacerbating this concern (Beaunoyer et al., 2020; Chan et al., 2021). Now, more than ever before, it is imperative that we implement teaching strategies and learning solutions that promote inclusivity and a sense of belonging. An issue that needs particular attention is that of equitable access to the learning environment, including unequal access to technology, hardware, and software, and the ways in which instructors can ensure that all learners have access to the materials they need to succeed, especially at times when learning contexts are rapidly changing and transforming.

Since the onset of the pandemic, many learners were, and continue to be, removed from their traditional classrooms, and thrust into new and unfamiliar online spaces. This was something they did not expect, nor were they well-prepared. Not all learners will have access to a regular Internet service or top-of-the-line software and hardware. Moreover, many will have connectivity issues including unstable, unpredictable, or generally low levels of access to the Internet; they may rely on data plans that may run low or run out before they have completed all their coursework; they may lack access to physical devices such as computers, tablets, printers, webcams, or other equipment; they may not have access to specialized software; or they may be unable to run certain applications or software on their devices. Although there may be community-based resources to address some of these access issues (e.g., free Internet at public libraries, stores, and coffee shops), these resources may not be accessible to all learners when they need them, or these may not be available at all in the event of community-wide closures.

Following are some ways to address accessibility, promoting an inclusive and equitable environment:

- Ask learners about their level of access to technology, because this will inform you of the technology choices for your courses. This may be done anonymously so that learners do not need to feel ashamed or embarrassed by their lack of access to technology.
- Offer flexibility or alternatives to learners when access is an issue. For those who anticipate or who have stated that they lack access, ask what they would need in order to participate more fully in the course generally or with regard to specific assignments.
- Provide a balance between asynchronous and synchronous tools. Because online learners are situated in multiple in time zones, consider the flexibility provided by asynchronous tools. While synchronous experiences are generally more responsive, these experiences can pose technical and logistical challenges, especially

when limited access is an issue. Asynchronous experiences can potentially reduce these challenges, and generate engagement since learners can access these at their own time and pace.
- Create an environment that includes and values *all learners*. Especially during an unstable or unpredictable time, stress is elevated, with many learners facing a variety of challenges that can impact their motivation, concentration, and performance. Moreover, some learners will be impacted in ways that they may not want to share with you. As such, offer all learners additional flexibility to meet deadlines and adjust their workloads accordingly.

DEVELOP A LEARNING COMMUNITY

In the online environment, social belonging and a sense of community are associated with increased engagement and motivation (Berry, 2017, 2019; Croxton, 2014; Moore, 2014; Schwartz et al., 2016). Developing a learning community has been at the heart of distance education since its inception, and the need to foster community in the online environment remains a focal issue by implementing strategies that will increase learner engagement not only with the course content and with the instructor, but also with peers. To create a collaborative environment that encourages and fosters a community of learning, Riggs and Linder (2016) explain that in the absence of a physical space, an *architecture of engagement* must be intentionally created. The implication is that it is an instructor's presence and thoughtful facilitation that will pave the way for the quality of the interaction and connections.

Establishing an online teaching presence contributes to learning and perception of community, thereby cultivating a "learning community" (Bloomberg, 2005). Being present means *being there* for your learners, and focusing your time and energy to help them achieve their goals. You are there, first and foremost as a guide to ensure that your learners are actively learning the subject matter and figuring out how to apply it appropriately. In addition to a guide, you also become a co-learner, a partner in the learning experience, by creating an environment that is conducive to active participation. In terms of the natural pursuit to connect, learners will often tend to utilize available forums in the LMS to connect with each other and share material and experiences. However, you should not solely rely on learners making connections for themselves, but rather be intentional in inviting interactivity by embracing all available opportunities for peer-to-peer learning and collaboration. In doing so, you begin to facilitate the types of learning experiences that will build community among your online learners.

FACILITATE GROUP WORK AND COLLABORATION

The following activities can contribute to learners' greater sense of belonging by connecting them to a broader learning community.

Facilitating Asynchronous Discussion Forums

Discussion forums (sometimes referred to as "discussion boards") are a significant part of online courses, facilitating communication and interaction as learners ask questions and respond to discussion prompts. The asynchronous format removes technical hurdles and ensures that learners are able to engage with peers and each other in a discussion-based class at a time of their own choosing, even without a strong Internet connection. This experience allows them to demonstrate their knowledge and also build a sense of community with their peers. Discussion forums can be used with small group activities, thereby replacing research-based assignments with opinion pieces, and incorporating thought-provoking topics. However, you should realize that this is not to be seen as a hands-off approach where the instructor can just observe and to some extent disengage. Rather, through discussion forums you have an opportunity to engage more fully with your learners by contributing your own opinions, explanations, and useful examples.

As the facilitator of learning, be sure to encourage and guide your learners toward achievement and success by ensuring that they are actively engaging with the subject matter and grasping the relevant concepts that are being taught. Develop thoughtful and clear questions that will generate dynamic interaction among your learners, engage them more deeply with the course material, and foster meaningful contributions from their peers. To generate increased interaction, you might consider assigning specific roles so that learners are provided with greater responsibility and autonomy, and an enhanced sense of community. For example, they might "role play" or you might ask them to undertake particular tasks, such as being a summarizer, a respondent, or a connector with outside resources. Overall, be sure to closely monitor the conversations—not just quality and timeliness—but also make sure that all discussions and communication are useful, relevant, appropriate, and that the tone of the conversation is inclusive and respectful. Remember that a successful discussion is not measured by the quantity of learner responses, but rather by the quality of those responses. As such, a high quantity of generic responses should not be construed as representative of a high-quality dialogue. Refer to Appendix N, *Online Support Resources*, a selection of curated resources for those seeking additional support and services. The resource *Engaging online students with synchronous and asynchronous learning tools* contains useful information regarding planning effective discussion boards (pp. 10–11); evaluating discussion forums (pp. 12–14); and equitable online facilitation (pp. 17–18).

Facilitating Synchronous Discussion Groups

As an alternative to asynchronous discussions, consider offering your learners the option to interact synchronously with their peers. In this way, they can move away from standard written replies and engage in real-time conversation about course material and pose questions without the constraints of a formal discussion forum or the pressure of being graded. Being open to your learners' input regarding how online discussions are driven will help you promote their autonomy while encouraging them to engage with the course material and their classmates in meaningful ways. This is also a good way to cater to those who prefer the spontaneity and organic nature of face-to-face discussions.

Refer to Appendix O, which includes a variety of collaborative applications to support and enhance teaching and learning. Numerous online collaborative tools can be usefully harnessed for the purpose of bringing learners together and encouraging a sense of community, including online productivity suites and social media platforms. Your LMS will undoubtedly also offer course-specific applications, thereby providing you with a variety of ways to create community by connecting learners with others who have similar interests, or who are working on common projects. Remain thoughtful and proactive in encouraging meaningful interaction and providing appropriate and supportive guidance. For example, if you are setting up synchronous meetings to bring groups of learners together, if you only turn on your camera and audio right at the start of class, that would be similar to walking in the door of an in-person class right at the scheduled start time and going straight into teaching. Whether in-person or online, those precious minutes before and after class are critical for answering questions and connecting with your learners. Therefore, sign in several minutes before class and greet learners as they come in. This period of time before the class actually begins also offers an opportunity for informal peer interaction and community building. Many synchronous tools that are currently available include virtual "breakout rooms" can be used to create learner–learner interaction for think-pair-share or team-based exercises. In this way, learners have the opportunity to collaborate in the breakouts and then join the larger group to debrief and report back.

Guidelines for Effective Synchronous Activities. Following are some key strategies pertaining to ensuring that online classrooms are accessible, and that you are envisioning an environment in which all of your learners can connect and thrive:

- Make sure that all directions are clear before you set up any synchronous meetings, and ahead of the meeting be sure to provide any worksheets or instructions that your learners may need.

- Record all synchronous sessions, and make these readily available. In that way, if your learners are unable to attend the synchronous session at the time that it is offered, or if they encounter connectivity issues during the livestream, they can play back the course recording when they're able to get back online.
- When a course uses video or multimedia content, provide a transcript so that even those with poor Internet connections have access to the written materials.
- Develop schedules and design coursework to meet the needs of all learners, wherever they may be. Make sure that synchronous sessions are offered at a wide variety of times to accommodate those in different time zones. It is also important that you try to use tools that can be easily accessed internationally.

Facilitating Peer Review

One way to achieve collaboration is to have learners engage in a group writing activity such as peer review, which can be conducted using Wikis or Google Docs. You can also consider setting up discussion forums for peer reviews in small groups because most LMSs have embedded discussion boards that can be used to engage learners in peer review. Peer review (discussed also in Chapter 3) involves learners formulating questions about their classmates' writing, and providing constructive feedback to one another on their assignments.

A common misstep that many instructors make in approaching peer review is to assume that learners already have the skills needed to conduct peer reviews, and that incorporating peer review is simply about asking learners to apply these skills to the tasks of reading and responding to one another's writing. Instead, instructors should approach peer review as an opportunity to identify and teach these skills and for learners to practice these by guiding and supporting them through the process. Moreover, this community-building approach is likely to be more successful if learners first practice peer review with shorter sample assignments, under the guidance of the instructor who will explain the value of the peer review process, and also educate learners about the evaluation criteria to be used. Even though learners as peer reviewers should not be asked to use the same criteria the instructor uses when grading papers, by participating in peer review they should gain a better understanding of those criteria. By using an explicit peer review worksheet and modeling peer review, you can provide your learners with the guidance necessary to provide one another with helpful and substantive feedback. In this regard, Appendix F offers *Guidelines for Conducting Peer Review*. Making the writing process more collaborative by way of peer-review activities provides learners with opportunities to learn from one another and helps them build connections, thereby fostering a learning community.

Facilitating Peer Dialogue Journals

Peer dialogue journals, a learning exercise developed by Bloomberg (2005), can be used to prompt reflections on course material, issues related to the course, and on new learning as a result of a specific course module or the entire course. In this type of journaling activity, two or more learners work collaboratively by sharing experiences via a common journal, examining and analyzing central questions and issues related to the course material, and offering each other insights and thoughts as the shared experience unfolds. Through their dialogue, learners build on each other's insights, reflections, and learning, and present each other with new ways of thinking and reasoning. The journal becomes an account of the learners' work in progress, but more essentially an opportunity for reflection on learning by providing *a shared experience* to critically and analytically engage with course content, or even to debate certain concepts and issues.

As with peer review, appropriate and explicit guidance from instructors is essential to gain the most out of this activity. Be careful not to assume that your learners will know how to engage in peer dialogue journaling. Rather, approach this activity as an opportunity to teach learners how to most meaningfully engage in this learning experience and use it for maximum benefit as well as an opportunity to collaborate with fellow learners. By using effective prompts in the way of critical questions that are related to the course content, you can provide your learners with a springboard to deep thinking and discussion. Remember that it is the quality of the discussion that is valuable, with deeper critical thinking and reflection giving way to deeper learning and more meaningful insights. The quality of prompting questions is therefore key to ensuring deep and meaningful discussion. Appendix G offers *Guidelines for Implementing Peer Dialogue Journals*.

FEEDBACK AS THE MEDIUM OF INSTRUCTION

In the online environment, the primary instructional delivery mode is written, audio, or video feedback, which creates the foundation for constructive learner–instructor interaction. *Your feedback is your teaching!* And, because you are not situated physically in a classroom with your learners, establishing a sense of *presence* through your feedback becomes an essential component to creating a successful online learning experience. In fact, in some online environments, feedback may be an instructor's only interaction with their learners, and when feedback is minimal or absent, it will negatively impact learner engagement.

Assignments, tasks, or activities are usually required regularly (mostly weekly) throughout a course because these are a measure of the learner's

Table 6.1. Basic Rules for Online Dialogue

Principle	Ground Rule
Respect	Ask questions, but do so respectfully
Honor	Share thoughts and ideas, but do so honorably and with integrity
Flexibility	Offer opinions and insights, but do so flexibly to encourage further dialogue
Courage	Be willing to engage in difficult conversations; do so in a healthy rather than destructive manner
Focus	Focus your conversations on the quality of the "work"; not on the "person" or their abilities and attributes

progressive and ongoing application of knowledge. Assignments may be written or in some other presentational format (such as PowerPoint, Prezi, YouTube, etc.). It is easy to fall into the trap of merely interacting with learners by grading assignments. But this is not sufficient! Your feedback on assignments, tasks, or activities *is the way by which you teach*. Consider each assignment as a window into your learner's thinking, and use this to recognize the deeper conceptual and content-related issues that must be addressed, including understanding and articulating ideas, demonstrating critical thinking, and also writing skills. In practice, this means viewing each learner on their growth trajectory, with the assignment as a measure of their progress, and you as the instructor guiding them toward improvement and success. Instead of just grading one assignment after another, your focus should be on how to facilitate engagement—through your feedback—and to help your learners develop and succeed! Table 6.1 includes ways to ensure that you are engaging in constructive and inclusive online dialogue and communication.

Deep Learning Versus Surface Learning

Let us pause for a moment to think about the type of learning that we hope to instill in our learners, and what essential knowledge we want them to derive from our teaching. Garrison and Cleveland-Innes (2005) suggest that learners typically employ a variety of approaches to learning, including *surface, achievement, and deep approaches*. *Surface learning* employs the least amount of effort toward realizing the minimum required outcomes. Surface learners are motivated to complete the task rather than assimilate the learning. While we might hope for more from these learners, we need to recognize that they might not be interested in deeper interaction or meaning. *Achievement learning* reflects an orientation to the external reward for demonstrated learning. Achievement learners are motivated by grades, and their focus is predominantly on activities that will result in the highest grades. Such learners will often be high achievers and may very likely have anxiety around grades and feedback. It is important to recognize that they may be challenged to accept critical feedback and may need additional support in terms of accepting instructor feedback and integrating it into their work. *Deep learners* embrace and digest course material in the search for meaning, significance, relevance, and applicability of knowledge. They focus on understanding and tend to actively seek clarity. In doing so, these learners will likely reach out to instructors independently, ask questions, and seek connection. Remember that through the feedback that we provide and the interactive strategies that we employ, we want to foster the *deepest approach to learning possible*, by helping all of our learners engage with the material in ways that are most meaningful to them. Table 6.2 offers ideas regarding the types of questions that can provoke deeper thinking, and hence deeper and more significant learning. Ask your learners questions about what it was about their course that was important or relevant to them, and why. In other words, your questions are not just content specific, but about their *interest in the content and what they may do with the content in their lives and careers.*

Table 6.2. Critical Questions to Promote Deep Thinking

Question Type	Description	Purpose	Examples
Closed	Serves to elicit a brief, often single-word response.	Gather information from learners, learner attention or knowledge, or reinforce key points.	• Do you agree or disagree with this statement? • Are you satisfied with that outcome?
Open-Ended	Serves to elicit detailed and complex responses to check understanding and apply information.	Draw out learner's thoughts, and encourage learners toward a deeper level of understanding.	• How and in what ways would you address this issue? • Why is it important to consider this idea? • What are the ways you can accomplish this task? • How are these concepts similar and/or different? • Can you explain this idea in your own words?

(continued)

Multimodal Teaching Strategies to Engage and Empower Learners

Table 6.2. (continued)

Question Type	Description	Purpose	Examples
Recall	Serves to elicit responses that are a response to or that refer to past experiences and prior knowledge.	Allow learners to recall key points, and reinforce key points through repetition and deeper thinking.	• How have you addressed this issue in the past? • What is the primary strategy recommended by the research we've been examining? • Based on previous experience, how do you interpret this question? • Can you think of another instance where this occurred?
Viewpoint	Serves to elicit higher-order thinking by connecting to learners' ideas and experiences. This usually requires analysis or evaluation.	Engage learners by inviting their perspectives and prompting them to autonomously make decisions and take a standpoint on significant issues or events.	• What is your understanding of this idea or concept, and why? • Of the many ways to complete this task, which do you think is the best or most effective?
Reflective	Serves to elicit higher-order metacognitive thinking by connecting to learners' ideas and experiences. This requires deeper critical reflection.	Ensure that deep learning actually occurs by providing a space to think critically and reflectively and engage in dialogue and/or action as a result.	• Why do you explain this idea in this way? • Can you think of different ways to approach this issue? • How did you arrive at this conclusion? • What have you learned that you can now apply in your life and/or professional practice?

Learners' Perceptions of Feedback

A study conducted by McLean et al. (2015) examined learners' perceptions of feedback, revealing four key points:

- **Feedback as telling**, where learners equated feedback with information that is fixed and not open to interpretation or to

adaptation. In this conception, the feedback comes from an "outside expert," and is focused on the here and now. It is in direct response to the task at hand without including any future implications.
- **Feedback as guiding,** where learners reported feedback as pointing them in the right direction. There is more to this type of feedback than just being told something. Learners thought about the feedback in terms of how it prompted them to give themselves feedback, and to reflect on what they did, and so they were beginning to see value in feedback.
- **Feedback as developing understanding,** where learners saw the information as explanatory, helping them to understand not just that they were doing something wrong, but why it was wrong. In addition, the feedback was seen as being relevant beyond the classroom and could be applied to learners' work, professions, and careers.
- **Feedback as offering a different perspective,** where the feedback was seen as offering another point of view, thereby introducing learners to other ways or alternative perspectives. Here, feedback could be viewed from different angles, and even be questioned. This feedback could be applied right now and also in the future, and was seen as useful for ongoing personal and professional development. This study revealed that these varying conceptions guide how learners think about and therefore respond to the feedback that they receive from their instructors. This is an important consideration as *we do want our feedback to be both usable and useful!* Questions, if well-articulated and thoughtful, have the potential to prompt critical thinking and foster deeper learning.

It is important to realize that while you are cognizant of providing feedback to your learners, you cannot necessarily assume *how they will receive it*. Moreover, you cannot expect or guess how your learners will know *how to apply* your feedback. Appendix D, *Learner Support Resource: How to Benefit from Feedback and Critique*, is a sample of what you may provide as a support for your learners to let them know more about the type of feedback that you will provide and how they are expected to address your feedback. A word on critique is warranted: Critique is *not* the same as criticism. Criticism involves judgment and faultfinding, while the purpose of critique is to evaluate a piece of work in order to increase understanding and offer the challenge necessary to improve and succeed. Essentially, *the goal of feedback is evaluative and corrective* in order to support the learning process and guide learners toward building new knowledge and increasing their skills. This is achieved by helping your learners understand where they meet established standards and identifying what they can improve upon going forward to meet specified standards or outcomes.

PREPARE TO PROVIDE FEEDBACK

Useful and usable feedback is critical to engaging and empowering all learners, creating a supportive learning environment, and preparing them to succeed in the current learning experience and beyond. To begin to get a feel for the type of **written feedback** that is required, refer to Table 6.3, which offers some basic ideas for adopting an interactive teaching approach.

In preparing to provide written feedback, there are a few key points to consider that apply to teaching generally, and that have direct and specific applicability to online instruction.

Table 6.3. Tips for Providing Engaging Written Feedback: A Brief Cheat Sheet

Tip	Underlying Reason
Show respect and warmth by addressing each learner by their correct name.	Using no name or an incorrect name creates "distance," and a sense of disconnectedness.
Teach by example. Ensure that what you are writing is well presented and grammatically correct. Proofread before sending it!	Errors in punctuation and grammar appear unprofessional and do not model the type of writing that we expect of the learner.
Make use of consistent writing style and font throughout.	Lack of consistency appears unprofessional and messy and does not model the writing conventions that are expected of the learner.
When you refer a learner to a resource (library, learning center, etc.), include links and information regarding making the connection.	Simply referring a learner to a resource does not ensure that they will know how to access the resource or obtain the necessary assistance.
Feedback should be clearly focused on the work at hand rather than on the learner.	Your goal is to provide critique that will assist and motivate the learner to improve on future assignments. Your goal is NOT to criticize or undermine the learner!
Feedback should be directly focused on the prescribed CLOs. Addressing the CLOs ensures that the feedback is actionable!	Feedback is first and foremost about the learner and their success. Attaining the learning goals is paramount so feedback must address the extent to which these goals are actually being met.
Provide affirmation and acknowledgment of work well done, as well as point out limitations and shortcomings that require ongoing improvement.	Instruction should include a balance of support and critique so that learners clearly understand the applicability of the feedback and are motivated to actually use it!

(continued)

Table 6.3. (continued)

Tip	Underlying Reason
Make sure to intersperse questions that encourage critical reflection.	Lecture mode is perceived by learners as distant and unengaging. Questions serve to draw your learners into the conversation and demonstrates that their ideas are valued by you.
Common courtesies such as the use of "please" and "thank you" are important aspects that add a positive tone.	Demonstrating respect goes a long way toward building strong teaching relationships, and hence engagement.
Always let the learner know that you are available to discuss your feedback, and their progress, and that they can contact you with any questions or concerns.	This welcoming "invitation" opens the door to ongoing dialogue and allows your learners the opportunity to feel free to engage with you and also plan ahead as needed.
End on a positive note by thanking the learner for their work, and conclude your feedback with a warm salutation such as "Thank you, Dr. B."	A negative tone will be perceived as disingenuous (or even offensive) and counteracts any attempts to engage learners. A warm informal salutation is preferable to ending with a generic phrase such as "Have a great day." To remain professional, always sign off with your title and name.

Ensure Teaching Presence

Being present means being fully tuned to the needs of the learner to whom you are providing relevant and **individualized feedback**, and fully focused on the task at hand. As discussed in previous chapters, teaching presence encompasses both social presence (collaboration and interaction among learners and instructors) and cognitive presence (sharing knowledge and engaging in dialogue and critical reflection with regard to the work at hand). The implication is that instructors are approachable and available to learners through ongoing and sustained communication, collaboration, and interaction. Be "in the moment" and "connected" to each of your learners by removing distractions. Provide feedback in a direct but conversational way. Along with your feedback always offer an invitation for the learner to contact you to discuss the feedback, receive additional clarification or information, or plan ahead. Your openness to setting up one-to-one synchronous conversations demonstrates your desire to connect, and displays your commitment to your learner's ongoing success, thereby further solidifying your presence. When teaching new ideas and concepts, try to consider how you can do so in ways that relate to the learner's interests and experiences. Be deliberate in frequently using the words "we" or "us" when talking about the work at hand, thereby establishing yourself as a co-learner and partner in the learning experience.

Address Growth Academic Mindset

While mindset was discussed in Chapter 5, we revisit this for a moment here, because it is important to consider the mindset of your learners in order to most effectively evaluate their work, offer relevant resources, and assign appropriate grades. It also means being mindful of your own mindset, and working to be as objective as possible when evaluating the work of your learners. Being conscious of encouraging a growth mindset in each of your learners will ensure that you focus your feedback on how they can improve, and that you are providing the necessary support and motivation to ensure their ongoing learning and development. Reflecting on your own mindset as an instructor also serves to address (and often reframe) your expectations and your approach in working with your learners, and offer feedback appropriately. Remember that feedback should always be focused on learners' improvement and progress, and should include necessary supports so they can hopefully reach their potential, and succeed. This means that you will likely realize that not all strategies will work the same with all learners. However, you will hopefully commit to providing encouragement and motivation so that all of your learners will continue working and persevere.

Lecture Versus Interactivity

It is easy to fall into the trap of simply lecturing, by adopting the role of "sage on the stage," with the expectation that learners just accept what we are teaching them. The "sage on the stage" characterization of the teacher's role is synonymous with a teacher-centered approach to education, in which the standard lecture is considered to be the principal mode of delivery. In this scenario, the learner is simply a passive notetaker, a receiver of content, and an accumulator of facts. While it is one of the most traditional methods of teaching, and is often regarded as an effective instructional method in a wide array of disciplines, lecturing in isolation is one of the most ineffective instructional methods when it comes to retention of information and long-term academic success. This is especially so in the online environment where learners can often tend to feel isolated and disconnected. A key principle of adult learning is that the learners seek to be self-directed and take ownership of their learning. As such, it is vitally important that instructors consider ways to incorporate interactive rather than lecturing approaches to sustain learner engagement, thereby deepening knowledge retention and overall academic performance. Interactivity occurs by actively engaging with your learners through ongoing and sustained communication and support.

Tone and Presentation

Much of the communication in the online environment is in written form; hence, your writing skills and ability to communicate through writing is critical. Connecting with learners by being "personable" is a matter of writing style, and instructors must be sensitive to how they come across in their writing. With verbal communication, our message comes across not just in terms of *what* we say but *how* we say it. The "how" is where nonverbal communication comes into the picture; that is, our tone, facial expressions, and body language. If verbal and nonverbal communication are in sync with one another, the message is effective and easily understood. However, written communication does not have the advantage of benefiting from nonverbal cues, and this can naturally create a challenge in establishing a positive and conducive learning environment. Moreover, giving critical feedback is especially difficult without nonverbal cues. Consider carefully how your learners may internalize and receive your feedback. In addition, consider how cultural differences can shape how communication is delivered and received, and recognize that even with all good intentions, the impact may be felt differently by your learners. In remaining aware of how your feedback is perceived and accepted, tone and presentation are therefore critical considerations.

Timeliness and Frequency

Finally, remember that the timeliness and frequency of your feedback and grading is critical. An expectation in the online environment is the timeliness of feedback, grading of submissions, and completion of assessments. Typically, learners submit an assignment and wait for the response and feedback from their instructor before starting work on the next assignment. Learners are more likely to implement feedback when it is evident that their instructor is present and attentive by responding to their work regularly and consistently. Your learners will be relying on your feedback to guide their learning, and if they are not receiving feedback consistently throughout their course, they will have difficulty identifying where to focus their efforts. Providing feedback as soon as possible, while the work is still fresh in learners' minds, is important in the online learning setting to ensure that they remain engaged and motivated. Delaying feedback may result in a learner not moving on to the next task or assignment. In recognizing that frequency is relative to a number of factors (type of course, term length, content, credit hours, etc.), it is recommended that you provide learners *at least* one opportunity a week to receive your feedback. Institutions set guidelines regarding timeliness policies. A common practice is to set 24–48 hours as a timeline to access, grade, and provide feedback for completed work. It is also advisable, and indeed essential, that you adhere to your institution's guidelines and policies regarding timeliness.

GUIDING PRINCIPLES FOR SUBSTANTIVE AND ENGAGING FEEDBACK

The way that you present and organize your feedback indicates that this has been thoughtfully compiled, and also models and exemplifies the quality of work that we expect of our learners, encouraging them to do the same in their work. There are some important steps that you can take to ensure high-quality feedback and increase the likelihood that your feedback will be well received, clearly understood, and usable. To achieve this, your feedback must be (1) meaningful and individualized; (2) balanced; and (3) developmental, forward thinking, and actionable. All of these criteria are essential to empower your learners to take ownership of their learning.

Feedback Is Meaningful and Individualized

Learners are more likely to persist in their online courses if the educational experience is personalized rather than generic (canned or prepared in advance). As a start, address each learner by name! Determining the needs of each learner depends on your *careful assessment* of their work, including the quality of previous course submissions and the extent to which your prior feedback has been addressed. Keeping these factors in mind will avoid a "routine checklist" approach to providing feedback, and ensure that you always remain mindful of the individual needs of each learner. To make your assessment systematic and thorough, there are some basic criteria or "teaching points" to consider.

Assignment Completion. Determine whether the learner has followed the assignment instructions and completed all necessary requirements. Let them know whether this was achieved or not. Be very clear in pointing out any areas that have been omitted.

Conceptual Understanding. Assess whether and to what extent the learner demonstrated that they understand the course content and are able to apply the appropriate materials and/or concepts. This is a priority, because if the learner does not have a good grasp of the course content, this is something to work on improving. To prompt your feedback, ask yourself the following questions: Did they think critically about the material? Did they achieve the objectives of the assignment? The answers to these questions will constitute the main focus of your feedback. If the learner displays a deep understanding of the material, be sure to acknowledge this in your feedback. Simply saying "good job" or "it is clear that you understand (or don't understand) the material" is not sufficient or meaningful. Instead, be specific and explain how you can tell that the learner understood the content, and how this content can be applied in real-world contexts or used in the learner's field of practice. Similarly, if the work displays a lack or limited understanding of the material, be sure to explain the material that the learner is struggling with as well as some appropriate support resources. This clarifies why they are not currently meeting expectations and also offers guidelines for improvement. Remember that learners do need to know where they stand regarding their mastery of the material, so they will know what to work on as they move forward.

Assignment Presentation. Assess and provide feedback about the ways in which the learner has presented their work. To prompt your feedback, ask yourself the following questions: Did the learner present the work in a professional and articulate manner? Did they adhere to the expected writing style and writing conventions? Is the writing clear and compelling, and are all sources correctly cited (this is essential to avoid plagiarism)? Is the writing grammatically correct? Help learners understand *why* these areas of improvement are important and direct them to the available resources for support.

Table 6.4 provides an overview of the "teaching points" that become the key criteria for assessment and feedback. By creating and developing your own toolbox, you can begin to collect a bank or repository of responses to frequently encountered misconceptions, errors, or blind spots. Feedback should address what learners have accomplished, but also help them develop useful work habits. Be intentional in providing ongoing support and encouragement to sustain motivation and engagement. You will be very thankful for your toolbox when you are teaching multiple learners at the same time as this will save you much time in the long run! Continue to add examples of ways to promote and reinforce good work habits that will aid learners with their future work. Remember that as you add to your collection of responses, be mindful at all times to "personalize" and "individualize" your feedback.

Feedback Is Balanced

Online instructors must intentionally work toward developing and implementing strategies that increase learner engagement. To sustain motivation and engagement, and to encourage a growth in academic mindset, feedback should of necessity incorporate a *balance of critique and support*.

Table 6.4. Streamlined Feedback Toolbox

Teaching Point	Feedback Examples	Reinforce Work Habits
Assignment Completion	"You have addressed some but not all of the assignment requirements. Going forward please be sure to read the instructions carefully so that you do not miss anything." "Please keep in mind that you need to cover all of the items that you are asked to address in the activity, since instructors are required to deduct points for incomplete answers or missing sections."	"Assignments are designed to help meet CLOs, so it is very important to read and follow all necessary requirements." "Assignments are designed to assist you to meet CLOs, so it is really important to follow assignment instructions. If something is not clear, please feel free to ask questions prior to working on the assignment."
Content Understanding	"You have a good beginning here but you are still missing the point—your study is not about implementing the program, it is about finding out what learners and faculty think about it." "Can you add a few sentences here to explain the reasons for this phenomenon?" "I am not sure what is meant by this. Please explain clearly." "I'd like to hear more about why you chose this idea. You cannot assume the reader is familiar with these ideas, so it would help to define these ideas."	"Carefully reading and taking notes on the assigned readings can help you prepare a top-notch paper. Be sure to make use of assignment resources that are included in the syllabus, that is, the readings (articles, books, etc.) that are provided." "Make notes of concepts or ideas that are not clear to you and then reach out to your instructor for clarification and explanation. Your instructor is here to assist, so always feel free to reach out if you are unsure of something."
Presentation	"I notice that you are having some difficulty with headings and subheadings. Please refer to the Writing Manual so that you can become familiar with academic writing requirements." "Citations are needed here to substantiate what you have written and to show where you obtained this information. Please add these citations	"To avoid plagiarism—even unintended plagiarism—all work that you use must be cited so that you give credit where credit is due. Lack of citations is not only unacceptable in academic writing, but it also undermines the quality of your work." "In a well-organized and cohesive paper, sentences and

(continued)

Table 6.4. (continued)

Teaching Point	Feedback Examples	Reinforce Work Habits
	as appropriate. Remember that citations must always be precise to avoid any errors." "This is very important information; you will need to have an in-text citation." "Whenever you refer to studies that have taken place, you will need an in-text citation for the studies that you are referring to." "In academic writing, paragraphs must be tight, crisp, and focused. Omit needless words, and avoid unnecessary clauses. Make sure all sentences are clear and direct so that there is no ambiguity or confusion on the part of the reader." "Please remember to be very specific in your writing so that the reader clearly understands your ideas. Each paragraph should be focused on one idea only."	paragraphs are thoughtfully assembled to support one or more points. To achieve this, carefully planning is key. The introductory paragraph sets the stage and explains the focus of the paper, followed by successive paragraphs each of which is focused on one aspect of the discussion. The concluding paragraph must synthesize and provide closure to the discussion." "Organization of ideas serves to make your discussion flow and unfold logically and smoothly, allowing your reader to follow and understand your train of thought and thus remain engaged." "To organize your ideas, think of a topic sentence for each paragraph. This sentence becomes the anchor, allowing you to stay focused as you develop your ideas. Starting with a topic sentence lets readers know what each paragraph will cover, which makes it easier to follow."
Writing Mechanics	"This is an incomplete sentence as the verb is missing. Please reword so this sentence is clearer." "This sentence includes grammatical errors. Please correct these." "Sentences should not start with an acronym or an abbreviation. You can either spell it out or rewrite the sentence."	"At the graduate level, and in academia generally, clear and concise writing is important. This conveys professionalism and academic competence. Always be sure to check for errors prior to submitting your assignments. You can do this by reading the paper out loud, or having a friend or colleague proofread for you."

(continued)

Table 6.4. (continued)

Teaching Point	Feedback Examples	Reinforce Work Habits
	"This is a run-on (overly long) sentence. Please reword this." "Split this long sentence into two. That would flow better."	"Formal writing guidelines must be adhered to in all academic work. This includes clear introductions, sentence construction, paragraph development, and effective conclusions. In order to maintain the attention of your reader, clarity and logical flow are essential."
Support and Encouragement	"Thank you, Mary, for your hard work. This is a great start! Please review my feedback and let me know if you have any questions. I look forward to working with you!" "Bob, thank you for your ongoing work on this. I appreciate your time and effort!"	"If something is not clear, it is important to speak up, in this and all other courses!" "Please always feel free to schedule a time to discuss your work with your instructors. They are here to support you and ensure your success!"

Critique. Use specific and substantive feedback regarding areas in need of improvement, explaining abstract concepts and ideas, and make suggestions for improvement where needed. Learners should clearly understand what needs improvement, and how they might go about addressing errors or limitations. Remember that errors can potentially become important teachable moments! In order to achieve this, feedback should provide "doable" next steps, so be sure to frequently incorporate relevant practical examples and work samples to aid progress along the way.

Support. While you should not shy away from pointing out and addressing areas in need of improvement, be sure also to affirm and acknowledge progress and accomplishments, by providing positive and constructive feedback as applicable. Affirming the strengths of the work balances the flaws or limitations. Recognizing good work and letting learners know what they did well is empowering and reinforcing, and encourages motivation, engagement, and ongoing learning. By commending them, you demonstrate acknowledgment and respect for their efforts, allowing them to recognize and be proud of the positive aspects of their work. Moreover, by providing supportive feedback, you build rapport and trust with your learners, so they feel comfortable with accepting critique and asking questions if needed.

Feedback Is Developmental, Forward Thinking, and Actionable

While your learners are expected to master the material in front of them, you also need to consider how the feedback that they are receiving now will benefit them with regard to their future assignments and activities. Hattie and Timperley (2007) produced an effective teaching model that reduces discrepancies between current understandings, actual performance, and desired goals. This model includes three components: feedback (how am I doing?); **feed up** (where am I going?); and **feed forward** (where to next?). Therefore, to ensure a developmental approach means providing clear feedback, actionable feed forward, and relevant feed up. Feedback motivates because it contains explicit information and guidance regarding progress and improvement. Feed forward includes information, suggestions, direct instruction, and resources that learners can *actually use* in order to improve and succeed. Feed up addresses the "why," thereby helping learners better understand the bigger picture regarding their future learning, in order to become more autonomous and self-directed in their educational pursuits. Following is a little more detail for each of these three components:

Feedback. Feedback motivates because it provides learners with information that they can use to succeed. Feedback affirms strengths and accomplishments, and describes characteristics of good work commensurate with meeting the CLOs, and also points out areas in need of improvement. Feedback should be clear, specific, and focused. Merely telling a learner "this needs work" does not provide guidance on how to improve. Remember that you do not want to offer just **informational feedback,** which is effective in domains with clear right or wrong answers. Rather, you want your feedback to be empowering and transformational. As such, one way to deliver developmental feedback is to make sure that you include not only clear and direct explanations, but also thought-provoking questions that will stimulate critical thinking, and foster deep learning and ongoing development. Engaging your learners by asking them questions that pertain to the subject prompts them to delve into the topic in their own way and really explore the subject matter that is being discussed. Incorporating questions in your feedback also offers a reflective opportunity for learners to express or explain themselves if necessary. Moreover, this practice models teaching as an interactive, dialogic, and collaborative process, enabling you to customize your learning materials and strategies, and helping to build working relationships.

Feed Forward. The second dimension of developmental feedback is to incorporate available resources that will help learners improve. This makes the feedback actionable! Feed forward says: "Here's what you can do to improve future work." Feed forward means incorporating resources that are relevant and current, and that will be helpful regarding improvement and success. These resources include Internet sites, links to social media, and audio or video material. To inspire participation and learning, learners need to be comfortable with the new material, be actively involved, and be able to analyze the material. In line with the key principles of andragogy (theory of how adults learn), instructors should make connections to real-world applications in their feedback and provide clarification when needed so that feedback is meaningful and learners understand its relevance and applicability. As such, feed forward makes your feedback actionable and has the potential to stimulate transfer of learning to future tasks. This is an important consideration given that we strive for our learners' ongoing and sustained improvement, not just in the courses we teach, but beyond our courses. Of course, providing too many resources can be overwhelming so be sure to prioritize and offer relevant resources only as needed.

Feed Up. The third dimension of developmental feedback facilitates ongoing learning and engagement, by clearly communicating the value of each learning experience. Feed up says: "Here's what you can do to improve future work, AND here's why it will help you." The power of explanation can be illustrated by way of the feedback that you offer on assignments, which should both "show" and "tell." In addition to providing clear and specific suggestions for how the learner can improve (feedback), and the resources that can be uses to achieve improvement (feed forward), instructors should explain *why* the knowledge gained through the assignment is important, and the reasons *why* it is important to make the recommended improvements. This piece is in essence the final "motivation step," designed to articulate and explain *why* the course content or material is significant to real-world applications, and how the suggested changes can promote success in both their educational pursuits and long-term goals. This feed up component is vital in terms of forward thinking, helping learners develop their understanding of the bigger picture by connecting the dots from assignment to assignment and course to course, thereby becoming more autonomous and self-directed in their educational pursuits. Refer back to Table 6.4, *Streamlined Feedback Toolbox*, where you will see that the useful work habits are in fact the *feed up* component of your teaching!

Streamlining Your Feedback

As you can see, thoughtful and intentional customization and personalization of feedback are essential to assist learners to improve and succeed. And while there are some basic principles regarding how to teach and instruct in the online environment in engaging and supportive ways, there are also a number of skills and strategies that you can learn to use in order to streamline your teaching without diminishing the quality thereof. Learning ways to streamline your teaching is important, considering the workload that you may encounter in working with multiple learners at any one time, which could become overwhelming if not efficiently managed. Refer to Appendix H, *Satisfactory Versus Unsatisfactory Written Feedback Samples* (includes comparative feedback samples to indicate what makes feedback acceptable or unacceptable), and Appendix I, *Samples of Feedback Commentary*.

A word of caution: Streamlining your feedback is a useful strategy especially with a high workload. However, this needs to be carefully applied so as not to offer "canned" feedback. While instructors often develop a collection of useful resources to streamline the teaching process, you should not rely overly on stock or **boilerplate feedback**. Learners are quick to realize when they receive feedback that does not directly apply or relate to their own work. This diminishes your credibility as an instructor and will impact the development of effective teaching relationships. As such, be mindful that you are customizing your teaching, and that all resources and tools are tailored and personalized to meet each of your individual learners where they currently are in order to help them improve and succeed.

MULTIMODAL TEACHING

The multimedia principle (Clark & Mayer, 2011) explains that to enhance learning and maximize engagement, online teaching should include multiple media and tools. Creating alternative ways of representing information in rich and dynamic ways, broadening learner engagement opportunities, and expanding the ways learners can express their learning and knowledge can be of great benefit. By providing multiple means of engagement, for input of information and their own output, we increase the likelihood that learners with different abilities, experiences, needs, interests, and passions will all find something to connect to. In doing so, we engage our diverse learner population more effectively, which has been shown to correspond to deeper learning, increased motivation and persistence, and improved learning outcomes. Always remember that technology is not a substitute for authentic interactions and engagement; it is essentially a tool to *facilitate engagement*.

Working in the online educational environment means that you will have access to a variety of tools and resources that may not be available or applicable in traditional classrooms. As such, the role of an online instructor can and should extend beyond verbal and written feedback to include audio and video feedback, which is vital to engage learners and ensure their academic development. The technology that is currently available allows you to increasingly diversify your instructional strategies to effectively and meaningfully engage your learners. Some learners are auditory learners, so audio and video feedback will most likely be more applicable and relevant than written feedback. While multiple methods of feedback are encouraged, and for teaching to be at its best, audio and video feedback need not necessarily be a substitute for written feedback for most learners, but rather a useful and stimulating addition.

Benefits of Using Audio and Video Tools

Overall, when instructors use audio or video technologies, they tend to provide more feedback in less time when they explain verbally what they are seeing in the work. Mostly, this is simply because we can speak much faster than we can type. When using text, we need to be careful about our writing, and so we also tend to spend time correcting errors and editing. Keep in mind, however, it is not just about doing your job as an online instructor more quickly or efficiently. *Rather, it is about making your feedback more effective for your learners.* It is therefore important to know how to effectively use these tools, both singly and in combination. Table 6.5. allows you to consider a few scenarios in which audio and video feedback might be an effective instructional approach.

Incorporating Technology to Provide Feedback

Most current LMSs provide basic content delivery mechanisms for blended learning and easily handle the delivery of a variety of media including text, video, and audio. "Feedback tools" in the online environment include multiple digital applications or extensions used to provide responses to your learners' work, and as technology advances, new tools are constantly emerging. As an instructor, you may have a variety of feedback tools already at your disposal, which are built into your institution's LMS. While technology has the potential to make course feedback more effective and more engaging, that will not just happen automatically. Technology must be thoughtfully applied, and not just used for the sake of using it. Remember that it is not the type of tool that matters, but *how you use it to* help you directly communicate and interact more effectively with your learners, thereby guiding their learning. It is critically important not to get bogged down with the technology, but to really think about pedagogy and engagement. These are the central tenets of education regardless of whether learning is face-to-face or online. Consider all of the ways that you can connect with your learners, and the exciting levels of engagement that takes place when providing written feedback, audio or video feedback. Remember, asset-based teaching is an approach to feedback that is focused mostly on strengths and talents.

Table 6.5. Benefits of Audio and Visual Feedback Tools

Instructional Goal	Benefit for the Learner
You want to be more connected and "present" for your learners. Online learners may want a personal connection with their instructor for a number of reasons. Some are new to online studies or they are insecure about their abilities. Others may feel uncomfortable "bothering" the instructor with questions or speaking up in front of their peers. Audio and video feedback allow you to thoughtfully personalize your feedback. Learners begin to see you as a real person, rather than just someone behind a computer screen. You become "human."	Less isolation

Learners may feel motivated to learn if they are able to see you and/or hear your voice providing them specific and personalized feedback. This may help them to feel less separated from you as an instructor and begin to feel more connected to you and to one another. The presence of voice reminds learners that the instructor is a "real person." Voice humanizes the instructor and can convey a better sense of care than text feedback because it is perceived to be more personal than text. |
| You want to avoid or minimize miscommunication. We've all received an email or text that came off as angry or offensive. The chances are that was not the sender's intention. If you find that learners seem to misinterpret your written communication, or if you receive evaluation data that show you are perceived as distant or impersonal, audio or video feedback may help to resolve this. Audio and video tools allow learners to hear your intonation, listen, and watch as you point out areas that require revision or improvement. | Ongoing dialogue: Audio and video feedback tends to begin a dialogue with your learners. This creates a collegial atmosphere and the sense of working through issues collaboratively and supportively with the instructor, rather than alone. |
| You want to demonstrate a process. Communicating to your learners exactly where an error occurred within their written discussion can sometimes be challenging. With screencast you show learners how to *actually* make recommended improvements by pointing to the exact location of the error and showing how this can be revised or corrected. You are able to speak to the learner as though they are sitting next to you, acknowledging good work, and making suggestions for revision and improvements. | Improved understanding: Written feedback can be misconstrued or misinterpreted, and learners can tend to read it as harsher than you intended. By providing feedback with your voice, learners can hear your motivational tone and understand that you are constructively directing their learning for purposes of improvement. You want to convey nuance, and with video feedback, you can show learners exactly what you mean. |

Asset-based teaching is in contrast to deficit-based teaching where your feedback would be focused mostly on limitations and inadequacies:

- **Written and audio feedback:** Through the use of **audio feedback**, you can expand on written feedback or offer insights that will help learners bridge the gap between the current and upcoming assignment, activity, or task. Additionally, weekly prerecorded audio or video clips can allow you to connect with your learners and draw their attention to an assignment for the week, or a long-term assignment they should be starting to consider. Remember to keep the content short and light, saving the heavy lifting for the accompanying syllabus, which lists all the resources and assignments for the week.
- **Written and video feedback:** Through use of video feedback, you can expand on written feedback, a tactic that often helps learners "get it" faster. With screencast (video by way of sharing your screen or the learner's screen) you can show learners how to *actually* make recommended improvements by walking your learner through the assignment, and provide detailed, one-on-one support.
- **Written feedback with an invitation to meet synchronously:** In addition to providing regular feedback on assignments or tasks, you may choose to meet synchronously with learners. Adding this synchronous option brings you and your learner together in real time to thoughtfully discuss the work. This makes the online learning experience virtually real and demonstrates **multimodal engagement** at its best!

Guidelines for Audio and Video Feedback

There are many types of multimedia that you can use in your course, including audio, video, voiceover presentations, and screencast. The more you get to know your learners and the more familiar you become with the available feedback tools, the richer and more meaningful your instruction will be. Following are some key pedagogical strategies to prepare and support learners with regard to **multimodal feedback**:

Preparation
- Know the features of your LMS and become familiar with the audio and video options. Making use of a headset with an external microphone will capture better audio, and improve the sound quality. You are also recommended to do some tests before starting your recording to ensure the quality of the sound.
- Develop a clear and thoughtful plan at the outset. Don't simply add a new tool at the last minute, without careful preparation. The

technology may have limits or issues that you should be aware of, including user maximums, download time, file sizes, associated fees, and so on. Become familiar with the tool and its limitations. And, plan carefully how you will use it.
- Make accommodations regarding ADA compliance as necessary. Using prerecorded teaching material will generate automatic closed captions that are needed for accessibility purposes. Automatic closed captioning is not perfect, so speak clearly and not too quickly to make sure that the content is as accurate as possible.

Learner Engagement
- Before you begin teaching a course, check with each learner regarding their preferred way of receiving feedback and honor their requests. For some learners, text feedback may be the preferred mode, so you will need to respect that. If auditory, consider a supplementary audio recording. If visual, consider a video recording or screencast.
- Make sure to let your learners know when you are offering video or audio or screencast feedback, and how to access this as they may need to download appropriate software. Remember to ensure technical support to avoid any stress regarding accessing feedback.
- As you teach a course, take notes on what technologies would or would not work in different situations. *Context is critical when it comes to using technology.* Consider the substance and purpose of your feedback. Try to vary your feedback techniques and select the most appropriate method for each assignment.

Audio and Video Application
- Use voice feedback to cover conceptual and content issues. Review what was done correctly and what still needs attention. Avoid using voice feedback for minor writing issues. The comments of your written feedback are a more appropriate way to address these.
- Video and audio feedback do not have to be perfect. Scripting and editing lose the spontaneity and humanism that you are seeking. Make your feedback sound like a natural conversation that you are having with each learner.
- Voice feedback can be somewhat nuanced and often misinterpreted as a result. It is not only *what* you say but *how* you say it. All content must be presented as bias-free and inclusive. Maintaining a respectful and engaging tone will ensure that your learners will feel comfortable participating in the course and engaging with the course content.

- Be sure that your feedback is focused and clear, making sure that the length of your presentation is appropriate. You cannot expect your learners to watch a very lengthy presentation. Be sensitive to learners' time and file-size constraints. Try to be concise and on topic in your feedback. This is not the time for a formal "lecture."
- Screencast is generally considered more effective than a "talking head" video, especially when you are explaining a complex process, because learners are able to both see and hear your explanation in real time. With screencast (video by way of sharing your screen) you are showing learners how to *actually* make recommended improvements. To facilitate engagement, speak to the learner as though they are sitting next to you, acknowledging good work, and suggesting any necessary improvements.
- Remember that there is such a thing as *too much information*. When creating videos, it is easy to overlook cognitive overload by presenting too much information too quickly. To avoid confusion, only talk about whatever it is you are pointing to on the video. When using screencast, use the cursor or a highlighting tool to point out exactly what you are talking about so that your voice and the image(s) align for the learner. This is called signaling, and it helps to reduce cognitive load.

ASSESSMENT AND GRADING

In Chapter 2, we covered how assessment entails defining what you want your learners to know or be able to do, providing learning opportunities to gain knowledge or skills, and then specifying ways to collect and analyze evidence of that learning. Because assessment is based directly on the CLOs, this ensures the integrity of the course content. Grading is the application of those assessments. Along with substantive feedback, you will also need to provide appropriate and understandable grades as an assessment of completed work.

Grading guidelines are designed to ensure that instructors and learners have a shared understanding of what is expected, and that learners will clearly understand the reasons for assigned grades. Using detailed analytic scoring rubrics will make your grading more transparent to learners, and also less prone to bias because you can more logically and transparently "justify" the grades that you assign. Rubrics also assist with streamlining your grading, making the process more organized, standardized, and accurate. Moreover, a rubric provides your learners with a clear understanding of the evaluation criteria before they even begin the assignment, task, or activity; helping them self-evaluate their work and identify areas for improvement. Carefully reviewing the grading guidelines and rubrics can help learners plan and complete their assignments to the best of their ability. You may choose to design your own rubrics, such as the one presented in Appendix J, *Sample Grading Rubric*. Most LMSs also have a built-in rubric tool, which offers time-saving features such as reusable comments and a total-points column that will automatically tally the points that have been assigned for each of the rubric's evaluative criteria.

Grading practices should always be logical and reasonable, because learners are more likely to accept grades that are thoughtfully applied. Clearly explaining or justifying how you arrived at a grade enables learners to understand the rationale for the assigned grade, rather than be confused or frustrated. Consequently, be sure to provide, to the extent possible, a grade justification that is clearly and directly related to assignment requirements and learning outcomes. This makes the grading rationale transparent and is more likely to be understood and accepted. Again, using a rubric can assist with making your grading clear, understandable, and transparent. You may refer to Appendix K for a *Sample Grade Justification Rubric*.

Let us turn for a moment on how you reflect your mindset and sense of teaching presence in the ways that you grade your learners' work. When you are grading and the work is well-done, you naturally develop a sense of closeness with the learner through their ideas. On the other hand, when you are grading a learner whose work is weak, poorly structured, or incoherent, try to remain focused on what is presented and not become drawn toward what "should" have been presented. In this instance, teaching presence and mindset are about what "is" rather than what is "not," and the focus should be on ways to assist and support the learner toward improvement and success. Remember that errors are teachable moments, so grade for growth and progress! Additionally, remember that **resubmissions** for poor work provide an opportunity to apply the feedback and revise as needed. This practice offers learners another chance to succeed by capturing teachable moments. Remember that the goal is ongoing improvement, and we want to offer opportunities for learners to perform at their best, thereby engaging and empowering them.

Tips for Getting Started

In reading this book, you are most likely relatively new to online teaching, so don't be afraid to ask for assistance and support. Technology is constantly evolving, and it is understandably difficult to keep up with every new feature and function. In the same way that you want your learners to reach out when they need help, there are people including instructional designers, educational technologists, and information technologists who are available to support you too. Table 6.6 provides some tips as you move forward with a "multimodal" frame of mind.

Table 6.6. Moving Forward: Some Final Tips

Start out with tools that your institution has in place!
One of the easiest ways to get started is to use the feedback tools integrated into your LMS. There is also most likely a plethora of resources available to you, including reference videos, dedicated support staff, and FAQs, so make use of these. The more familiar you are with the available feedback tools, the better these will work for you and your learners.
Mix it up, as one size does not fit all!
There is no single universal best practice for providing feedback. Be sure to vary your approach, using a mix of written, audio, or video content. Context is critical when it comes to using the technology and providing feedback. The feedback tool should fit the learner AND the specific assignment.
Make sure that your choices are accessible for everyone!
As with all course design, it is imperative that accessibility be taken into consideration when providing feedback. A broad range of learners benefit from accessible feedback tools, not just those with particular needs. If you create audio or video feedback, ensure all learners can access it. If you are unable to provide captions or transcripts, ask learners if they prefer written feedback. If the tool incorporates automatic captioning, make sure you speak clearly.
Ask your learners!
Learners will appreciate being able to tell you how they feel about your teaching methods or other aspects of the course, especially when granted anonymity. Asking what they think about your feedback practices or the use of a specific technology can be done via a survey or a poll. By asking for their views, you are helping empower your learners, and in the process, you are learning more about which feedback methods will work best for them. Their ideas can, and indeed should, help guide your instructional choices when you next teach the course.

CHAPTER SUMMARY AND SYNTHESIS

The primary instructional delivery mode is written, audio, or video feedback, which creates the foundation for constructive and meaningful learner–instructor interaction. While there is no formula for providing feedback, there are certain pointers that can assist you: Your feedback should be balanced (a mix of support and critique) and developmental, forward thinking, and actionable (to ensure progress and improvement). Importantly, feedback must also be individualized, so even though you may draw from your toolbox in order to make your work less labor intensive, the quality of the feedback should not suffer. Throughout this chapter, there is a strong focus on respectfully addressing diversity and inclusion, and ensuring that this is infused throughout one's teaching practice. Because online learning can certainly be a lonely and isolating experience, a key goal is to make the learning environment conducive to active participation, by implementing strategies that will increase learner engagement. Plan how to best engage learners and make their learning more meaningful by making use of a combination of tools. Remain flexible and keep an open mind so you do not overlook the ways that different technologies can enhance or limit learners' interactivity. Be aware of the ways that *you* like to communicate and present information since you may tend to overuse those techniques. Thoughtful facilitation methods and combinations of options will ensure inclusivity, leading to greater engagement and persistence.

Throughout the learning experience, be sure to consider all of the ways that you can connect with your learners and instill motivation. Promote an ongoing "I can do this" attitude by providing recognition, support, encouragement, and constructive feedback. Your role as an instructor must extend beyond grading assignments to include verbal and written encouragement, which is vital for academic and personal development. The technology that is currently available allows you to increasingly diversify your instructional strategies to engage and motivate all of your learners! Finally, note that whatever mode of feedback you use, always remember to *offer your learners direction* on how to improve. Doing your job correctly means giving credit for good work, and offering constructive suggestions for improvement. In that way, you are teaching through engaging meaningfully with your learners. This practice will certainly enable motivation and positive progress on future tasks and activities. As always, in your role of "reflective practitioner," be sure to take the time to reflect on your teaching practices for purposes of ongoing performance improvement!

CHAPTER 6: REFLECTION CHECKPOINT

Multimodal Teaching Strategies to Engage and Empower Learners

- How will I know whether I am being inclusive in my instructional approach?

    TIP: Think of how you are addressing the various elements of diversity of your learners to meet everybody's needs. Are you approaching your teaching from a "multimodal" stance? To what extent are you intentionally aware and respectful in your approach to engage and empower all learners to have a voice, so that nobody feels excluded, unheard, or undermined? Pay close attention to how you understand and address equity and inclusion.

- How do I reflect my awareness of presence in my teaching practice?

    TIP: What does "presence" mean to you? What are all of the different ways that you can communicate and display teaching presence?

- How can I be sure that I am reaching and attending to all of my learners throughout the course?

    TIP: Remember to address all needs, abilities, and interests. Be aware of how your positionality influences the way you "show up," interact, and communicate. No matter how open and approachable you may be, it is important to recognize that as instructors we still have both advanced education and power.

- How can I encourage self-efficacy and a sense of autonomy in my learners?

    TIP: What are you doing to enhance your learners' beliefs regarding their capabilities and capacity to achieve success and meet learning outcomes? In what ways are you providing encouragement? What type of mindset do you promote? Do you invite dialogue? Do offer your learners a chance to follow up with you or approach you for clarification? Do you convey a steadfast belief in their ability to learn and improve?

- How does my own mindset impact the mindset of my learners?

    TIP: What mindset do you hold, and why? What assumptions inform your mindset? How and in what ways are you ensuring that your learners believe that they have the agency and capability to set and pursue their own goals and complete their work successfully? Do you focus comments on learners' written work overwhelmingly on the problems? Or do you highlight their successes and then strategically identify those items the learner can prioritize for improvement? When learners do not perform well on an assignment, do you assume that they aren't working hard enough or aren't motivated? Or do you assume that they're working hard but may require scaffolding to improve their skills? When learners provide incorrect answers on an exam, do you think to yourself, "Where on earth did they get that idea?" Or, do you think, "How do I teach that differently in the future to address that misconception or error?"

- How do I know that my feedback is positively received?

    TIP: Be aware of the tonal messages in your written and audio feedback. Is your communication professional yet also personable? Is your tone respectful, encouraging, and instructive? Could your comments be misinterpreted in any way? Is there any way that a learner could be hurt, offended, or confused by what you have written or said?

- How can I be sure that my feedback is balanced as well as developmental, forward thinking, and actionable?

    TIP: Are you including a mix of support and critique? Think back to the three "Fs": feedback, feed forward, feed up. Are you addressing all of the many components of feedback? Don't forget to include the "motivation step"!

- How can I incorporate feedback most effectively?

    TIP: Review the guidelines provided regarding written, audio, and video feedback. Make a conscious effort to reach and engage with all learners by way of multimodal touchpoints.

- How can I be sure that my learners are improving from the feedback that I provide?

    TIP: Think about your assessment of whether learners are meeting CLOs and improving over time. Think about the impact of your instruction, and how you could be doing anything differently. Consider the ways in which you can make assessment and grading transparent and therefore well-received. Learning and engagement are ongoing and so you should be checking in and monitoring each of your learner's progress and achievements (or lack thereof) continuously!

What are YOU willing to try out to make a difference to your practice?

Part II Synthesis

A positive culture for online learning begins with excellence in preparation of instructional design and development. Instructors want and need practical strategies, access to and ease in using the technology, and the ability to design, develop, and customize instructional materials. The chapters of Parts I and II address all of the components that make up the online learning experience, including design, development, and delivery. Part I introduced you to the "setup cycle," with the approach to design and development of materials being divided into three interconnected parts: determining and selecting CLOs is the starting point for course design; developing content that includes all types of media as well as tasks, activities, and assignments that learners are required to complete throughout their course; planning for assessment of learning that is necessary to monitor progress and plan ahead. Part II covered the ways in which you can offer learning experiences that support and enhance learner engagement based on an "engagement cycle." The cycle includes welcoming, onboarding, and supporting learners, building working relationships, teaching through those relationships, and building community. A central aspect to promoting learner engagement, and in turn ongoing success, is the establishment of teaching presence, and throughout the chapters of Part II, you explored effective practices for intentionally enhancing teaching presence in order to deliver engaging and empowering learning experiences. You build capacity for your learners to be able to think critically and push boundaries, thereby promoting a growth academic mindset. You avoid uncertainty by providing prompt feedback and creating a safe environment where learners feel valued and able to share their ideas. And, you instill self-efficacy, autonomy, and confidence by providing the tools needed to empower your learners to take ownership of their learning and ongoing development.

As with all learning environments, it is imperative that instructors maintain a reflective stance to think more deeply about their work, make changes as needed, and ensure a successful learning experience both for themselves and their learners. The chart that follows, Table II.1, summarizes all of the multiple touchpoints of learner engagement that have been addressed throughout this book. This comprehensive "cheat sheet" is an opportunity to remain alert, check in again, and remind yourself to address these engagement touchpoints.

Table II.1. Engaging and Empowering Your Learners: A Comprehensive Action Checklist

Prepare to Teach Your Course		
Action Task	Rationale	Action Steps!
1 Compile your welcome letter (see Appendix C).	Your letter is an important first piece of the puzzle in making initial contact and developing a working relationship with your learners. This letter introduces you and ensures that all course requirements and expectations are clearly delineated. The goal of the welcome letter is to be welcoming, supportive, and engaging!	• Customize the letter for each course so your message is specific and not generic. • Introduce yourself and provide a brief overview of the course content. • Explain institutional policies and procedures (academic integrity, timeliness, grading). • Provide details regarding your availability ("office hours") and contact information. • List all available support resources and include direct links for ease of access.
2 Record and upload your welcome video.	Your "this is me" welcome video is a powerful tool to help "put a face to a name," giving learners an opportunity to see and hear you. The video is brief, spontaneous, and informal. Having learners share their own introductory videos offers networking opportunities and builds community.	• Upload a brief video in each course. • Convey clearly that you are here to help! • Remove all old or outdated welcome messages, and make sure to only keep the most current version in all courses. • Encourage learners to share an introduction video with you and their group or cohort.
3 Ensure technology support.	Most LMSs have the capability to embed technology aides to highlight course content, send notifications, and provide reminders. Your goal is to make sure that all technology aids are in place and all content is accessible.	• Review the course and syllabus each time you teach a course to ensure that all technology aids and learning content are clear, intuitive, and easy to navigate. • Reach out for technical support regarding necessary revisions or corrections.

(continued)

Table II.1. (continued)

		Initiate Working Relationships	
	Action Task	Rationale	Action Steps!
1	Initiate the first point of contact (see Figure II.1).	This is an important first point of contact that will set the stage for the new course. Up until now, the learner may have heard from advisors and other staff. Now they will hear for the first time directly from you, their instructor!	• If your welcome materials are not embedded within the course, send an email with your attached welcome letter. • Address each learner by name. • Direct learners to the syllabus where they will find all necessary course information. • Ask learners to contact you, and explain how to schedule a synchronous meeting.
2	Schedule and conduct a synchronous meeting.	It is important that this meeting takes place in "real time" to establish a real connection with learners right from the start! Remember that not everyone will want this personal level of interaction so you will need to be mindful to engage with learners according to their comfort level and needs.	• Introduce yourself in real time! • Inform learners how and when to participate and what choices they have. • Remind learners to access their course daily and complete assignments on time. • Share time-management skills. • Ask relevant questions to get to know your learner, their mindset, and past experience. • Explain the importance of addressing feedback on assignments as this will guide their ongoing improvement and success.

(continued)

Table II.1. (continued)

	Action Task	Rationale	Action Steps
3	Offer a learning contract (see Appendix E).	The contract provides a formal way to structure learning goals and keep learners focused on course requirements and deliverables. This contract begins to establish empowerment by offering learners a sense of ownership and establishing clear goals and timelines that they have a hand in determining.	• Set up learning contracts as appropriate. (This may not apply to all learners or all courses.)
4	Assess your learner's needs and address these accordingly.	Your course will be more engaging by thoughtfully adapting your teaching practices to meet each individual's needs. This is an opportunity to leverage what you know and ensure that the course content is relevant for each individual.	• Determine learners' strengths and limitations so you can always build capacity. • Make necessary adjustments for accommodations or modifications. • Determine which assignments are best suited to certain types of feedback (audio, video, written, or combinations).
	Enhance Engagement and Empowerment Throughout the Course		
	Action Task	Rationale	Action Steps!
1	Remain present, available, and accessible (see Figure 4.1).	Teaching Presence relates to instructors interacting with learners, and establishing collaborative and supportive working relationships. Positive perceptions of instructor involvement lead to higher levels of achievement and greater likelihood of course completion.	• Show learners throughout the course that you are committed to their success. • Emphasize in your feedback on weekly assignments that you are available for a synchronous meeting if additional clarification is needed. • Respond to all communication as soon as possible so learners are not left "hanging." • Alert learners to all course updates.

(continued)

Table II.1. (continued)

2	Build ongoing engagement through authentic relationships.	Engaging early and often is essential to maintaining teaching presence and building relationships. Relationships develop through onboarding and ongoing support. Being open with your learners while still maintaining professional boundaries can help them to trust you and feel comfortable in approaching you for assistance or support when necessary.	• Maintain open lines of communication with each of your learners throughout the course. • If a learner requests a change in the schedule or an accommodation, consider and honor the request. • Build capacity by allowing learners a sense of autonomy and "ownership" of the course materials. • Instill a growth academic mindset through an empowered "I can do this attitude."
3	Embrace diversity and inclusion.	Learners come from a variety of social and cultural contexts, and bring varied life experiences. Being culturally responsive in your teaching means communicating effectively and empowering learners to celebrate diversity. An inclusive educational experience means understanding learners' contexts and unique needs. Addressing diversity and inclusion must be infused throughout your practice, requiring recognition of power and positionality.	• Your task is to create a safe and supportive learning environment for all learners. • Encourage those who identify with a marginalized or underrepresented culture to showcase, through their coursework, their own values, beliefs, and traditions. • Consider the ways in which all forms of diversity and personal identification can impact the teaching relationship. • Be aware of how you "show up" and communicate with your learners. • To address power and positionality, reflect on how your biases, and lack of knowledge and exposure can impact your learners.

(continued)

Table II.1. (continued)

4	Provide multimodal feedback/ instruction (see Tables I.1, 4.1. and 6.1–6.6, and Appendixes H and I).	Research in the field of distance education emphasizes the centrality of engagement and its impact on learner performance. As such, incorporating multimodal strategies to engage meaningfully with all learners serves to strengthen your instructional approach. Integrating video and audio materials with written feedback provides an optimal learning experience. Technology allows you to increasingly diversify your instructional strategies to engage learners.	• Provide weekly substantive feedback (written, audio, or video modes). • Feedback must be individualized. • Address each learner by name. • Feedback should be balanced, pointing out good work, followed by limitations and a clear indication for improvement. • Ask critical questions to stimulate deep learning. • Provide helpful and applicable resources. • Ask questions to encourage critical thinking. • Encourage a growth mindset by focusing on how learners can develop and improve. • Reiterate weekly that you are available for synchronous meetings to discuss feedback.
5	Ensure equitable and transparent grading (see Appendixes J and K).	Grading guidelines ensure that learners understand the reasons for assigned grades, and also assists them to self-evaluate their progress and identify areas for improvement. Rubrics make grading more transparent to learners and also less prone to bias.	• Grading practices should always be logical, reasonable, and transparent. • Provide a grade justification that is directly related to assignment requirements. • When possible, allow for resubmission of assignments that do not meet academic standards. These are teachable moments!

(continued)

Table II.1. (continued)

6	Instill ongoing motivation.	Learners often need reminders to be able to see beyond the present. They also like to hear that their instructor believes in them. This creates a welcoming and trusting learning environment where learners will feel valued and motivated to do their best.	• Incorporate motivational strategies throughout your course, including acknowledgment of perseverance, and opportunities for resubmission of work. • Nurture a passion for learning to establish an ongoing achievement and motivation. • Encouragement includes check-ins through emails, phone calls, and video messages. • Make the path for success realistic by setting attainable goals.
7	Employ relevant support and resources.	Throughout the course, be sure to maintain engagement and ongoing development. You do this by providing additional layers of support that will serve to enhance motivation and academic performance.	• Develop a "toolbox" of resources that you can draw from and share as needed. • Familiarize yourself with support resources (writing center, library, and support personnel), and direct learners to these. • Alert learners to opportunities for ongoing development (literature and conferences).
8	Nurture a sense of community.	Community is associated with increased engagement. Convey that online learning is not "alone learning." Learners should never feel alone on their learning journey, but rather part of a thriving, learning community.	• Encourage collaborative learning opportunities (e.g., peer review, journals, discussion boards). • Help learners envision being active and contributing members of an academic learning community. • Seek ways for learners to feel part of the larger community through available communication channels and networking opportunities.

(continued)

Table II.1. (continued)

Monitor and address ongoing progress and development.	Because the learner population is diverse, you will encounter multiple needs and academic skill sets. Carefully monitor progress and identify and assist those who are struggling.	• When you notice someone is struggling or disengaged, reach out immediately. • Make accommodations as needed. • Notify administration of at-risk learners so progress can be monitored and addressed. • Provide additional resources and support (e.g., learning center, accommodations).

Part III

TAKING STOCK: A REVIEW OF MULTIMODAL ENGAGEMENT

The forced shift to online learning that occurred as a result of the pandemic has heightened the significant disparities at both the individual and institutional levels, exacerbating existing barriers not just to technology but to library services, as well as other services that enable a holistic learning experience, such as, but not limited to, advising, career guidance, and emotional support services. These barriers disproportionately impact learners from marginalized communities in significant ways. Almost a year later, we have developed a greater understanding not just with regard to inherent limitations, but also of what is possible, thereby setting up the future educational landscape for some significant shifts in order to address widespread unequal access and affordability to information and communication technologies. The focus going forward will certainly be on reducing educational disparities, increasing equitable access, and providing meaningful learning opportunities for all. There will also undoubtedly be greater acknowledgment of the value and impact of increased engagement, participation, and collaboration. It is more important now than ever before that our efforts to create inclusive learning environments go beyond words and translate into measurable actions.

As the growth of online programs continues to rapidly accelerate, concern about success and retention has increased. While models for understanding persistence in the face-to-face learning environment are well established, there is a need for establishing effective frameworks or taxonomies for evaluating online learning experiences in light of the unique characteristics of the online environment and the online learner. Ongoing and current research indicates that attrition rates are significantly higher than in face-to-face programs. As such, the development of models to explain and assess learner engagement in the online environment is imperative so that barriers can be recognized, and that progress can be appropriately monitored and addressed.

INSTRUCTOR VOICES

"I suggest that new online faculty let go of some of their expectations around the 'typical' classroom and 'typical' engagement."

"Trying to impose an on-ground format to an online model will frustrate you and your students. Online learning poses unique challenges and also unique opportunities!"

"It can be easy to underestimate the amount of work that it takes to build in authentic engagement with students, especially if you are accustomed to a more traditional model. Double the time you think you need. You'll still feel like it isn't quite enough."

"As work, home, and school schedules blend and fuse, it means you have to be flexible and patient. Think carefully about your teaching practice; what is working and what you might need to change?"

"Recognize that as the instructor you do not have all the answers, and that your students have a variety of lived experiences that will serve to help you learn and grow in your role."

CHAPTER 7

Revisiting Your Engagement Strategies

As the demand for access to high-quality online programs rapidly accelerates, concern over retention and learner success is increasing. Models for understanding learner persistence in the face-to-face environment are well established; however, many of the same variables are not present in the online environment or may manifest in significantly different ways. As such, there is a significant need for establishing effective frameworks or taxonomies for evaluating online learning experiences in light of the unique characteristics of the online environment and the online learner. With attrition rates significantly higher than in face-to-face programs, the development of models to explain and assess learner engagement in the online environment is imperative. This chapter presents a set of **engagement indicators** as a means of assessment. For each of the engagement indicators, an instructor reflection checkpoint is included to ensure reflexivity. An additional assessment tool in the form of a rubric that was specifically designed for evaluation and self-evaluation (a form of reflective practice) is included as Appendix L, *Engagement Evaluation Rubric*.

ENGAGEMENT INDICATORS

To foster meaningful connections at all stages of the educational journey, support mechanisms must be established to prepare learners for their responsibilities in meeting learning outcomes. With the rapid expansion in online courses, it is essential to ensure that a diverse population of learners can learn in flexible ways to meet their needs. If learners' needs are not accommodated, they are likely to experience transactional distance, including feelings of isolation and disconnectedness, possibly leading them to withdraw completely from their course or program. Reducing transactional distance is critical to online learners' success and is accomplished as a joint effort between institutional administrators, instructional designers, and instructors. While it is incumbent upon instructional designers to plan and develop courses that incorporate learner-centered pedagogies in the pursuit of active online engagement, it is *the role of instructors* to work toward intentionally developing and maintaining engagement of their learners *throughout* the course or program (Bloomberg & Grantham, 2018; Khan et al., 2017; Lehman & Conceição, 2010; Major & Sumner, 2018; Mohr & Shelton, 2017; Riggs & Linder, 2016). Research consistently indicates that there is a clear link between instructor engagement, learner engagement, and actual learning. However, engagement may not occur spontaneously without instructors' intention and effort. To create a collaborative environment that encourages a community of learning, Riggs and Linder (2016) explain that in the absence of a physical space, an *architecture of engagement* must be intentionally created. When used wisely, interactive technologies can serve to foster meaningful connections, not only with the course content and with the instructor, but also with peers.

Numerous educational agencies, including the Online Learning Consortium (OLC) and the Institute for Higher Education Policy, have provided general guidelines and benchmarks for online education. It is clear that best practice recommendations and strategies for teaching in online environments emphasize the need for interactivity that includes teaching presence, learner collaboration, and the facilitation of a learning community. From a review and analysis of some of the most prominent best-practice reports, the author has distilled key Engagement Indicators (EIs) for a successful and productive online learning experience. The EIs incorporate relevant theoretical principles and are grounded in the research-based literature related to online learning. These are also derived from the conceptual framework (based on the practical drivers of good online teaching) that was introduced in the preface, reinforced in the introduction, and woven throughout all of the chapters to become infused in practice.

A framework can be a useful conceptual and organizational tool, especially for those instructors who are learning to navigate the online teaching environment and incorporate best practices regarding facilitation. Frameworks can sometimes describe work at a conceptual level, orienting instructors with regard to what needs to be done, but not necessarily with the implementation. The framework presented here operates at the implementation level in that it allows for a thorough consideration of the critical elements inherent in the construct of engagement, and affords an opportunity for instructors to select and apply the indicators of engagement to their teaching practice. The engagement indicators, which are outlined below, provide valuable information regarding the distinct dimensions of the construct of engagement, and can be used to look for, check, and improve teaching practices. In line with the view of the instructor as a "reflective practitioner," each of the EIs is accompanied by a set of reflective questions to encourage you to think more deeply about your current practice, and what might be done differently. These questions may also be used as discussion points for further exploration with colleagues who also teach in online environments.

Revisiting Your Engagement Strategies

Figure 7.1. Multimodal Engagement: Key Contributing Factors

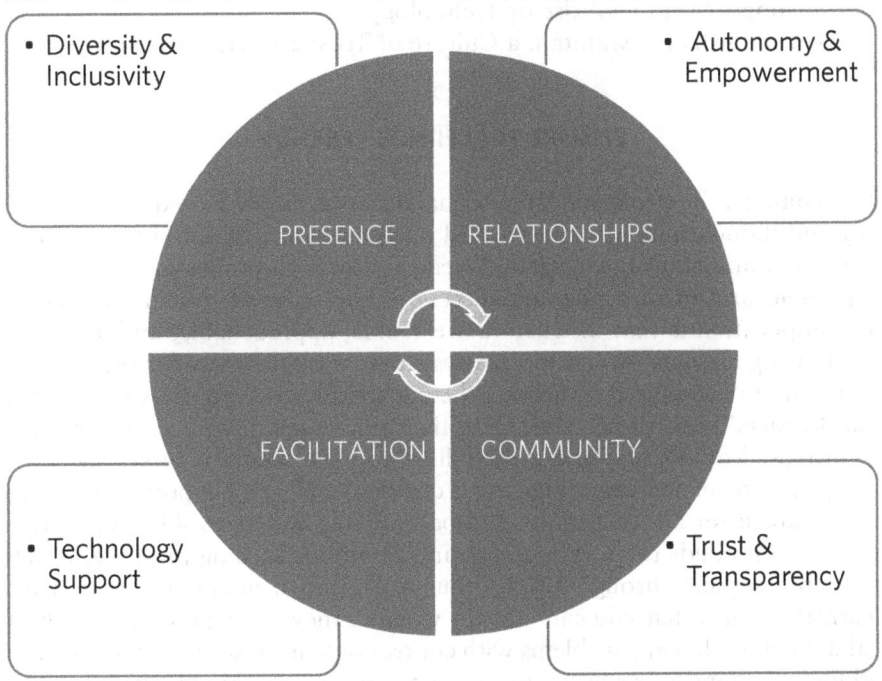

Based on the content of this book, the EIs are encapsulated within eight categories. As you will see, while these categories are distinct in and of themselves, they do overlap because in reality the online learning and teaching experience is holistic yet complex and multidimensional. All of these factors work in unison to create an optimal online learning experience. This penultimate chapter serves as an opportunity to revisit the concept of engagement, and consider the multiple ways that you can meaningfully engage with your learners. The chapter is based on a set of checklists that address ways to review and appraise multimodal engagement strategies, serving in effect as a broad checklist for the entire book. Figure 7.1 represents a conceptual model for multimodal engagement, indicating eight key contributing factors, with each factor encompassing multiple touchpoints:

1. Ensure Teaching Presence
2. Nurture Working Relationships
3. Apply Effective Facilitation Practices
4. Create a Sense of Community
5. Address Diversity and Inclusivity

6. Embrace Learner Autonomy and Empowerment
7. Support Learners' Use of Technology
8. Establish and Maintain a Culture of Trust and Transparency

ENSURE TEACHING PRESENCE

To counteract the effects of transactional distance, you will need to intentionally and thoughtfully incorporate and implement strategies to keep learners motivated and actively engaged. A central aspect to promoting learner engagement, and in turn ongoing success, is the sense of teaching presence. The implication is that instructors are visible, approachable, and available by showing learners—in multiple ways—that you are "there for them," and that you are committed to helping them learn and succeed. Research shows that learners' positive perceptions of their online instructor's presence leads to increased motivation and greater likelihood of course completion. Your task, right from the beginning, is to create a safe and supportive learning environment for all learners, and to be available and accessible. Supportive preparation builds rapport and is an indication of teaching presence, which must be ongoing throughout the course. Sustained interaction with your learners ensures that you can address whether they are experiencing technical difficulties, having problems with course content, or whether they require additional support or specific resources to complete required activities. The ways in which you communicate and interact with your learners will sustain teaching presence.

- ✓ Offer supportive onboarding preparation including welcome materials and clear contact information.
- ✓ Develop a working relationship with each learner at the start of a course by inviting them to a synchronous introductory meeting.
- ✓ Facilitate and manage ongoing and sustained interaction by way of available modalities (synchronous and asynchronous).
- ✓ Acknowledge and reinforce progress and achievement through your feedback on assignments.
- ✓ Emphasize in your feedback on weekly assignments that you are available for a synchronous meeting if additional clarification is needed.
- ✓ Participate in online discussions, and make timely and thoughtful posts to discussion threads.
- ✓ Maintain open lines of communication with each of your learners throughout the course.
- ✓ Communicate clearly at all times both verbally and in writing.
- ✓ Respond promptly to all questions and concerns so learners are not left "hanging."

- ✓ Monitor learners' progress throughout the course, and raise alerts as necessary.
- ✓ Reach out to those who have not completed course requirements and offer support as needed.
- ✓ Connect learners with specific needs to appropriate resources and available services.
- ✓ If you are going to be away then let your learners know, and inform them of who will be able to assist them during your absence.

> **Reflection Checkpoint: Ensure Teaching Presence**
>
> - In what ways am I intentionally working to ensure teaching presence?
>
>   TIP: There are multiple strategies that you can use to make yourself more visible, accessible, and available in the online environment in order to engage with and support your learners.
>
> - What forms of teaching presence feel natural to me?
>
>   TIP: What are your strengths? What do you feel are your teaching competencies?
>
> - In what way/s do I find establishing teaching presence challenging or difficult?
>
>   TIP: What are your weaknesses or challenges with regard to relating to and working with learners? In what ways might you be "holding back"? Which teaching competencies do you feel that you would like to improve upon?
>
> Refer to Chapters 3–6, which cover best practice strategies for engaging learners, from content design and development, and throughout course delivery. Think carefully about your current practice and what you might consider doing differently to be more visibly "present" and engage even more meaningfully with your learners.

NURTURE WORKING RELATIONSHIPS

We can work toward a more inclusive educational experience when we take time to understand our learners' contexts and unique needs by building authentic working relationships with them, empowering them to take ownership of their learning, to think more critically and reflectively, and to develop as self-directed lifelong learners. We do this by thinking of our learners as partners. Positive relationships create a sense of safety, making it easier for learners to ask questions, challenge ideas, share experiences, and engage in thinking that helps them grow and develop. Building positive relationships also enables you to learn more about your learners' backgrounds, cultures, and personalities, and with that knowledge, you can better address their needs. Building rapport and ongoing communication with your learners must be intentional and consistent. Creating and maintaining meaningful teaching relationships takes insight, care, and effort. Being present and engaging in dialogue is the key means of developing *intentionally structured* online working relationships, with interactivity occurring through ongoing communication and dialogue. By skillfully using technology in a variety of ways, you can ensure that all learners, particularly those who are less vocal, have the opportunity to participate equitably in all learning activities. With any online learning experience, technology is a key part of maintaining relationships with your learners. We start the relationship process by working on ourselves, and reflecting on our role as a teacher by examining how our personal and cultural experiences inform our teaching practices and potential biases.

- ✓ Provide welcome materials that include contact information; clearly delineated course expectations and requirements; and institutional policies.
- ✓ Offer an initial synchronous introduction to welcome and meet each learner and provide clear and helpful responses to any questions or concerns.
- ✓ Connect with all learners who respond positively to your invitation to meet. Remind those who do not respond that you are available to meet as needed.
- ✓ Communicate clearly so that learners will understand what is expected of them and be able to plan and organize their time in order to meet course requirements.
- ✓ Provide learners with access to communicate directly with you in mutually suitable ways.
- ✓ Show your learners that you are paying attention to their progress early in the course by noting achievements and offering support and resources when needed.
- ✓ If a learner requests a change in the schedule or an accommodation, consider and honor the request.
- ✓ Initiate conversations with learners and offer opportunities to meet synchronously, especially with those who are struggling and need additional support and guidance.
- ✓ Encourage learners to view their online experience as a *collaborative learning experience*, with you as the instructor, guiding, supporting, and motivating them along the way.
- ✓ Think of your learners as partners! Convey your role as facilitator, mentor, and co-learner rather than "sage on the stage" by being careful not to lecture or talk down to them.

- ✓ Instill in your learners a sense of autonomy, whereby they feel as though they are active participants in a dynamic working relationship.
- ✓ Model appropriate and acceptable ways in which learners are expected to communicate and interact online.
- ✓ Model responsibility and accountability by returning assignments and/or grades within the communicated established time period.
- ✓ Respond timely and directly to unanticipated problems or concerns, and attempt to resolve these.
- ✓ Seek feedback and remain receptive to ongoing feedback from your learners regarding many ways to make the course material more meaningful, relevant, and accessible.

Reflection Checkpoint: Nurture Working Relationships

- In what ways am I intentionally working to build, develop, and maintain working relationships with all of my learners?

    TIP: There are multiple strategies that you can employ to build relationships and engage with your learners. Have you tried different approaches? Which strategies do you find most useful and effective in building trustworthy and constructive relationships? Conversely, what strategies have proven to be ineffective? Why?

- How do I "show up" to my learners?

    TIP: What image of "teacher" do you value? How do you define the role of "teacher" or "instructor"? Do you adopt the role of "sage on the stage" or "co-learner"? Are you conveying the message that instructor and learners are "partners" in a shared experience? What do you see as the characteristics of good teaching? Why?

- What methods am I making use of to communicate with my learners?

    TIP: Are you attending to individual needs and addressing these needs accordingly? What are your strengths and what are your weaknesses regarding the ways in which you relate to and communicate with your learners? Which teaching competencies do you feel that you would like to improve upon?

    Refer to Chapter 5, which covers best practice strategies for engaging with learners to build positive working relationships. Think carefully about your current practice and what you might consider doing differently to engage meaningfully by building supportive relationships with your learners.

APPLY EFFECTIVE FACILITATION PRACTICES

As a facilitator, it is your responsibility to *learn from and with learners*, thereby basing your teaching on a learner-centered model. Your role in this context becomes the "guide on the side," or "learning partner," as opposed to a "sage on the stage" or a "sit and get" approach to teaching. Presenting yourself as a *co-learner* goes a long way to building trust, respect, collaboration, and motivation. Because of the diversity that characterizes the learner population, you will encounter multiple different needs and academic skill sets, so you will need to carefully and continually monitor progress and identify and assist those who are struggling, failing, or disengaged. Be aware of any cultural biases embedded in your teaching and presentation styles, and in your expectations, as ignorance of these biases can prevent you from seeing opportunities for more effective avenues of interaction with all of your learners. Move away from a grading-based orientation of teaching to a coaching-based orientation, which means viewing each learner as on their growth trajectory. In the online environment, the primary instructional delivery mode is written, audio, or video feedback, which creates the foundation for constructive learner–instructor interaction. In the online environment, *your feedback is your teaching*, and establishing a sense of presence through your feedback becomes an essential component of engagement. Through your feedback, you want to foster the *deepest approach to learning possible*, by helping all of your learners engage meaningfully with the material.

- ✓ Be aware of any cultural biases that may be embedded in your teaching, presentation, and expectations.
- ✓ Clearly explain all course goals and requirements.
- ✓ Provide collaborative learning opportunities
- ✓ Provide opportunities for critical thinking and reflection. This offers learners space and time to think about their own learning and progress.
- ✓ Remind learners that questions are welcome and that you are available for discussion as needed.
- ✓ The technology that is currently available allows you to diversify your instructional strategies to engage learners, so thoughtfully incorporate multimodal tools.
- ✓ Make sure that your learners understand how they are expected to use or address your feedback.
- ✓ Allow learners to develop products that are meaningful to them, personally and/or professionally.
- ✓ Help learners to construct their own meaning by modeling and explaining when needed, providing options, and using examples or illustrations to clarify difficult points.

- ✓ Provide prompt and frequent feedback on assignments or drafts or work in progress as needed.
- ✓ Present feedback in a professional and organized manner.
- ✓ Offer your learners *direction* on how to improve so that the feedback that you provide is *actually actionable*. This means giving credit for good work and offering constructive suggestions and resources for improvement.
- ✓ Provide ongoing encouragement by asking targeted questions in your feedback on assignments in order to stimulate critical thinking.
- ✓ Offer flexible deadlines as needed to motivate learners and accommodate individual needs.
- ✓ Direct learners to available discussion forums that encourage group collaboration and dialogue.
- ✓ Provide ongoing support for learning, research, resources, and guidance by directing learners to relevant library services.
- ✓ Monitor progress and utilize support services and resources for those who are struggling, failing, or disengaged (tutoring services, writing center, learning center, career counseling, and so on).
- ✓ Be aware of all policy and processes that are in place to support ADA requirements, and be prepared to address accommodations as needed.

Reflection Checkpoint: Apply Effective Facilitation Practices

- In what ways is my teaching approach helpful and supportive to my learners?

    TIP: There are multiple strategies you can employ to engage with your learners. Which strategies do you find most useful and effective in supporting learning and ongoing improvement?

- How do I describe "effective online teaching"?

    TIP: What are the characteristics of good teaching? Which teaching principles apply specifically to online teaching, and why? How do you want to "show up" for your learners?

- How can I adopt a multimodal teaching approach in order to engage all my learners?

    TIP: The technology that is currently available allows you to increasingly diversify your instructional strategies. Become familiar with all of the modalities offered by your LMS. Make sure to move beyond just offering written feedback! Your learners will want to both see and hear you!

> Refer to Chapter 6, which covers multimodal strategies for engaging and empowering your learners. The way in which you teach becomes the structure on which to model and maintain a working relationship in which the learner feels valued and respected, and is motivated to learn and persevere. Think carefully about your current practice and what you might consider doing differently to more effectively and impactfully engage your learners through your instructional approach.

CREATE A SENSE OF COMMUNITY

As educators transition from traditional classrooms to virtual meeting spaces and online classrooms, it is important to create a community of online learners through meaningful interactions and social technologies. Online learning should not be thought of as "alone learning." Between an engaging instructor and various support services and resources, learners should never feel alone, but rather a part of a learning community. The notion of a learning community is predicated on the value of connection and collaboration among learners and instructors, where interaction and participation are ongoing, regular, and focused around common and shared goals. Shared collaborative experiences allow learners and instructors to value the other's perspectives, thoughts, and ideas, thereby *learning with and from one another*. When learners sense their school environment to be supportive and caring, they are more likely to develop a sense of "connectedness" and "community," and this is associated with increased engagement. A primary goal is to make the online learning environment conducive to active participation by implementing strategies that will increase learner engagement not only with the course content and with the instructor, but also with peers. Online interactive technologies, used wisely, can serve to foster meaningful interactivity, social connectedness, and community. Your style of facilitation, and your intentionality and thoughtfulness as you work alongside your learners, will play a significant role in the nature and frequency of interactions, and in the creation of a thriving and dynamic learning community.

- ✓ Convey a clear message that online learning is not considered "alone learning."
- ✓ Set a positive tone that will pave the way for the quality of the interaction by modeling appropriate social norms and ways to interact.
- ✓ Be intentional in inviting interactivity and social connections to ensure that learners have opportunities to reach out to instructors, advisors, and peers.

- ✓ Integrate synchronous collaboration tools that are meaningful and accessible.
- ✓ Facilitate collaboration by creating accessible opportunities for learners to actively participate and communicate with each other.
- ✓ Encourage collaborative learning opportunities such as peer review, peer dialogue journals, blogs, discussion boards, and appropriate social media platforms.
- ✓ Consider the wealth of interests and experiences within the room, and be proactive in inviting learners to find familiar elements in their assignments.
- ✓ Help learners envision the value of being members of an academic learning community.
- ✓ Inform learners about all of the ways that they can share and receive resources and support, including services such as library, writing center, learning center, and so on.
- ✓ Engage learners with the program and the institution, thereby creating a broader sense of community. This can include leadership and advisors, and can include remote as well as onsite opportunities if available.

Reflection Checkpoint: Create a Sense of Community

- How do I conceptualize a "learning community"?

    TIP: Sociocultural theories of learning view the interactions of individuals in social environments as essential to the construction of knowledge. Think about the ways that people learn best through sharing and collaboration.

- What is it about community that encourages and fosters learning?

    TIP: Think about the online environment and the sense of isolation that can occur. In what ways are connections important to learners?

- What can I do as an instructor to create a sense of community?

    TIP: Think about different learner-instructor and learner-learner interactions. How can you encourage these interactions, both formal and informal? What types of engagement and motivational strategies could you use? What will learners gain from these shared opportunities?

    Refer to Chapters 3 and 6, which cover best practice strategies for creating community, both in terms of course design and the delivery of content. Think carefully about your current practice and what you might consider doing differently to ensure that you are engaging your learners in community-building and collaborative learning opportunities.

ADDRESS DIVERSITY AND INCLUSIVITY

All learners have a right to work within an equitable environment, without barriers to participation and communication. The forced shift to online learning that occurred as a result of the pandemic has heightened the significant disparities at both the individual and institutional levels, exposing how too many learners are on the wrong side of the digital divide. Now, more than ever before, it is imperative that we implement teaching strategies and learning solutions that promote access, inclusivity, and a sense of belonging. To remain inclusive, it is crucial to address and accommodate the diverse needs of learners from different cultural backgrounds, and to consider any necessary adjustments to your teaching practice. An individual's ability to learn is often influenced by their sense of belonging, and, without an intentional focus on inclusive teaching practices, instructors can unknowingly alienate certain learners, thus causing them to withdraw mentally, emotionally, or physically. It is also important to recognize that as instructors, we do have both advanced education and power, a concept referred to as *positionality*. The ways in which power and privilege impact the online classroom cannot be overlooked, and integrating the principles of diversity, inclusion, and equity into your teaching practice is essential to ensure learning, progress, and success. To help learners feel valued and develop their authorship is to offer them voice and choice in their learning. This includes choosing topics that are interesting and culturally or professionally relevant to them, and offering opportunities to demonstrate their learning in different ways, choosing their readings within a topic or theme, and allowing them to provide input regarding assessment criteria. Your task is to create a safe and supportive learning environment for all learners, because the value of an engaging and inclusive climate is critical. Adopt a growth mindset by conveying the expectation that every learner will succeed!

- ✓ Consider the ways in which race, ethnicity, gender, sexual orientation, socioeconomic class, disability status, or other cultural factors impact learning and teaching.
- ✓ Try to understand the ways that learners who identify as minorities can feel as they engage with you as their instructor (positionality).
- ✓ Consider how you "show up" as an instructor and relate to and communicate with your learners.
- ✓ Be aware of the ways in which your own biases, prejudices, stereotypes, assumptions, and lack of knowledge and exposure can impact your learners and their learning. Be self-reflective!
- ✓ Identify topics and readings that address equity and inclusion in order to offer your learners both a voice and a choice regarding their own learning.

- ✓ Offer multiple modes of communication so that learners can select what works best for them and suits their purposes.
- ✓ Make accommodations regarding different needs and the ways that people learn differently.
- ✓ Adapt your assessments to recognize a greater diversity of learners' assets and skills.
- ✓ Ensure equitable and transparent grading practices.
- ✓ Ensure that assignment requirements are not exclusive of any culture or circumstances, by encouraging learners to showcase, through their coursework, their own values, beliefs, traditions, and "stories." Let them know that their voices count!
- ✓ Remind learners that their personal values and strengths matter by helping them discover the value of the course content to their lives.
- ✓ Acknowledge and accept the personal and/or professional experiences that learners incorporate in their work.
- ✓ Be aware of all institutional or organizational policies and processes that are in place to support ADA requirements, and take all the necessary steps to address these requirements and make accommodations as needed.

Reflection Checkpoint: Address Diversity and Inclusivity

- Why is it important to move away from the idea that there is a "prototypical learner"?

    TIP: Who are today's learners in the global online environment? What are all the aspects of diversity? Think about the importance of being inclusive. Think about what it means to be equity minded?

- What is implied by "culturally responsive teaching"?

    TIP: Think about the different aspects of culture and how culture can impact learning. Think about your role as a facilitator of learning. What are your responsibilities? In what ways can you appreciate the multiple intersecting identities that learners bring to the classroom and supporting them with a curriculum that affirms and embraces diversity? In what ways, if any, are you offering your learners both a "voice" and a "choice"?

- Why are issues of access so important to consider?

    TIP: Online learning is mediated by learners and the devices that are used to access this learning. The wealthy have access to better technological systems and larger and more private spaces to participate. In addition to

> concerns related to economic inequality, the "digital divide" also includes a need to address accommodations for those with learning disabilities.
>
> - How can I make every learner feel that they belong?
>
>   TIP: Creating a sense of belonging is not just about being friendly or kind. It's about grasping the ways that some of your learners experience a classroom as foreign, intimidating, or hostile. It's about providing a consistent psychosocial, intellectual, and emotional counternarrative to the microaggressions, imposter syndrome, and stereotype threat your minority learners may experience. How can you regularly demonstrate to all learners that their specific backgrounds, experiences, and perspectives are valuable? How do your course activities ask or expect learners to connect the content to their lived experiences?
>
> - What do I do in my practice to be inclusive?
>
>   TIP: What are some of the elements of an educational experience that can exclude certain groups of learners, particularly minority groups? How does this occur? What steps can you take to avoid being exclusionary?
>
> - What are the dangers of exclusivity?
>
>   TIP: Think about the power that you have as an instructor. Think about the notion of positionality, and how you acknowledge this in your teaching practice. In what ways can you address your positionality? Why is this so important?
>
> Refer to Chapters 3-6, which cover best practice strategies for addressing diversity and engaging all learners. Being inclusive occurs from content design and continues throughout course delivery. Are you ready to be more intentional about making your syllabus, course content—including assignments and assessments—more equity-minded, so that this mirrors the full range of learner identities in your online classrooms? Think carefully about your current practice and what you might consider doing differently to engage with all of your learners so that nobody is excluded, ignored, disrespected, marginalized, or alienated—even unintentionally.

EMBRACE LEARNER AUTONOMY AND EMPOWERMENT

You build capacity by allowing learners a sense of autonomy and "ownership" of the course materials. Valuing learner autonomy, while at the same time providing structured and supplemental support, goes a long way toward sustaining ongoing motivation. Presenting yourself as a *co-learner* contributes to building trust, respect, collaboration, and motivation. Develop in your learners, right from the start, an empowered sense of self-motivation and an "I can do this attitude"—in essence, a growth academic mindset. Those with a fixed mindset will avoid challenges or give up easily, and tend to ignore or reject feedback, while those with a "growth mindset" hold the attitude that intelligence can be developed through experience and effort. Having a growth academic mindset leads to the desire to learn and the tendency to embrace challenges, persist in the face of setbacks, and learn from constructive feedback. By nature, adults do not want to be viewed as passive receptors of knowledge, but rather as active participants in the educational experience. Therefore, by avoiding the "sage on the stage" or "sit and get" approach to teaching, you empower your learners to be autonomous. This encourages a sense of empowerment, agency, ownership of learning, and ongoing motivation.

- ✓ Be aware of your own mindset: A "fixed mindset" can create an atmosphere of judgment, and you may tend to give up on learners who are not performing well.
- ✓ Be intentional in encouraging a growth mindset in your learners to ensure that you focus your feedback on how they can improve.
- ✓ Provide the necessary support and motivation to ensure ongoing learning and development.
- ✓ Instill in your learners a sense of autonomy, whereby they feel as though they are active participants in a working relationship.
- ✓ Involve learners in setting their own goals regarding their educational journeys by creating a big picture and having their next steps in mind. There is power in planning!
- ✓ Encourage learners to draw on their own personal and professional experience in developing assignments and tasks.
- ✓ Provide opportunities for learners to choose appropriate ways to present assignments and tasks.
- ✓ Engage with learners to help them actively develop a repertoire of good study habits and **learning strategies**.
- ✓ In addition to long-term goals, set goals within the context of immediate assignments. This enhances competence and an ongoing sense of achievement.
- ✓ Ensure that learners are not dependent on external rewards by nurturing their passion for learning and establishing an ongoing sense of achievement and intrinsic motivation.
- ✓ Ensure that learners develop new ideas and understanding through interaction and collaborative work.
- ✓ Provide ample reflection opportunities so that learners can better understand their learning and progress, and intentionally plan ahead.

> **Reflection Checkpoint: Embrace Learner Autonomy and Empowerment**
>
> - Why is it important to encourage self-direction and autonomy?
>
>   TIP: Think about the characteristics of the adult learners. Then think about the principles of teaching that address those characteristics. Try to think more deeply about what it is on the part of the instructor that facilitates learning.
>
> - In what ways is my teaching helpful and supportive to learners in terms of empowering them?
>
>   TIP: There are multiple strategies that you can use to empower your learners. Which strategies are you most familiar with? Which strategies will you look forward to using? Why?
>
> - How do I describe an "empowered learner"?
>
>   TIP: What are the implications of empowerment? How and in what ways will an empowered learner "show up" in society? Why is this important?
>
>   Refer to Chapters 4-6, which cover best practice strategies for engaging and empowering learners. Think carefully about your current practice and what you might consider doing differently to empower your learners so that they can move forward in making productive changes in their own lives, in the lives of others, and in their communities.

SUPPORT LEARNERS' USE OF TECHNOLOGY

Engaging with your learners is mostly going to occur within the LMS that is used to manage their work and provide feedback on assignments. Ability to use technology to build teaching relationships and community depends greatly on the type of technology available, and some platforms can lead to greater interaction and connectivity among users. Your familiarity with the LMS will help make connecting with learners both easier and more effective. While the institution provides guidance to both learners and instructors regarding the use of all forms of technologies used for course delivery, instructors must be available for ongoing support. Since technology is critical for learning and engagement, managing all forms of available support will ensure a successful learning experience. Moreover, technology is rapidly changing and transforming, so it is essential that both you and your learners are updated and informed.

- ✓ Right from the beginning, become familiar with your current LMS and all the available tools in order to promote meaningful and ongoing engagement.

- ✓ Stay updated regarding all available technology and seek assistance if needed.
- ✓ Ensure that throughout the duration of the course/program, all learners have access to appropriate technical assistance and technical support.
- ✓ Be aware that not all learners have the same technological proficiency or access to materials, resources, and connectivity. The "digital divide" is real!
- ✓ Provide support for all learners who may have limited online experience and who may have limited technical proficiency or access.
- ✓ Be prepared to intercede on behalf of your learners in cases of technical assistance needs by directing them to appropriate and available support services.

> **Reflection Checkpoint: Support Learners' Use of Technology**
>
> - Why is ongoing technical support so important?
>
>   TIP: Think about all the functional aspects of the online learning experience. Think about what would happen if an online learner had no access or limited access to the necessary technology.
>
> - How can I ensure that I am responsive to learners' technical needs?
>
>   TIP: Learners that may need technical support the most are those who may have limited proficiency such as older learners or those who may not have access to Internet services, computers, and connectivity. Many learners may not even have access to basic electricity!
>
> Refer to Chapter 6, which covers best practice strategies for remaining attentive to all learner needs and ways to provide support structures to address these needs. Think carefully about your current practice and what you might consider doing differently to remain aware of learner needs so you can continue to support all learners to be successful.

ESTABLISH AND MAINTAIN A CULTURE OF TRUST AND TRANSPARENCY

At all times throughout their educational journeys, learners should feel that they are learning within a safe and supportive environment. Gain and maintain the trust of your learners as their supporter and advocate. Making the path for success seem realistic, doable, and achievable minimizes potential barriers to learning. Convey that you are here for your learners and are committed to assisting them to be successful. Also convey that you are curious about their experiences, viewpoints, and perspectives. Being open with your learners while still maintaining professional boundaries can help them feel more comfortable in trusting your teaching and in approaching you for assistance or support when necessary. Trust ensures that learning can occur in a place where it is safe to make mistakes. Help learners understand that errors are a natural part of learning; in this way you create valuable teachable moments. Transparency is another a critical component in the exchange of information, both in verbal and written forms, including assessment and grading practices. To avoid confusion, frustration, or anxiety, it is critical to help learners understand your feedback and grading because in this way you help them self-evaluate their progress and identify areas for improvement. As the instructor, it is your responsibility to continually monitor and ensure that all communication and interaction is productive, thereby creating a positive, trustworthy, and inclusive environment.

- ✓ Put yourself in the shoes of your learner to understand their perspective and reality. Although professional relationships entail boundaries, it is critically important to demonstrate empathy.
- ✓ Be aware of any stereotypes and generalizations on your part, as these undermine your credibility.
- ✓ Ensure that the learning environment and experiences are set up for valuing diversity and individual strengths.
- ✓ Encourage those who identify with a marginalized or underrepresented culture to showcase, through their coursework, their own values, beliefs, and traditions.
- ✓ Let learners know how to communicate with you, and acknowledge their preferred methods of communication too.
- ✓ Make sure that all communication is productive to ensure a positive and inclusive learning environment.
- ✓ Maintain open lines of communication with your learners throughout the course.
- ✓ Be consistent and very clear in what you say to your learners.
- ✓ Be aware of what your learners are saying to you. If you sense a double message, ask for clarification.
- ✓ Use questions to demonstrate your interest in what learners say and to promote critical thinking.
- ✓ Respond as soon as you are able when learners contact you. Leaving learners "hanging" is extremely discouraging.
- ✓ Let your learners know if you will be away, and let them know who will be available to assist them during your absence.
- ✓ Set clear course goals and explain learning outcomes.
- ✓ Clarify all instructions, expectations, and course requirements as needed.

- ✓ Indicate that you are always available to discuss your learners' work and your feedback.
- ✓ Help learners overcome fear of failure by conveying the message that errors are a natural part of learning and that we learn through correcting these.
- ✓ Carefully review the grading guidelines to help learners understand the grading criteria and therefore plan and complete their assignments to the best of their ability.
- ✓ Explain clearly how you arrived at a grade so that learners can understand the rationale for assigned grades.
- ✓ Use rubrics whenever possible to make grading more transparent to learners and less prone to bias because you can justify the assigned grades.
- ✓ Consider and honor requests regarding changes in schedule, accommodation, or teaching modality.
- ✓ Listen to your learners' feedback and be open to receiving and addressing it so that you can act on the feedback YOU receive, and use it to improve your teaching.

Reflection Checkpoint: Establish and Maintain a Culture of Trust and Transparency

- What am I doing to create a culture of trust and transparency?

    TIP: Think about all the different aspects you need to be aware of right from the start and throughout each course.

- What are the different ways to address diversity so that the learning experience is fair for all learners?

    TIP: Think about the importance of being inclusive. Think about what it means to be equity-minded? What steps are you taking in striving to be inclusive and respectful of all learners?

- Are my grading criteria clear—and also thoughtful and reasonable?

    TIP: We know that clear grading criteria—whether in the form of a rubric or a narrative—is key to learners' success. In order to think more deeply about how we're grading, we also have to ask ourselves what assumptions we have about our learners. What do we think they already know? Why do we think this? What do we prioritize in an assignment or activity, and more importantly, why is that the priority? Do our priorities align with the learning goals or CLOs? The answers to these questions should be transparent to learners too as they embark on their assignments.

- What can lead to lack of trust on the part of my learners?

  TIP: Think about what you would hope for from your instructor and what type of treatment you would expect. Put yourself in the shoes of your learner to really understand their perspective and reality. Although professional relationships entail boundaries, it is important to demonstrate empathy. Be aware of any stereotypes and generalizations on your part, as these undermine your credibility. Check in with yourself regularly as a means of increasing your own self-awareness. Be aware of any assumptions that you might be making, and seek additional information from your learners as needed.

  Refer to all of the chapters of Part I and Part II, which cover strategies for engaging and empowering learners, from content design and development through course delivery. Think carefully about your current practice and what you might consider doing differently to more meaningfully engage with your learners, and provide them with a safe and trustworthy learning experience.

CHAPTER SUMMARY AND SYNTHESIS

Engagement has been presented as a central multimodal construct throughout this book. In this chapter, eight sets of EIs are presented as a practical model to determine the extent to which engagement has been established and maintained throughout a course. These indicators are based on and derived from the essential drivers of success that apply to the online learning context, and which have been detailed in the previous chapters. Indicators include teaching presence, diversity and inclusivity, positive working relationships, application of effective teaching practices, technology support, learner autonomy and empowerment, creation of community, and culture of trust and transparency. Each of these sets of EIs is accompanied by reflective questions to stimulate deeper insights and awareness of the multiple touchpoints that each engagement indicator encompasses. Revisiting multimodal engagement, as laid out in this chapter, offers you the opportunity to again think more critically about your own practice and the strategies that you employ to maximize your engagement touchpoints with each learner. This is also a chance to consider employing additional engagement strategies to enhance your practice.

For learners to thrive, instructors must remain self-reflective and attuned to all the many ways of meaningfully engaging with their learners. Think of your learners as your partners! Ongoing reflective practice is therefore strongly encouraged to critically examine the effectiveness of your engagement strategies on multiple levels as you work to instill deep learning by providing empowering learning experiences.

CHAPTER 8

Instructor as Reflective Practitioner

Online instructors can assume different roles, including facilitator, course designer, content manager, subject matter expert, and mentor. Moreover, the common tasks of an online instructor course can fall into either or both of the following two areas: course design and teaching. The idea that has been emphasized in this book is that engaged online learning is "instructor facilitated and student owned" (Schroeder-Moreno, 2010). Highly effective instructors drive the process of engaging and empowering learners, resulting in deeper learning and increased opportunities for success and achievement. The objective of this book is to provide online instructors or aspiring online instructors with the knowledge, skills, and understanding to design and/or teach in the online environment, and to engage and empower learners so that they develop and build capacity as they strive to achieve their goals.

Throughout this book, you have been prompted to stop, think, and reflect. In this final chapter, we circle back to the concept of reflective practice. Having read this book, you hopefully now clearly understand the complex challenges and barriers to learning that exist in the online environment. You now also know more about how to go about facilitating meaningful and engaging online learning experiences, and you have begun to develop and apply the necessary competencies and skills to engage and empower your learners, thereby opening the way to facilitate deep learning and increase opportunities for success and achievement. Reflection is a vital skill that is central to the capacity to learn from experience and to apply that learning to professional practice. This chapter is an opportunity to reflect on and consolidate what you have learned in this book, and to think about applying your knowledge and skills in your own real-world context, thereby driving the process forward.

REFLECTIVE PRACTICE

Reflective practice involves examining actions in order to challenge beliefs and assumptions. Reflection is a critical component in learning, and is the basis of the philosophy and work of educational reformer John Dewey.

Reflective thought, according to Dewey, includes **experiential learning**, the process of questioning one's experiences and, in the process, developing critical thinking skills. Dewey believed that reflection enables effective problem solving and enhances learning, and he explained reflection on experience as a "learning loop," that becomes an integral element of thoughtful action. While developed in the early part of the 20th century, Dewey's work (1916, 1933, 1938) is very much in evidence in present-day social constructivist teaching. Moreover, the use of reflective practice is a pedagogical cornerstone for interactive discussions that replaces standard lecturing, whether in a traditional face-to-face classroom or in the online learning environment. Subsequently, this body of theory has been developed by Boud, Keogh, and Walker (1985), and Schön (1983, 1987) who developed the notion of the instructor as a "reflective practitioner." Indeed, reflection is an important component of deep learning, and just as it applies to our learners, so it applies to our own teaching practice. Schön (1987) defined the process of reflection as "knowing-in-action," and presents the following questions:

- What do I do?
- How do I do it?
- What does this mean for myself as a professional as well as those I serve (my learners)?

Self-reflective practice should come full circle, by adding a final question:

- What have I learned, and what will I therefore do differently in the future?

This final question prompts us to ensure that our reflections are actionable, and to make the necessary changes in our practice that will facilitate growth, development, and ongoing improvement.

Theories of reflective thinking and reflective practice have been further refined by Brookfield (1995, 1998) and Mezirow (1991, 1994, 2000), who have examined in greater detail the notion of critical reflection. Whereas reflection encourages looking at issues from different perspectives, thereby maximizing opportunities for learning, "critical reflection" takes the notion of reflection a step further, in that it is concerned not just with the "how-to" of action, but the "why"; that is, the reasons for and the consequences of what we do. Mezirow (2000) explains that exploring our inherent assumptions and biases within a reflective context enables a deeper understanding of the ways in which these inform and shape teaching practice. Research consistently shows that critical reflection and metacognition ("thinking about our thinking") facilitates the transfer of knowledge and skills, so building ways for instructors to reflect on their practice is a valuable way to help them to apply their knowledge and skills to other experiences and their workplace.

Rodgers (2020) writes about reflection as it relates to "teaching presence," explaining how reflective teaching is grounded in a living and evolving philosophy of practice. She sees four supporting purposes in practicing reflection: the development of perception, the development of acceptance of "what is", alignment of teaching practice with one's values, and alignment of teaching practices with the purpose of education. Overarching these is an attitude of inquiry and critique regarding what one might be doing better. There are various stages in the process of facilitating reflective practice, including awareness (focusing on an issue or situation that will stimulate critical thinking); critical analysis (developing a deeper and more critical examination of the situation issue at hand); "thinking on your feet" by examining knowledge, challenging assumptions, and imagining and exploring different alternatives); and synthesis (the process of integrating new knowledge and experiences, developing a new perspective, and hopefully making the necessary changes in practice based on the new perspective).

IMPLICIT BIAS

As learning environments become increasingly globalized, instructors must continually seek to reduce barriers to education in order to provide a high quality of education for all learners. With increased diversity comes a high level of responsibility for educators, who must be able to communicate effectively with learners of multiple cultural backgrounds, address their needs, and at the same time empower learners to celebrate their unique identities. Increased awareness of multiple and intersecting factors will help us teach in ways that better include and support our culturally diverse learners—especially those of marginalized or underrepresented cultures—thereby creating inclusive learning experiences and facilitating achievement and success for all.

Do you perhaps have a bias, yet do not fully recognize or acknowledge it? Have you ever been in a professional setting and felt prejudice or discrimination? Have you ever engaged in a conversation with a colleague that appears to expose a bias that you were unaware existed in either yourself or the other person? While there are explicit beliefs that we outwardly exhibit through our verbal statements and actions, there are also *implicit beliefs* that reside in our subconscious, and that we may not be aware of. While our implicit beliefs go unstated, they may still be conveyed. Such implicit associations have the ability to taint the manner in which we make decisions as well as interact with others. Raising your awareness to your own biases can enable you to counteract and lessen the impact of potential invisible barriers when making decisions.

- Implicit biases are as pervasive as those that are explicit.
- Implicit and explicit biases are related but distinct mental constructs.
- The implicit associations we hold do not necessarily align with our declared beliefs or even reflect stances we would explicitly endorse.
- We instinctively tend to hold implicit biases that favor our own "in-group," although research has shown that we can still hold implicit biases against our "in-group."
- The implicit associations that we have formed can be gradually *unlearned* through a variety of intentional "de-biasing" techniques.

It is also important to explore the effect of accountability through a reduction of bias on decisionmaking effectiveness. This type of exploration—through self-reflection—is especially important when those decisions have the potential to significantly impact the lives of others, and in this case, our learners.

Reflective practice, then, is the ability to reflect on one's thinking and behavior so as to engage in a process of continuous learning by examining your practice and making any needed changes. Engaging with your learners via self-reflection *with renewed or rejuvenated practice* is the key message! This has significant benefits with regard to increasing self-awareness and developing a better understanding of others. Reflective practice encourages active engagement in work experiences, by guiding our thinking and helping to examine our assumptions, and thereby opening new possibilities. We can indeed become better instructors if we explore questions about our practice in a meaningful and intentional way. Therefore, the concept of reflective practice has broad application in the field of education, for learners, for instructors, and for those who train, teach, coach, or evaluate instructors.

FINAL REFLECTION

This concluding chapter offers a final opportunity to reflect on lessons learned, and how to move forward with facilitating meaningful, engaging, and inclusive online learning experiences. Here is one more opportunity for you to stop, think, and reflect.

Instructor as Reflective Practitioner

> **FINAL REFLECTION CHECKPOINT: SYNTHESIS AND KEY TAKEAWAYS**
>
> As an instructor, you are also an active learner and a "reflective practitioner" who carefully considers your role as an educator and takes the time to better understand the factors, strategies, and practices that can help to foster and promote engagement and empowerment. You have the potential to help shape lives! What work could be more valuable?
>
> **Did you know?**
>
> List what you came in wanting to know:
> 1. _____
> 2. _____
> 3. _____
> 4. _____
> 5. _____
>
> **Now you know!**
>
> You now know from reading this book that there is a strong link between instructor engagement, learner engagement, and actual learning. Reflect on your role as an online instructor. What do you bring to the table? What are your key strengths with regard to building learner capacity? What type of mindset do you hold, and why? Is yours a fixed mindset or a growth mindset? What are your assumptions regarding learning and development? What are your expectations regarding your learners, and why? How do you "show up" as an instructor who is truly present? In what ways does your awareness (or lack thereof) impact your ability to create inclusive learning experiences?
>
> **What do you still want to know?**
>
> What would you like to continue working on to ensure that you are an excellent instructor? What aspects of your practice may need improvement? Remember that as an instructor, you are a learner too, and lifelong learning is ongoing! Be sure to continue to stop, think, and reflect. And, be willing to take action! Therefore, think carefully about your current practice and what you might consider doing differently to engage and empower your learners as you move forward.
>
> **Commit to continuous improvement!**
>
> A hallmark of good teaching is the desire to keep learning and improving. Be sure to bring that zeal and enthusiasm into your online classroom. Demonstrate your commitment to your learners' success by pursuing your own professional development. Invest time and energy into developing as an online instructor, and remember that even small efforts can have a

significant impact. Remember that there are many ways that you can continue to develop in a professional capacity, including accessing educational materials, attending professional development offerings, and interacting with fellow online instructors to share resources, learn from their approaches, and contribute your own ideas. Interacting with others who are grappling with the same teaching issues can certainly lead to significant insights and ideas.

What are some ways to ensure that you will continue to learn, and strive to improve your practice?

Glossary

Both research and technology are developing and evolving at a rapid pace. To ensure that a book such as this does not fall in the trap of time, and to maintain relevance and currency, be aware that some of the specific current technologies that are in use and that are included in this book may in the near future become outdated or need to be updated.

Accessibility: Equal access to education is mandated by law and is grounded in the hope that all people will indeed have equal access. When designing a course, be cognizant of building in accessibility from the start, and make sure that all content is accessible; that it supports all learners and ensures inclusion; and that it provides multiple opportunities for engagement and interaction. Instructors are required to recognize which tools and formats (document and media) support accessibility and which do not. The pandemic and resulting digitalization of education has redefined the discussion around accessibility and inclusion, highlighting the challenges confronting educational institutions in their efforts to provide equal teaching conditions and meet the specific needs of underrepresented communities. Essentially, the pandemic intensified and exacerbated a challenge that already existed, with the disadvantages that some learner populations have been facing now becoming more visible—and indeed glaringly obvious.

Active learning: This refers to actively participating in learning activities and contributing to discussions, and has become an essential consideration for best practice research in online education. Active engagement, problem solving, and solution exploration puts the learner as the focal point, allowing the learner to construct knowledge rather than passively absorb it. Whereas traditional pedagogies are teacher-centered, with the instructor as the focal point, active learning places the learner at the center of the learning experience, and therefore has significant applicability to engagement strategies in online education.

Adult learning principles: As an instructor, you should understand how adults learn and under what conditions adults learn best. Adult learners bring experiences and self-awareness to learning that younger learners do not. Malcolm Knowles, a pioneer in adult learning, developed the theory of andragogy based upon a set of assumptions regarding adult learners. These assumptions evolved to become the "principles of adult learning," on which to base teaching practice.

Adult learning theory: Theories of learning contribute to a comprehensive understanding of learning in adulthood. Knowledge of how adults learn allows instructors be more careful listeners, understand individual differences, and thereby attend to each learner as an individual, facilitating significant learning. (*See also* Andragogy, Transformative learning theory)

Andragogy: Defined by Knowles (1984) as "the art and science of helping adults learn," andragogy builds upon the theory of constructivism that suggests that learning is an active process, whereby learners construct meaning based on their own experiences. Andragogy is based on a number of assumptions regarding the adult learner, and from each of these assumptions, Knowles drew numerous implications for the design, implementation, and evaluation of learning activities for adults. (*See also* Pedagogy)

Assessment (of learning): Assessment is an ongoing systematic process aimed at understanding and improving and enhancing learning. The results of those assessments are used to make informed decisions about the improvement of learning, teaching, instructional methods, and planning ahead. Assessments are derived directly from the learning outcomes. All forms of assessments must be inclusive of all learners and their many types of diverse experiences and characteristics. The terms *assessment* and *evaluation* are sometimes used interchangeably. Assessment refers to learner assessment, and evaluation refers to program and product evaluation; you assess learners and you evaluate products and processes. In addition to a final assessment, it is recommended that shorter assessments of different types are administered periodically throughout a course to enable learners to assess their ongoing progress. (*See also* Direct and indirect assessment, Evaluation, Formative assessment, Multimodal assessment, Summative assessment)

Assessment methods: Assessment of learning can be conducted using a variety of available instruments and methods, including rubrics. (*See also* Rubrics)

Assignment: Completing tasks or activities is typically required in most courses as these are a measure of the learner's progressive and ongoing application of knowledge. Assignments may be textual (written) or in some presentational format (such as PowerPoint, Prezi, a diagram, etc.). Assignments provide a "window" into the learner's thinking, and the instructor uses these to understand the deeper conceptual and content-related issues that must be addressed.

Asynchronous: Asynchronous tools include communication and teaching methods that do not occur in real time, accounting for time zones, and allowing learners to access content at the time, pace, and place of their choosing. This option also creates an accessible archive of past materials. One disadvantage is that learners may feel dissatisfied or unmotivated without the social interaction between their peers and instructors. A further disadvantage is that course material may be misunderstood or misconstrued without real-time interaction and without the opportunity to ask questions "in the moment." (*See also* Synchronous)

At-risk learner: Refers to a learner who requires temporary or ongoing intervention in order avoid failure to succeed academically. Your administration should be notified of these learners so that their progress can be monitored and addressed.

Audio feedback: As opposed to written feedback, this type of instruction is delivered by way of auditory modes so that the learner can actually hear it instead of just reading it, such as video and screencast. Audio feedback can often be used to complement written feedback. Audio feedback enables instructors to expand on written margin notes and offer additional insights to assist learners.

Auditory learner: An individual whose learning preference is by way of hearing instruction, as opposed to viewing it, as would be the case with written instruction. Audio materials are provided by way of audio or video technologies. (*See also* Visual learner).

Barriers to learning: Challenges that stand in the way of achieving success. Barriers take numerous forms in the online environment and may be related to the learner, to the instructor, the technology, or to the actual course material.

Best practices: As in best in class, this refers to a method or technique that has consistently shown results superior to those achieved with other means, and that is used as a standard or benchmark. Sometimes also referred to as "effective practices."

Blended learning: A combination of face-to-face and online learning, as in hybrid courses or learning experiences. Currently, there is an increasing number of blended learning programs that include a significant distance learning component. (*See also* Hybrid course)

Bloom's Taxonomy: The theory of behaviorism (usually associated with Ivan Pavlov, B. F. Skinner, and Edward Thorndike) focuses on how people behave. Behaviorism led to the development of taxonomies of learning to define the elements of learning. Benjamin Bloom (1956) was among the early psychologists to establish a taxonomy of learning that related to the development of intellectual skills. A higher-order thinking skill is one that requires more thinking power—or *cognitive effort*—than lower-order thinking skills. Given that well-written CLOs should be measurable, certain verbs are associated with the different levels of the taxonomy. The taxonomy is based on six key elements: Creating, Evaluating, Analyzing, Applying, Understanding, Remembering. (*See also* Problem-based learning)

Boilerplate feedback: Refers to the use of standard or stock feedback that is not individualized to address particular and current needs. While instructors often develop a "toolbox" of resources to streamline their instructional approach, they should be mindful of individualizing their teaching. Tools must be customized to meet learners where they currently are, in order to help them succeed.

Cognitive presence: This relates to instructors and learners being able to construct meaning through sustained discourse (dialogue and critical reflection) within a community of inquiry. Cognitive presence can be demonstrated by inviting active participation and interaction. (*See also* Presence, Social presence, Teaching presence)

Collaboration: By way of interdependent contributions of group members toward a shared goal, collaboration provides opportunities for learners to work together on assignments, build knowledge collectively, and support each other's understanding. Collaborative learning opportunities can involve either group discussions or group projects.

Collaboration tools: Asynchronous and synchronous tools, as well as a combination of tools, can be incorporated for online course delivery. Appendix O includes a selection of applications to support and enhance online teaching and learning. (*See also* Asynchronous, Online tools, Synchronous)

Collaborative learning: Interaction within online educational environments has long been advocated as conducive to learning, whether interaction between learners and instructors, learners and course content, or learners and their peers. The collaborative construction of knowledge that occurs as a result of the interaction within an online environment requires intentional responsiveness on the part of the instructor. In order to provide the best possible learning experience, a primary goal is to make the learning environment conducive to active participation and interaction.

Communication: Refers to a method of engaging in dialogue and interaction. Communication can be formal or informal, and involves an exchange of information. There are many forms of communication currently in use, including synchronous (real time) and asynchronous (electronic) options.

Community of Inquiry model: This model, developed by Garrison et al. (1999, 2001, 2003), views learning as a function of three interdependent elements that pertain to online learning environments: social presence, cognitive presence, and teaching presence. The model identifies teaching presence as a complex construct that addresses transactional distance, thereby creating a conducive learning environment. Optimal learning is said to occur in a learning community or community of inquiry, where learners and instructors work collaboratively in constructing knowledge to derive academic benefit. (*See also* Presence, Teaching presence)

Competencies: Online instructors are expected to acquire strong competencies (skills and abilities) to be successful in designing and delivering a high-quality learning experience. A fundamental competency is that instructors embody a learner-centered approach with their role as "facilitator." Key competencies include understanding how learning occurs, effective facilitation practices, establishing teaching presence, applying engagement strategies, and familiarity with existing and emerging technologies.

Constructivism (also referred to as constructivist learning): Lev Vygotsky, John Dewey, and Jean Piaget focused on constructivism to explain teaching and learning as complex phenomenon whereby knowledge is actively constructed by way of interaction among learners and teachers. In the latter part of the 20th century, the major learning theories, especially cognitive theory and social constructivism, began to overlap. For example, Lave and Wenger (1991) and Wenger (1998) promoted concepts such as *communities of practice* and *situated learning*. The position of these authors is that learning involves a deepening process situated in, and derived from, participation within a learning community of practice. Their work is evident in many studies, including those related to online education.

Course content: Refers to the material that comprises a course. (*See also* Course material, as these terms are used interchangeably)

Glossary

Course development: Coherence and alignment are critical features of successful course development. Both of these concepts draw on the literature on learning, teaching, and instructional design. Learning outcomes establish the foundation of a course. Following that, you will move to assessment, which mirrors the course learning outcomes, and then develop appropriate and engaging course content to foster deep (as opposed to surface) learning.

Course delivery: Online courses require different means of content delivery from classroom courses. Instructors must master the tools of technology, and serve as a content specialist and a facilitator of learning. Whether they are teaching in fully online or hybrid environments, there are many resources and ways to deliver course content, including traditional textbooks, online publisher resources, e-textbooks, web-based multimedia and open-educational resources, podcasts and video materials, and original content files that are added to the course site within the LMS.

Course design: The success of any course is determined by how well the course is planned and built prior to its delivery. To effectively design, develop, and deliver an online course that engages and empowers learners, thoughtful planning is essential, particularly in an online environment. Your vision for the course, the approach you use to design, develop, and deliver the course, as well as your expectations for learner success will shape the course.

Course guide: Used interchangeably with syllabus, an outline of the course, including all relevant information and details so as to be a preview of the course itself. (*See also* Syllabus)

Course learning outcomes (CLOs): This is one brief sentence that clearly states or signifies what learners should know or be able to demonstrate at the conclusion of a course. CLOs focus on the intended learning that will occur by using concrete, measurable action verbs. (*See also* Institutional learning outcomes; Program learning outcomes)

Course material: Refers to the content that comprises a course. To engage with the online content and to be motivated to learn, learners must of necessity perceive its value. The instructor's role should be focused on making connections to link the subject matter to prior experiences and relevant content, helping learners identify and set meaningful and realistic goals, and adapting the course content to their interests and needs so that they understand its applicability to their own lives and goals. (*See also* Course content)

Critical reflection: Whereas reflection encourages looking at issues from different perspectives, thereby maximizing opportunities for learning, the notion of "critical reflection" addresses not just the "how-to" of action, but the "why"; that is, the reasons for and the consequences of what we do. Mezirow (2000) explains that exploring our inherent assumptions and biases within a reflective context enables a deeper understanding of the ways in which these inform and shape our teaching practice.

Critical thinking: Philosopher and educator John Dewey (1938) defined critical thinking as: "Active, persistent, careful consideration of a belief or supposed form of knowledge in light of the grounds that support it and the further conclusions to which it tends." Critical thinking involves three interrelated phases: discovering the assumptions that guide our choices and actions; checking the accuracy of these assumptions by exploring different perspectives, viewpoints, and sources; and making informed decisions. It is important for teachers to model critical thinking by asking questions that foster reflectivity and encourage critical thinking.

Critique: Critique is different from criticism. Criticism involves judgment and faultfinding, while the purpose of critique is to evaluate a piece of work in order to increase understanding. The goal of feedback critique is evaluative and corrective, to help learners understand where they meet established standards and aid them in identifying what they can do better going forward.

Culturally responsive teaching: With diversity comes a great deal of responsibility for educators who must be able to communicate and interact meaningfully with a wide array of cultural backgrounds. Increased awareness of diversity helps us teach in ways that better include and support our culturally diverse learners—especially those of marginalized or underrepresented cultures—thereby creating inclusive learning experiences.

Culture: Culture, as defined by anthropologists, is the sum total of all learned behavior. It is passed down from generation to generation through individuals and human groups, exerting a profound influence on behavior, attitudes, learning, how we solve problems, how we interact with each other as social beings, the values we carry with us, and the beliefs that we hold. Cultural uniqueness is manifest on many different social levels, shaping the many and varied ways that we make meaning of our experiences in the world.

Deep learning: Garrison and Cleveland-Innes (2005) suggested that learners employ a variety of approaches to learning, including *surface, achievement, and deep approaches*. *Surface learning* employs the least amount of effort toward realizing the minimum required outcomes. *Achievement learning* reflects an orientation to the external reward for demonstrated learning. Achievement learners are motivated by grades, and their focus is predominantly on activities that will result in the highest grades. *Deep learners* embrace and digest course material in the search for meaning, significance, relevance, and applicability of knowledge. Such learners will be able to demonstrate that they understand the course content and they are able to apply the appropriate materials and/or concepts. (*See also* Significant learning)

Differentiation (Differentiated Instruction): One classic way to differentiate instruction is to create different paths for learners to demonstrate their learning. To address all learning needs and abilities, there are three ways that educators can differentiate based on the assigned task: content, process, or product. By offering learners some choice in how they can demonstrate their learning, we help them to tap into their natural creativity, curiosity, and intrinsic motivation. Because they are drawn to tasks that are personally relevant and challenging, such as creating multiple pathways to approach their own learning (process), demonstrating their learning (product), or customizing their learning (content), learners will deepen their understanding and increase their personal and academic engagement.

Glossary

Digital divide: Any uneven distribution in the access to, use of, or impact of information and communication technologies between any number of distinct groups. These groups may be defined based on social, geographical, or geopolitical criteria, or otherwise. In addition to concerns related to economic inequality, the digital divide also includes a need to address proper access and accommodations for those with learning disabilities.

Direct and indirect assessments: Assessments can include a variety of direct and indirect measures. Direct measures include examinations, research papers, essays, and presentations. Indirect measures include surveys, focus groups, and exit interviews. Assessments can occur at the end of a learning experience (summative assessment) or sometime during the learning experience itself (formative assessment). (*See also* Formative assessment, Summative assessment)

Disability: Disabilities can include learning disabilities, mobility impairments, ADD or ADHD, and other health and medical-related impairments. Invisible disabilities, also known as "hidden disabilities" or "nonvisible disabilities," are those that are not immediately apparent or obvious. Typically, these are chronic illnesses and conditions that can significantly impair the normal activities of daily living. Online education is a viable option for individuals with disabilities by offering benefits in terms of flexibility that may not be as readily available in a face-to-face delivery format. As such, it is imperative to comply with the Rehabilitation Act of 1973, the Americans with Disabilities Act of 1990 (ADA), the Americans with Disabilities Act Amendments Act of 2008 (ADAAA), and Section 508 of the Rehabilitation Act, as amended in 1998, so that learners with disabilities have equal access to online course content.

Discussion boards: Sometimes referred to as discussion forums, an asynchronous mode of communication where dialogue does not occur in real time. These are used in online courses to both prompt learner engagement and build community.

Disengagement: Learners often feel disconnected from faculty, peers, and resources, and tend to become detached and often completely removed from their institution's culture and traditions, leading to a sense of disengagement. (*See also* Engagement)

Distance education: Undoubtedly one of the most rapidly growing subsections of education, embracing emerging social needs (especially since the pandemic) and based on evolving technological advancements. Distance education is the broad term of reference that encompasses all forms of learning and teaching in which those who learn and those who teach are for all or at least most of the time in different locations. The terms *distance education* and *distance learning* are used interchangeably in the literature, a usage that needs to be treated with caution, however, since institutions and instructors are the agents of change and control educational delivery, while learning is ultimately the responsibility of the learner.

Diversity: Diversity refers to anything that sets one individual apart from another, including the full spectrum of human demographic differences and the different ideas, backgrounds, and opinions that people bring. Diversity includes the spectrum of qualities and characteristics that differentiate individual people, and it is the combination of these qualities that makes each person unique. To ensure inclusion and equity, addressing diversity on multiple levels is critical. Learners come from a variety of backgrounds, including individual differences (personality, prior knowledge, and life experiences), and group/social differences such as race/ethnicity, class, gender, sexual orientation, country of origin, ability, and cultural, political, religious, or other affiliations. Each learner is unique, and in seeking to reduce barriers to education, a high quality of education must be provided to everybody no matter their background or past educational experiences. (*See also* Inclusion)

Education: This book's approach is to foster the deepest learning possible, by helping learners engage with the material at the level that is most meaningful to them. The idea that education is about the "transmission" of knowledge from an expert to a novice is problematic. Knowledge is more than a "transmission" of information, but rather is meaningfully constructed when one brings their prior understanding to interact with new ideas, experiences, and environments. (*See also* Learning)

Emotional presence: Defined by Cleveland-Innes and Campbell (2012) as "the outward expression of emotion, affect, and feeling by individuals and among individuals in a community of inquiry, as they relate to and interact with the learning technology, course content, students, and the instructor" (p. 283).

Empowerment: Empowerment is both process and outcome. Empowerment theory emphasizes the importance of issues related to control. For instance, it draws attention to power structures, such as who has control in a given situation, the teacher or the learner, and how an imbalance in control might impact individuals. Similar to Bandura's notion of developing self-efficacy (1977, 1986), empowerment is achieved through an experience that results in increased self-determination, self-efficacy, intrinsic motivation, and engagement. (*See also* Engagement, Teaching through empowerment)

Engagement: Recognized as essential for learner satisfaction and course completion, engagement is considered one of the most significant factors impacting academic performance. The idea promoted throughout this book is that engaged online learning is "instructor facilitated and student owned" (Schroeder-Moreno, 2010). Research consistently indicates a clear link between instructor engagement, learner engagement, and actual learning. Engagement may not occur spontaneously without instructors' intention and effort, and there are multiple ways to enhance engagement through facilitation techniques. (*See also* Disengagement)

Engagement indicator: A means of assessment to measure the extent to which instructors are providing an engaged learning experience. Indicators provide valuable information regarding the distinct dimensions of the construct of engagement and can be used to look for, check, and improve teaching practices.

Equity: Fair and equal treatment of all peoples despite their background or previous educational experiences and the creation of opportunities for historically underserved populations to have equal access to and participate in educational programs. (*See also* Diversity, Inclusion)

Equity-minded: The perspective or mode of thinking exhibited by those who call attention to patterns of observed inequity. They are typically willing to take responsibility for the success of their learners, and work to actively and critically reassess their own practices by remaining race-conscious and being acutely aware of the social and historical context of exclusionary practices in education.

Evaluation: The terms *assessment* and *evaluation* are also used interchangeably; therefore, it is important to ensure that you and your colleagues are using the terms in the same way. Typically, assessment refers to learner assessment and evaluation refers to program and product evaluation. (*See also* Assessment)

Exclusion: Refers to the antithesis of inclusion that calls for the ways in which all learners have access and are treated equitably. Exclusionary practices ignore or alienate learners. (*See also* Inclusion)

Experiential learning: This theory draws on the work of John Dewey, Kurt Lewin, and Jean Piaget among others. It was Dewey who first put forward the idea that learning was concerned with experience rather than just the acquisition of abstract knowledge; that experience exhibits the principles of continuity and interaction so learners can connect what they are learning with their experiences and also see possible future implications. Malcolm Knowles, drawing on Dewey's theory, posited that "adults accumulate an increasing reservoir of experience that becomes an increasingly rich resource for learning" (1984, p. 44). He also observed that adults tend to define themselves by their experiences. More recently, numerous adult educators have underscored the fundamental role that experience plays in learning and how we develop from and through our experiences.

Face-time technologies: Tools that allow for synchronous "real-time" communication and interaction, which is extremely valuable in the online environment. The anonymous feeling of the online environment makes it easier for learners to participate minimally or completely withdraw. Without face-to-face contact, instructors cannot observe nonverbal cues that indicate when learners are frustrated, anxious, or disengaged. There are currently multiple face-time technologies in use, and with the rapid growth of online learning, new tools are regularly emerging. (*See also,* Synchronous)

Facilitator: Traditionally, it was accepted that teachers have knowledge and expertise in a particular field, and that they impart that knowledge through a variety of means to their learners. In contrast, a facilitator does not operate under the traditional concept of teaching, but rather adopts a learner-centered model, assisting learners through self-exploration, reflection, and dialogue. Unlike the lecture style, facilitators ask learners to question and explore ideas rather than simply have the answers given to them. Research shows that strict content delivery, or what is often referred to as "sit-and-get" does not have the same effect on learner achievement. The instructor's role as facilitator is "guide on the side," or "learning partner," as opposed to "sage on the stage," a phrase first coined by Alison King (1993).

Feedback: In the online environment, the primary instructional delivery mode is written and/or audio feedback. Feedback motivates because it provides learners with information that they can use to succeed. Positive feedback affirms strengths and accomplishments, and describes characteristics of good work commensurate with meeting learning outcomes. Providing useful and timely feedback is critical to engaging learners, creating a supportive learning environment, and preparing them to succeed. Instructors are expected to provide feedback that is useful and engaging, and that encourages critical reflection and a growth academic mindset. (*See also* Feed forward, Feed up)

Feed Forward: This refers to incorporating resources that are relevant and current. Feed forward says: "Here's what you can do to improve future work, and here's why it will help." These resources, including Internet sites, links to social media, and audio or video material, should be thoughtfully provided to be of maximum support to learners. (*See also* Feedback, Feed up)

Feed Up: In addition to providing clear and specific suggestions for how the learner can improve (feedback), and the resources to achieve success (feed forward), instructors should explain *why* the knowledge gained through an assignment is important, and *why* it is important to make the recommended improvements. Feed up helps learners understand the underlying purpose of their work, helping them to better understand what it means to be successful on a task. In line with the principles of andragogy, instructors should make connections to real-world applications so learners understand its relevance and applicability, so that they can self-evaluate and become more autonomous in their learning. Feed forward has the potential to stimulate transfer of learning to future tasks. (*See also* Feedback, Feed forward)

Fixed mindset: The assumption that intelligence, abilities, and talents are fixed traits that cannot be significantly developed or changed. This is in contrast to a growth mindset that assumes that intelligence, abilities, and talents can be developed and enhanced through effort and learning. (*See also* Growth academic mindset)

Formative assessment: Formative assessment occurs during a course, informing the learner of their progress and alerting the instructor about providing opportunities for learners to improve. The feedback that is provided from these assessments is critical to success, offering opportunities for learners to practice new skills or demonstrate knowledge. Conducting a formative assessment also offers instructors the opportunity to use the data to help you better adjust your instruction to meet the needs of your learners. Research shows that frequent short assessments improve retention and learning, and serve to create a climate of academic integrity. (*See also* Summative assessment)

Grade: In U.S. higher education, this is usually a letter ranging from A through D (with F for failure) that indicates the quality of a learner's work and performance in a given course.

Grading: Assigning an assessment by way of numerical values that indicate a learner's level of achievement. Grading should be tied to and aligned with course learning outcomes. All grading criteria must be equitable and clear.

Growth academic mindset (also referred to as growth mindset): Carol Dweck (2007) explains that as opposed to a "fixed mindset," learners with a "growth academic mindset" assume that intelligence and other abilities can be developed, and that feedback is helpful in enhancing development. A growth academic mindset leads to the desire to learn and the tendency to embrace challenges and seek to improve from receiving constructive feedback. Instructors with a growth academic mindset find it rewarding when they witness their learners' progress and achievement. Instructors with a growth mindset are therefore more likely to look for ways to set learners up for success by providing necessary support and encouragement so they will keep working and persevering.

Growth trajectory: Viewing a learner on a growth trajectory implies that an assignment is a measure of a learner's progress on that trajectory. The assignment is a "window" into the learner's thinking, and the instructor uses that to understand the deeper issues that must be addressed as the learner moves progressively along their growth trajectory.

Hybrid course: Courses or learning experiences that are delivered by way of a combination of online and face-to-face technologies. (*See also* Blended learning)

Implicit bias: Implicit bias tends to be more subliminal than other types of more outright and vocal bias, prejudice, and discrimination. Most people recognize issues such as outright and vocal racism and discrimination and can cite examples of how those are harmful. However, there are also some forms of less obvious or implicit bias, and checking on this is essential, especially within the educational environment and workplace. Scholars at Harvard University have been studying implicit bias in a wide range of ongoing research surveys.

Inclusion: Diversity includes the many characteristics and attributes that make individuals different, where inclusion includes the social standards and behaviors that help people feel accepted. Inclusion refers to the ways in which all learners have access and are treated equitably, and is the act of respecting, supporting, and valuing others for who they are and treating everybody with respect and dignity, leading to a sense of belonging. Inclusivity implies the active, intentional, and ongoing engagement with diversity—in the curriculum and in communities (intellectual, social, cultural, geographical) with which individuals might connect—in ways that increase awareness and empathy regarding the complex and multifaceted ways in which individuals interact within systems and institutions. (*See also* Diversity, Exclusion, Inclusive pedagogy, Universal Design for Learning framework)

Inclusive pedagogy: Describes curriculum and teaching approaches that encourage learners to have a sense of belongingness. Belonging refers to the experience of being treated and feeling like a full member of a larger community where you can thrive. This includes course materials that represent a variety of perspectives that can be meaningfully applied in a diverse set of real-world scenarios; and teachers meeting learners where they are and helping them to meet course learning outcomes, and eventually to be able to contribute to their field of study. We can work toward a more inclusive educational experience when we take time to understand our learners' contexts and unique needs through building authentic working relationships with them. (*See also* Diversity, Inclusion)

Individualized feedback: This is crafted thoughtfully for each learner, in order to meet their specific and unique needs, as opposed to boilerplate or stock feedback, which is highly discouraged.

Informational feedback: This type of feedback is effective in domains with clear right or wrong answers when tested immediately after training. With informational feedback, people are told whether their answers are right or wrong. Such informational feedback may be a simple right-wrong response (minimal feedback) or it may include an elaboration. However, you want your feedback to be more than just informational; you want it to transformative and empowering.

Institutional learning outcomes (ILOs): The knowledge, skills, abilities, and attitudes that all learners are expected to develop as a result of their overall learning experiences, including all courses and programs that they attend at a given institution. (*See also* Course Learning Outcomes, Program Learning Outcomes)

Instructional design (ID): Also known as instructional systems design (ISD), this is the practice of systematically designing, developing, and delivering instructional products and experiences. The instructional design process consists of determining learners' needs, defining end goals and objectives, designing and planning assessment tasks, and designing teaching and learning activities to ensure the quality of the instruction. A positive culture for online learning begins with excellence in preparation of instructional design, development, and delivery.

Instructional strategies: These are the techniques that instructors use to help learners become independent and self-directed in their educational pursuits. (*See also* Online instruction, Teaching strategies)

Interaction: Moore (1989) identified three types of interaction inherent in online courses: (1) learner–learner interaction, (2) learner–instructor interaction, and (3) learner–content interaction. The online learning experience is enhanced by the quality and frequency of the interaction between learners and instructors, as well as consistent learner–learner interactivity.

Journal (also referred to as reflective journal): A reflective journal is a means for learners to reflect on new knowledge learned in a course, and solidify their learning experience as they progress and learn new material. Journaling also offers learners an opportunity to formulate new opinions and perspectives, and provides them a risk-free venue to explore, think, and practice skills. A reflective journal is an account of the work in progress, but more essentially an opportunity for reflection on the learning experience, providing learners with a means of engaging critically and analytically with course content. (*See also* Peer dialogue journal)

Knowledge: The question of what it means to know something and what constitutes "knowledge," has been debated by philosophers for centuries. Consider Neil Postman's definition of knowledge as "organized information—information that is embedded in some context; information that has a purpose, that leads one to seek further information in order to understand something about the world. . . . When one has knowledge one knows how to make sense of information, knows how to relate information to one's life, and, especially, knows when information is irrelevant" (1999, p. 93). The notions of "contextualizing" information, leading one to "seek" further information, knowing how to "make sense" of information, and how to "relate" that information—these are examples of "acting upon" knowledge. The goal is to foster knowledge that can be useful and usable with regard to application to life experiences.

Learner-centered: The view that the learner is at the heart of the learning experience, as opposed to teacher centered. There is a shift of focus of instruction from the teacher to the learner. (*See also* Student-centered)

Learner mindset: The learner mindset includes learners' self-concept and self-efficacy beliefs, as well as their persistence at learning tasks. The beliefs that adults have about themselves as learners can have a cyclical relationship with achievement (i.e., previous academic achievement fosters particular beliefs, which in turn encourage future achievement). When adults are aware that learning involves effort, mistakes, reflection, and refinement of strategies, they are more resilient when they struggle. (*See also* Fixed mindset, Growth academic mindset)

Learning: Garrison and Cleveland-Innes (2005) suggest three broad approaches to learning: surface, achievement, and deep learning. Surface learning employs the least amount of effort toward realizing the minimum required outcomes; learners are motivated to complete the task rather than assimilate the learning, and they might not be interested in deeper meaning. Achievement learning reflects an orientation to the external reward for demonstrated learning; learners are motivated by grades and may be challenged to accept critical feedback. Deep learning embraces the search for meaning; learners will likely ask questions, and seek connections. In terms of this book's approach, we want to foster the deepest learning possible, by helping learners engage with the material at the level that is most meaningful to them. Programs and workplaces that recognize adults' developmental diversity, and that support adults' learning and development, will be especially effective. (*See also* Education)

Learning accommodations: The term, sometimes referred to as learning modifications, is used to describe an alteration of environment, curriculum format, or equipment that allows an individual with a disability to gain access to content and/or complete assigned tasks. Accommodations allow those with disabilities to pursue a regular course of study. Regarding ADA issues, you will need to make accommodations to address learners' specific needs. Before you begin a course, check with each learner regarding their preferred way of receiving feedback, and honor their request.

Learning community: Optimal learning is said to occur in a learning community or community of inquiry, where learners and instructors work collaboratively to derive academic benefit. Creating strategic opportunities to connect informally and formally has the potential to foster a culture of inclusivity and connection, thereby developing a productive learning community. Developing learning communities has been at the heart of distance education since its inception, and the challenge of fostering community remains a focal issue.

Learning contract: Learning contracts give ownership to learners over their learning at the outset of a course, prompting them to reflect on how they learn, and establishing clear goals and timelines. The contract provides a formal way to structure learning goals and activities, which helps to minimize misunderstandings and poorly communicated expectations. For instructors, learning contracts serve as an outline for independent study units and as a tool to aid assessments.

Learning management system (LMS): Online classes typically take place via your institution's LMS, a platform that includes communication, content delivery, and assessment tools to facilitate the teaching-and-learning process. The LMS is used for the administration, documentation, tracking, reporting, and delivery of educational courses or programs. The LMS is an integrated web platform that houses the collaboration tools used for course content as well as learner management tools (e.g., grades, rosters, and course calendars). Instructors can use the LMS to teach classes, administer tests, store data, and communicate with learners. Familiarity with the LMS and its many features will help make connecting with learners both easier and more effective. There are currently numerous LMSs available to address online education contexts, including Google Classroom, Blackboard, Moodle, Desire2Learn (D2L), and Canvas, among others. Be aware that LMSs are continually updated and new LMSs are periodically being produced.

Learning outcomes: Statements that identify observable behaviors or actions on the part of learners that demonstrate that the intended learning objective has occurred. Outcomes occur at course, program, and institutional levels. Selecting appropriate and relevant learning outcomes is the starting point for course design. Learning outcomes are sequenced, connected to program competencies, general education outcomes, and professional accreditation standards, and must be specific and measurable. (*See also* Course learning outcomes, Institutional learning outcomes, Program learning outcomes)

Learning preferences: Everyone learns differently and course content should be presented in a variety of ways to facilitate individual preferences. To accommodate a variety of preferences, it is best to design alternative activities to reach the same objective and offer learners the option of selecting those options that they would prefer.

Learning strategies: Refers to learners' incorporation and use of select the appropriate instructional strategies to accomplish their tasks and meet their educational goals.

Learning theory: A theory typically describes, explains, and/or predicts phenomena. Learning theories have been developed to explain how people learn. There are currently many adult learning theories, including andragogy, self-directed learning theory, transformative learning theory, and experiential learning. The literature on learning theories is complex and extensive, and the theories are distinct, each providing a unique lens on the subject of how adults learn.

Massive Open Online Courses (MOOCs): Online courses with the option of free, open registration (i.e., without specific participation restrictions) and unlimited (massive) participation. Learners can choose to take noncredit hour courses offered free of charge through MOOCs without being enrolled in the university. MOOCs have been adopted by higher education to increase school enrollment, and provide multiple course credentials, such as certificates and credit-bearing online degrees.

Mentor: A guide, coach, or facilitator who works alongside their learners, as opposed to a "lecturer" or "expert." The goal is for an instructor to serve and be seen as a collaborative partner in the learning experience, actively guiding the learner along their educational journey.

Metacognition: Thinking about one's thinking. Refers to one's planning, monitoring, and evaluating one's own cognition when accomplishing tasks, integrating ideas, justifying decisions, and applying new learning. "Learning how to learn" implies developing skills and habits of self-reflection that will ensure that learning will continue after the current educational experience, and will be applied in future contexts.

Microaggression: Sometimes, people speak or behave in a manner that is not blatantly offensive but is intended to be hurtful and dismissive. This type of behavior is called a microaggression, a term identified by Pierce (1970). There are several subtypes of microaggressions that discriminate against members of marginalized, minority, or underrepresented groups. Microassaults are conscious and intentional actions or slurs, such as using racial epithets, displaying offensive symbols, or deliberately serving a person belonging to the dominant group before serving someone from another group. Microinsults are verbal and nonverbal communications that subtly convey rudeness and insensitivity and demean a person's identity or affiliation. Microinvalidations include communications that subtly exclude, negate, or nullify the thoughts, feelings, or experiences of a person from a marginalized group. (*See also* Implicit bias, Oppression, Positionality)

Module: The most common unit of organization for an online class is a module. Instructors use modules to organize class materials into topics, units, or sections. Modules are typically ordered sequentially and contain all necessary course materials and learning activities.

Motivation: Refers to the significant role in determining how much effort learners will invest in their studies to complete the course and achieve its outcomes. Motivation is a result of both intrinsic and extrinsic drivers. The impact of motivation on persistence and engagement plays a key role in determining overall success or failure. The need to better understand how to motivate learners in online courses is worthy of ongoing research. Many of the same issues in traditional face-to-face courses can apply in the online environment, but online learning presents its own set of challenges, as well as opportunities.

Multimedia principle: The multimedia principle (Clark & Mayer, 2011) implies that online learning should not be solely text-based, but include multiple media, such as audio and video materials that include varied examples. This principle underscores the importance of attending to different learning preferences in order to be inclusive of all learners. Developing multiple effective and meaningful online engagement strategies is therefore critical.

Multimodal assessment: Assessments can include a mix of objective tests and quizzes, projects, self-assessments, and reflections. Proctored assessments can also be used as necessary. These require coordination with your institution's or organization's protocol, and learners must be provided with clear directions, requirements, and procedures. (*See also* Assessment)

Multimodal engagement: Defined by Bloomberg and Grantham (2018) as follows: Instruction (verbal and written) is expected to include multiple methods of engagement to create a positive learning environment that encourages motivation and persistence. Instructors should maintain frequent communication with learners; offer opportunities for ongoing interaction to discuss feedback, address concerns, and plan; and make accommodations to address learning styles by personalizing teaching and using appropriate tools or modes of instruction. Multiple methods of engagement throughout a course helps create a positive learning environment that encourages motivation and persistence, and instructors are encouraged to make use of all available tools. Multimodal engagement is relational since it is a dyadic experience, from teacher-to-learner *and* learner-to-teacher.

Multimodal feedback: Feedback should employ multiple modes of instruction. While voice and audio feedback are highly encouraged, these modes should not be a substitute for written feedback, but rather an adjunct and support for the written feedback.

Multimodal learning: There is no "one-size-fits-all," and the needs of each individual are paramount. It is important to realize that people from different cultures may learn the same things, but they may tend to learn them *in different ways*. We need to be prepared for that reality and proactively create multimodal learning experiences that recognize and acknowledge the different and diverse ways that individuals think and learn by providing inclusive learning opportunities that do not favor any one group of learners over another.

Navigation: Refers to the ways in which the user moves through the course content. Navigation in the online environment includes the use of tools and technology that is specifically designed for this purpose. Using consistent design features and protocols will enable intuitive and easy navigation. To make navigation easier, instructions, materials, and assignments should be found in a consistent, predictable place in every course.

Nontraditional Learner: A majority of adult online learners are juggling greater responsibilities than learners of yesteryear. The stereotypical college learner who lives on campus and whose sole responsibility is to be a learner rarely exists, as such, "nontraditional." According to the National Center on Education Statistics (2019b), 43% of full-time undergraduate learners and 81% of part-time undergraduates work a paid job in addition to taking classes. As working learners balance the demands of school and a job, they may be unable to attend the office hours set by their professors and may struggle to balance the requirements of both school and work. Many learners are also parents, working full-time, and therefore spending less time on school-related activities.

Online instruction: There is no specific formula or method for online instruction, and there are many complex facets to consider. The approach that you use should provide meaningful guidance and direction ensuring measurable outcomes. (*See also* Instructional strategies, Teaching strategies)

Online learning: The use of the term online learning is frequently interchanged with terms such as e-learning (electronic learning), virtual learning, distributed learning, network-based learning, and web-based learning. Each of these terms refers essentially to a wide set of applications and educational processes that are characterized by the separation of teachers and learners in space and time, and the use of information and communication technologies and tools. These definitions will continue to evolve as technology undergoes rapid and ongoing change.

Online learning context: Refers to the online learning environment under consideration. Knowing about the online learning context will contribute to a greater appreciation of the factors that contribute to effective teaching and learning, including learner skills and learner supports.

Online learning experience: Refers to the learner's actual educational experience. Understanding this experience will contribute to a greater appreciation of the factors that contribute to effective teaching and learning, including learner skills and learner supports.

Online tools: The teaching and assessment methods or applications that are employed by the instructor to facilitate learning and engagement. (*See also* Asynchronous, Collaboration tools, Rubrics, Synchronous)

Oppression: An intersectional definition of diversity honors the fact that our different identities afford us more or less power and more or less oppression and need to be considered in all that we do. It is therefore important to pay close attention to the nuances that exist due to racial inequity and White supremacy, classism, heterosexism, ableism, and other forms of oppression that will impact individuals. (*See also* Implicit bias, Microaggressions, Positionality)

Pedagogy: Teaching or instructional approach and methods. Usually used in reference to teaching children, with andragogy being the term that is used to refer to the teaching and instruction of adult learners. (*See also* Andragogy)

Peer dialogue journal: Developed by Bloomberg (2005) as a means to explore learning experiences by examining and analyzing central questions and issues related to the course material. Peers become partners in conversation about issues related to the course material. As they share and exchange ideas and thoughts, they are engaged in a process of reflecting on their knowledge and experience as it unfolds. Through their dialogue, learners build on each other's insights, reflections, and learning, and present each other with alternative ways of thinking and reasoning. (*See also* Journal)

Peer learning: Refers to learners learning with and from each other by collaborating on projects, tasks, or activities. Learners coteach each other by providing resources, support, suggestions, tips, and relevant materials.

Peer mentoring: A peer mentor is in the unique position of understanding what another learner is facing because they have recently been through most of the same experiences themselves. Peer mentors are usually alumni or learners in more advanced courses.

Peer review: Peer review involves having learners give feedback to one another on their assignments. Making the writing process more collaborative through peer review gives learners opportunities to learn from one another, offer constructive feedback, and clarify the goals of the assignment. Peer reviews can be useful for any assignment that the instructor plans to have learners revise or build upon. Peer review can often be helpful after learners have completed a first draft of the assignment.

Persistence: The extent to which learners remain in the course or program based on their motivation and satisfaction.

Positionality: The social and political context that creates your identity in terms of race, social class, gender, sexuality, and ability. Positionality implies how your identity influences and potentially biases your understanding and outlook on the world, and the ways in which you interact and communicate with others. Consider how ongoing power structures, such as White privilege, White fragility, and class privilege, frame the ways that individuals and groups view and engage in or navigate within the American culture. (*See also* Implicit bias, Microaggressions, Oppression)

Preassessment: Refers to an assessment that would occur prior to the start or at the beginning of a course or learning experience.

Presence: Presence is essentially a state of being or "nearness" in space or time; a state or condition of "now." This important component must be established in order to initiate learning in the online environment and sustain interaction as a vehicle for building and maintaining learner engagement. Rodgers and Raider-Roth (2006) defined presence as ". . . to come into relation, into connection, with learners, their learning, subject matter and oneself" (p. 284). According to the Community of Inquiry model introduced by Garrison et al. (1999, 2001, 2003), online learning occurs as a function of four primary elements: cognitive presence, social presence, teaching presence, and emotional presence. (*See also* Cognitive presence, Emotional presence, Social presence, Teaching presence)

Problem-based learning: Presented with a specific problem, learning is more meaningful by applying new knowledge to evaluate, analyze, and eventually solve the problem. This has long been regarded as an effective technique to develop higher-level thinking skills. (*See also* Bloom's Taxonomy)

Program learning outcomes (PLOs): PLOs describe what learners are expected to know and be able to do when they have completed a program. These relate to the skills, knowledge, and competencies that learners will acquire as they progress through the program. The PLOs are stated as concise descriptions of the impact the program will have on learners and are linked to CLOs and ILOs. (*See also* Course learning outcomes, Institutional learning outcomes).

Progress assessment: Commonly referred to as formative assessment. It is recommended that instructors administer shorter assessments of different types periodically throughout the course to enable learners to self-assess their ongoing progress, in addition to a final assessment.

Rapport: Refers to the establishment of a sense of personal connection, whereby relationships are characterized by mutual understanding and communication.

Reflection: Defined by Boud et al. (1985) as "a generic term for those intellectual and affective activities in which individuals engage to explore their experiences in order to lead to new understandings and appreciation" (p. 19). Schön (1983, 1987) regarded reflection as having two components: reflection-in-action and reflection-on-action. Reflection includes thinking about something while engaged in doing it, having a feeling about something, and practicing according to that feeling. (*See also* Critical reflection, Self-reflection)

Reflective practice: This involves examining actions in order to challenge beliefs; it has its origins in the work of John Dewey, one of the forefathers of adult education. (*See also* Reflective practitioner, Self-reflection)

Reflective practitioner: A term developed by Boud et al. (1985) and Schön (1983, 1987) to characterize an excellent educator. Reflection is an important component of deep learning and also applies to teaching. As with andragogy, underpinning reflective practice is the theory of constructivism, where learning is viewed as an active process involving reflection on current and past knowledge and experiences to generate new thinking and learning. (*See also* Reflective practice)

Relationship building: With interactivity at the very heart of effective online learning experiences, a central element in facilitating engagement is developing and maintaining working relationships with learners. The process of building a relationship cultivates a culture of learning, demonstrates a commitment to learners' success, and builds a learning community.

Resubmission: The opportunity as provided by the instructor for a learner to revise and resubmit an assignment for purposes of ongoing improvement and success.

Rubrics: A scoring rubric is a method of classifying and categorizing identified criteria for successfully completing an assignment or task and to establish levels for meeting these criteria. A well-designed rubric will describe the definitions of each component being assessed and indicate the qualities by which levels of performance can be differentiated regarding each of the identified criteria. This becomes a working guide for both learners and instructors. (*See also* Online tools)

Sage on the stage: Research shows that strict content delivery by way of lecturing does not have the same effect on adult learners' achievement. Rather than perform the role of the "sage on the stage" (a term first coined by Alison King [1993]) in working with adult learners, the instructor's role should be that of "guide on the side"—a facilitator of learning and a coach or mentor who works alongside their learners to promote achievement and academic success.

Scaffolding: A way to support to learners as they work toward mastery. Tasks are broken into manageable subtasks, designing learning to be incremental. Minimizing cognitive overload has its roots in cognitive psychology and instructional design. Scaffolding can improve any learning experience and is particularly important in the online context that carries with it the high risk of isolation.

Screencast: A way of using video on a computer that is accompanied by a voiceover. Screencasts are considered more effective than a "talking head" video, especially when you are explaining a complex process, because learners are able to both see and hear your explanation in real time.

Self-directed learning (SDL): The concept emerged from the humanist philosophy of Carl Rogers and was further developed by Malcolm Knowles (1975, 1984). The foundation of this approach to learning and teaching is on the freedom and responsibility of the individual learner to construct their own learning experiences. This approach was a rejection of an excessively teacher-centered traditional educational experience that too often demonstrated little trust and respect for the competency of individuals to take responsibility for their own learning.

Self-efficacy: Defined by Bandura (1977, 1986) as the innate belief in one's individual capability to accomplish or complete given task, job duty, or project.

Self-reflection (or self-reflexivity): Learning and growth occur through self-reflection or self-reflexivity; that is, the ongoing process of reflecting on our teaching practice, and what we can do to improve that practice through new insights and awareness. This should be not a once-off occurrence, but remain an ongoing best practice. (*See also* Reflective practice, Reflective practitioner)

Sense of community: Online interactive technologies, used wisely, can serve to foster meaningful interactivity and social connectedness. Instructors' ability to use technology to build a sense of community must be intentional and sustained throughout the learning experience.

Signature assignment: The signature assignment aligns with all or most of the course learning outcomes and represents the application of learning gained throughout the course. Because of its importance within the course, this assignment should be composed first (with the possibility of some revision later in the process). The weekly activities are composed after the signature assignment and should support learners in demonstrating incremental proficiency toward the signature assignment. This assignment does not have to occur in the final week of the course; it could occur in the penultimate week, saving the final week for sharing and reflection.

Significant learning: Considered to be "deep" rather than "surface" learning, whereby the learner is engaged in critical thinking and reflection to address conceptual understanding. Significant learning is not just about knowing more but knowing *differently*, leading to greater self-awareness and self-understanding, critical reflection, meaning making, and perspective change. A key focus is on reflection and action as a means to bringing about significant changes in thinking and knowing. (*See also* Deep learning)

Social presence: Refers to the ways in which communication and interaction contribute to creating a positive online learning environment as participants present themselves as "real people." There are three forms of social presence: affective (the expression of emotion, feelings, and mood); interactive (evidence of reading, attending, understanding, and thinking about others' responses); and cohesive (responses that build and sustain a sense of belongingness, group commitment, or commitment to common goals and objectives). (*See also* Cognitive presence, Presence, Teaching presence)

Student-centered: Also known as learner-centered education, this encompasses methods of teaching that shift the focus of instruction from the teacher to the

Glossary

learner, placing the learner's needs and interests at the forefront of the learning experience. (*See also* Learner-centered)

Summative assessment: Refers to assessments that are included at the end of a learning experience or set of learning experiences as a final and complete evaluation of the achievement of learning outcomes. This can range from a single course to an entire curriculum. Ideally, the summative assessment is the sum of all the smaller formative assessments. (*See also* Formative assessment)

Syllabus: Used interchangeably with course guide, this is the entire course outline that lays out all the course requirements and expectations, course content, schedule of assignments, and lists of required and supplemental resources. A well-designed syllabus or schedule provides a structure for planning and success. It is important that learners come to think of the syllabus as both a motivator and a source of vital information, serving as a "road map" of the entire course. (*See also* Course guide)

Synchronous: Synchronous tools include real-time communication methods. Use of synchronous tools requires instructors to coordinate with learners and set times and dates to meet so that all learners have equal access. Immediate personal engagement increases motivation, reduces isolation, and enhances engagement. While synchronous experiences can be more responsive, this method of instruction is more resource-demanding, and can present technical and logistical barriers. (*See also* Asynchronous, Face-time technologies)

Teachable moment: An event or experience that presents a good opportunity for learning. Instructors create "teachable moments" by explaining the value of learning through errors and trying to help learners overcome their mistaken view of errors as failures. In doing so, they are conveying the message that errors are a natural part of learning, and that understanding the error is an opportunity to improve.

Teaching presence: Teaching presence implies that instructors remain visible, approachable, and available to assist learners. This occurs by actively interacting with learners, and establishing collaborative and supportive working relationships. Given the challenges of the online course structure, and the potential for teaching presence to influence learner motivation, an area of importance becomes how online instructors' support and feedback on learners' work can influence motivation and ongoing engagement. Learners perceive teaching presence through the course design and the ways in which the instructor guides and supports them throughout the course. (*See also* Presence)

Teaching strategies: The techniques teachers use to help learners become autonomous and self-directed. These strategies become learning strategies when learners independently select the appropriate ones and use them effectively to accomplish tasks or meet goals. (*See also* Instructional strategies, Online instruction)

Teaching through empowerment: An instructional approach that is promoted throughout this book, whereby learners are provided with the agency and autonomy to actively engage in the learning experience. This enables them to make decisions and implement changes in their own personal and professional lives, and ultimately in the lives of others and in their communities. If we want learners to be creative and self-directed, we need to move beyond engagement to empowerment. This requires a paradigm shift: The empowered learning environment is a shift from giving choices to inspiring possibilities; from making the subject interesting to tapping into learner interests; and from taking assessments to being provided with opportunities to assess one's own learning and to reflect on their learning and work. (*See also* Empowerment)

Technology: Broadly defined as the tools and mechanisms that may be used to solve real-world problems and achieve some value. Instructors need training and support to develop the necessary skills to use available technologies to teach in the online environment. Ability to use technology to build teaching relationships and a sense of community will depend on the type of technology available, and some platforms offer greater interaction and connectivity than others.

Transactional distance: One of the foundational theories in distance education is Moore's (1997) transactional distance theory, which emerged from his doctoral research in 1996 about educational programs where instructors and learners were physically separated from each other. Moore postulated that distance was a pedagogical phenomenon, rather than a function of geographic separation. The impact of transactional distance can cause online learners to participate minimally, disengage, or completely withdraw, and it is incumbent upon instructors to incorporate and implement strategies that will keep learners motivated, engaged, and supported.

Transformative learning (Transformational learning): Refers to a theory of how adults learn, developed by Jack Mezirow (1991, 1994, 2000) and further refined by other adult educators including Kegan (2000) and Cranton (2016). This type of learning encompasses an enhanced level of awareness of the context of one's beliefs, a critique of the assumptions underlying these beliefs, an assessment of alternative perspectives, a decision to negate an old perspective, and an ability to change behavior. Perspective transformation involves an empowered sense of self, a more critical understanding of how assumptions and experiences have shaped beliefs and knowledge, and strategies and resources for action based on new perspectives.

Underrepresented Groups: Populations, communities, or cultures that are underserved in that they have inadequate access to social services. Typically, these are minority groups that may have been discriminated against or denied access. The term vulnerable is often used interchangeably with underserved.

Understanding by Design (UbD): Developed by instructional designers and educators Wiggins and McTighe (1998), this is a curriculum planning approach that employs a "backward design"; that is, the practice of beginning with the end in mind and focused on *teaching to achieve understanding*. Selecting appropriate and relevant learning outcomes (what the learner should know and/or be able to do) is the starting point for course design; following which you determine how learners will demonstrate that learning (e.g., create assessments) and then develop teaching materials and course activities to achieve that.

Universal Design for Learning framework (UDL): Upon the creation of the Americans with Disabilities Act (ADA), there was an increased awareness of the challenges faced by those with disabilities, which resulted in a greater understanding of the need for accommodations. This increased awareness resulted in the concept of Universal Design for Learning (UDL). The focus on designing architectural features of the physical world that could be accessible to all users, regardless of ability and without accommodation, embodies UDL. Course designers and instructors can implement UDL with specific strategies in order to provide multiple means of engagement that make learners (1) interested in learning, (2) focused and persistent even when it gets tough, and (3) self-motivated and reflective in their learning (CAST, 2018). The UDL framework indicates that supports will benefit all learners, not just those with disabilities (CAST, 2018). (*See also* Diversity, Exclusion, Inclusion)

Usable knowledge: Knowledge that is directly relevant to learners and can therefore be useful with regard to application to life experiences. (*See also* Knowledge)

Video feedback: Refers to instructional feedback that is delivered by way of video technologies. Through use of video or screencast feedback, you can expand on written narrative feedback. (*See also* Written feedback)

Visual learner: An individual whose learning preference is by way of reading or viewing instructional materials, as opposed to hearing these. Visual learners' preference is to learn from written material and imagery that can actually be viewed. (*See also* Auditory learner)

Welcome letter: An informative and engaging welcome letter should be customized for each course, including a description of the course and the overall goals. The letter should demonstrate the instructor's accessibility, and specify course expectations and all relevant institutional policies and procedures.

Welcome video: A brief video introduction is an impactful way to build a relationship with online learners and is a powerful tool to help put a face to a name right from the start, making learners feel connected and supported. The video is typically less formal than a welcome letter.

Written feedback: The primary instructional delivery mode is written feedback on assignments. Providing balanced, meaningful, and individualized written feedback is critical to engaging learners and preparing them to succeed. Written feedback should include substantive summary comments pertaining to the overall quality of the work, as well as targeted margin comments regarding specific aspects of the work. (*See also* Audio feedback)

References

Anderson, L. W., & Krathwohl, D. R. (Eds.). (2001). *A taxonomy for learning, teaching, and assessing: A revision of Bloom's Taxonomy of Educational Objectives*. Longman.

Bandura, A. (1977). Self-efficacy: Toward a unifying theory of behavioral change. *Psychological Review, 84*(2), 191–215.

Bandura, A. (1986). *Social foundations of thought and action: A social-cognitive view*. Prentice-Hall.

Beaunoyer, E., Dupere, S., & Guitton, M. L. (2020). COVID-19 and digital inequalities: Reciprocal impacts and mitigation strategies. *Computers in Human Behavior, 111*, Article 106424. www.ncbi.nlm.nih.gov/pmc/articles/PMC7213963/

Beckett, D. (1998). Disembodied learning: How flexible delivery shoots higher education in the foot, well, sort of. *Electronic Journal of Sociology*. www.sociology.org/content/vol003.003/beckett.html

Berry, S. (2017). Building community in online doctoral classrooms: Instructor practices that support community. *Online Learning 21*(2). http://dx.doi.org/10.24059/olj.v21i2.875

Berry, S. (2019). Teaching to connect: Community-building strategies for the virtual classroom. *Online Learning, 23*(1), 164–183. https://files.eric.ed.gov/fulltext/EJ1210946.pdf

Bettinger, E. P., Fox, L., Loeb, S. & Taylor, E. S. (2017). Virtual classrooms: How online college courses affect student success. *American Economic Review, 107*(9), 2855–2875. https://files.eric.ed.gov/fulltext/ED580370.pdf

Bialowas, A., & Steimel, S. (2019). Less is more: Use of video to address the problem of teacher immediacy and presence in online course. *International Journal of Teaching and Learning in Higher Education, 31*(2), 354–364. https://files.eric.ed.gov/fulltext/EJ1224346.pdf

Bigatel, P., Ragan, L. C., Kennan, S., May, J., & Redmond, B. F. (2012). The identification of competencies for online teaching success. *Journal of Asynchronous Learning Networks, 16*(1), 59–77. https://files.eric.ed.gov/fulltext/EJ971040.pdf

Black, G. C. (2020). Who are today's college students?: Understanding the 21st century higher education digital learner. In A. W. Thornberg, D. F. Abernathy, & R. J. Ceglie (Eds.), *Handbook of research on developing engaging online courses* (p. 13). IGI Global.

Bloom, B. S. (1956). *Taxonomy of educational objectives handbook: Cognitive domains*. David McKay.

Bloomberg, L. D. (2005). Learning from a distance: Creating connected communities through peer dialogue journals. *Perspectives: The New York Journal of Adult*

References

Learning, 3(2), 33–44. www.transformationed.com/journal/perspectivesonline vol3.2.html

Bloomberg, L. D. (2014). *The coaching handbook: A guide for online faculty coaches.* Unpublished manuscript.

Bloomberg, L. D. (2020a). Coaching faculty to teach online: A single qualitative case study at an online university. *International Journal of Online Graduate Education, 3*(2), 1–22. http://ijoge.org/index.php/IJOGE/article/view/45

Bloomberg, L. D. (2020b). *Contributions to Transitioning to online teaching and learning as a result of COVID-19. Resource for the higher education community.* Series of articles developed for SAGE Publications. https://us.sagepub.com/en-us/nam/strategies-and-tips-for-successful-online-teaching

Bloomberg, L. D. (2020c). Transitioning rapidly to online teaching: Ten tips to prepare instructors for success. *International Journal of Online Graduate Education, 3*(2), 1–12. http://ijoge.org/index.php/IJOGE/article/view/46

Bloomberg, L. D., & Grantham, G. (2018). Teaching in graduate distance education: Perspectives on evaluating faculty engagement strategies, *International Journal Online Graduate Education, 1*(2), 1–24. http://ijoge.org/index.php/IJOGE/article/view/18

Boud, D., Keogh, R., & Walker, D. (1985). *Reflection: Turning experience into learning.* Kogan Page.

Brookfield, S. D. (1995). *Becoming a critically reflective teacher.* Jossey-Bass.

Brookfield, S. D. (1998). Critically reflective practice. *The Journal of Continuing Education in the Health Professions, 18,* 197–205.

Brookfield, S. D. (2006). *The skillful teacher: On technique, trust and responsiveness in the classroom.* Jossey-Bass.

CAST. (2018). *Universal design for learning guidelines (Version 2.2).* National Center on Universal Design for Learning. Retrieved from http://udlguidelines.cast.org; https://www.cast.org/impact/universal-design-for-learning-udl

Center for Advanced Research on Language Acquisition, University of Minnesota (CARLA). (2009). *What is culture?* Retrieved from www.carla.umn.edu/culture/definitions.html

Center for Excellence in Universal Design. (1997). *The 7 principles.* http://universaldesign.ie/What-is-Universal-Design/The-7-Principles/

Cervero, R., & Wilson, L. (2001). *Power in practice: Adult education and the struggle for knowledge and power in society.* Jossey-Bass.

Chan, R. Y., Bista, K., & Allen, R. M. (Eds.). (2021). *Online teaching and learning in higher education during COVID-19: International perspectives and experiences.* Routledge.

Clark, R. C., & Mayer, R. E. (2011). *E-learning and the science of instruction: Proven guidelines for consumers and designers of multimedia learning* (3rd ed.). Wiley.

Cleveland-Innes, M. & Campbell, P. (2012). Emotional presence, learning, and the online learning environment. *International Review of Research in Open and Distance Learning 13*(4), 269–292.

Cole, A. W., Allen, M., Anderson, C., Bunton, T., Cherney, M. R., Draeger, Jr., R., Featherston, M., Fisher, V. C., Motel, L., Nicolini, K. M., & Peck, B. (2017). Student predisposition to instructor feedback and perceptions of teaching presence predict motivation toward online courses. *Online Learning, 21*(4), 245–262. https://doi.org/10.24059/olj.v21i4.966

Cole, A. W., Lennon, L., & Weber, N. L. (2019). Student perceptions of online active learning practices and online learning climate predict online course engagement. *Interactive Learning Environments*, 1–15. https://doi.org/10.1080/10494820.2019.1619593

Cope, B., & Kalantzis, M. (2015). The things you do to know: An introduction to the pedagogy of multiliteracies. In B. Cope & M. Kalantzis (Eds.), *A pedagogy of multiliteracies: Learning by design* (pp. 1–36). Palgrave Macmillan.

Cranton, P. (2016). *Understanding and promoting transformative learning: A guide to theory and practice*. Stylus.

Croxton, R. A. (2014, June). The role of interactivity in student satisfaction and persistence in online learning. *MERLOT Journal of Online Learning and Teaching, 10*(2), 314–325. https://jolt.merlot.org/vol10no2/croxton_0614.pdf

Cutri, R. M., & Mena, J. (2020). Faculty readiness for online crisis teaching: Transitioning to online teaching during the COVID-19 pandemic. *European Journal of Teacher Education, 43*(4), 523–541. https://www.tandfonline.com/doi/full/10.1080/02619768.2020.1815702?scroll=top&needAccess=true

Damary, R., Markova, T., & Pryadilina, N. (2017). Key challenges of online education in a multi-cultural context. *Procedia Social and Behavioral Sciences, 237*, 83–89. www.sciencedirect.com/science/article/pii/S1877042817300344

Deci, E. L., & Ryan, R. M. (1985). *Intrinsic motivation and self-determination in human behavior*. Plenum Press.

Dewey, J. (1916). *Democracy and education: An introduction to the philosophy of education*. Macmillan.

Dewey, J. (1933). *How we think. A restatement of the relation of reflective thinking to the educative process* (Revised ed.). D. C. Heath and Co.

Dewey, J. (1938). *Experience and education*. Macmillan.

Dirkx, J. M. (2008). The meaning and role of emotions in adult learning. *New Directions for Adult and Continuing Education, 120*, 7–18.

Dweck, C. (2007). *Mindset: The new psychology of success*. Random House.

Edwards, R. & Usher, R. (2000). *Globalization and pedagogy: Space, place, and identity*. Routledge/Falmer.

Ellis, H. (2019). A nontraditional conundrum: The dilemma of nontraditional student attrition in higher education. *College Student Journal, 53*(1), 24–32. www.projectinnovation.biz/index.html

Fredricks, J. A., Blumenfeld, P. C., & Paris, A. (2004). School engagement: Potential of the concept: State of the evidence. *Review of Educational Research, 74*, 59–119.

Frey, W. H. (2018). *Diversity explosion*. Brookings Institution Press.

Fry, R., & Parker, K. (2018, Nov. 15). Early benchmarks show 'post-millennials' on track to be most diverse, best-educated generation yet. *Pew Social Trends*. www.pewsocialtrends.org/2018/11/15/early-benchmarks-show-post-millennials-on-track-to-be-most-diverse-best-educated-generation-yet/

Garrison, D. R., Anderson, T., & Archer, W. (1999). Critical inquiry in a text-based environment: Computer conferencing in higher education. *The Internet and Higher Education, 2*(2–3), 87–105. https://doi.org/10.1016/S1096-7516(00)00016-6

Garrison, D. R., Anderson, T., & Archer, W. (2001). Critical thinking, cognitive presence, and computer conferencing in distance education. *The

References

American Journal of Distance Education, 15(1), 7–23. https://doi.org/10.1080/08923640109527071

Garrison, D. R., Anderson, T., & Archer, W. (2003). A theory of critical inquiry in online distance education. In M. G. Moore & W. G. Anderson (Eds.), *Handbook of distance education*, 113–127. Erlbaum.

Garrison, D. R., & Cleveland-Innes, M. (2005). Facilitating cognitive presence in online learning: Interaction is not enough. *American Journal of Distance Education, 19*(3), 133–148. www.tandfonline.com/doi/abs/10.1207/s15389286ajde1903_2

Gratz, E., & Looney, L. (2020). Faculty resistance to change: An examination of motivators and barriers to teaching online in higher education. *International Journal of Online Pedagogy and Course Design, 10*(1), 1–14.

Hattie, J., & Timperley, H. (2007). The power of feedback. *Review of Educational Research.* 77, 81–112. https://doi.org/10.3102%2F003465430298487

Karchmer-Klein, R. (2020). *Improving online teacher education: Digital tools and evidence-based practices.* Teachers College Press.

Kegan, R. (2000). "What 'form' transforms? A constructive-developmental approach to transformative learning." In J. Mezirow & Associates (Eds.), *Learning as transformation: Critical perspectives on a theory in progress.* Jossey-Bass.

Kentnor, H. E. (2015). Distance education and the evolution of online learning in the United States. *Curriculum and Teaching Dialogue, 17*(1 & 2), 21–34. https://digitalcommons.du.edu/cgi/viewcontent.cgi?article=1026&context=law_facpub

Khan, A., Egbue, O., Palkie, B., & Madden, J. (2017). Active learning: Engaging students to maximize learning in an online course. *The Electronic Journal of e-Learning, 15*(2), 107–115. https://files.eric.ed.gov/fulltext/EJ1141876.pdf

King, A. (1993). From sage on the stage to guide on the side. *College Teaching 41*(1) (Winter), 30–35. https://doi.org/10.1080/87567555.1993.9926781

Knowles, M. S. (1975). *Self-Directed Learning: A Guide for Learners and Teachers.* Associated Press.

Knowles, M. S. (1984). *Andragogy in action: Applying modern principles of adult learning.* Jossey-Bass.

Knowles, M. S. (1986). *Using learning contracts: Practical approaches to individualizing and structuring learning.* Jossey-Bass.

Knowles, M. S., Holton III, E. F., & Swanson, R. A. (2015). *The adult learner: The definitive classic in adult education and human resource development* (8th ed.). Routledge.

Ko, S., & Rossen, S. (2017). *Teaching online: A practical guide* (4th ed.). Routledge.

Krathwohl, D. (2002). *A revision of Bloom's Taxonomy: An overview.* EBSCO Publishing. www.depauw.edu/files/resources/krathwohl.pdf

Lave, J., & Wenger, E. C. (1991). *Situated Learning: Legitimate peripheral participation.* Cambridge University Press.

Learninghouse. (June, 2019). *Online college students 2019: Comprehensive data on demands and preferences.* https://49hk843qjpwu3gfmw73ngy1k-wpengine.netdna-ssl.com/wp-content/uploads/2019/06/OCS-2019-FINAL-WEB-Report.pdf

Lehman, R. M. (2006). The role of emotion in creating instructor and learner presence in the distance education experience. *Journal of Cognitive Affective Learning, 2*(2), 12–26.

Lehman R. M., & Conceição, S. C. (2010). *Creating a sense of presence in online teaching: How to "be there" for distance learners*. Jossey-Bass.

Major, A., & Sumner, J. (2018). Reducing transactional distance: Engaging online students in higher education. *The EvoLLLution*. https://evolllution.com/revenue-streams/distance_online_learning/reducing-transactional-distance-engaging-online-students-in-higher-education/

Martin, F., & Bolliger, D. U. (2018). Engagement matters: Student perceptions on the importance of engagement strategies in the online learning environment. *Online Learning, 22*, 205–222. https://files.eric.ed.gov/fulltext/EJ1179659.pdf

Martin, F., Budhrani, K., Kumar, S., & Ritzhaupt, A. (2019). Award-winning faculty online teaching practices: Course design, assessment and evaluation, and facilitation. *The Internet and Higher Education, 42*, 34–43. https://files.eric.ed.gov/fulltext/EJ1211042.pdf

McGahan, S. J. (2018). Reflective course review and revision: An overview of a process to improve course pedagogy and structure. *Journal of Educators Online, 15*(3), 141–157. http://files.eric.ed.gov/fulltext/EJ1199111.pdf

McKinsey & Company. (2020a, May 7). *To emerge stronger from the COVID-19 crisis, companies should start reskilling their workforces now*. www.mckinsey.com/business-functions/organization/our-insights/to-emerge-stronger-from-the-covid-19-crisis-companies-should-start-reskilling-their-workforces-now#

McKinsey & Company. (2020b, October 26). *Reimagining higher education in the United States*. www.mckinsey.com/industries/public-and-social-sector/our-insights/reimagining-higher-education-in-the-united-states#

McLean, A. J., Bond, C. H., & Nicholson, H. D. (2015). An anatomy of feedback: A phenomenographic investigation of undergraduate students' conceptions of feedback. *Studies in Higher Education, 40*(5), 921–932. www.facultyfocus.com/articles/teaching-and-learning/students-perceive-feedback/

McTighe, J., & Wiggins, G. (1998/2005). *Understanding by Design*. ASCD. https://www.ascd.org/ASCD/pdf/siteASCD/publications/UbD_WhitePaper0312.pdf

McTighe, J., & Wiggins, G. (2014). *Improve curriculum, assessment, and instruction by using the Understanding by Design framework*. ASCD. www.ascd.org/ASCD/pdf/siteASCD/publications/ASCD_UBD_whitepaper.pdf

Mezirow, J. (1991). *Transformative dimensions of adult learning*. Jossey-Bass.

Mezirow, J. (1994). Understanding transformation theory. *Adult Education Quarterly, 44*(4), 222-244.

Mezirow, J. (2000). Learning to think like an adult. Core concepts of transformation theory. In J. Mezirow & Associates (Eds.), *Learning as Transformation: Critical perspectives on a theory in progress* (pp. 3–33). Jossey-Bass.

Mohr, S. C., & Shelton, K. (2017). Best practices framework for online faculty professional development: A Delphi study. *Online Learning, 21*(4), 123–140. files.eric.ed.gov/fulltext/EJ1163625.pdf

Moore, K. D. (2015). *Effective instructional strategies: From theory to practice*. SAGE Publications.

Moore, M. G. (1989). Three types of transaction. In M. G. Moore & G. C. Clark (Eds.), *Readings in principles of distance education* (pp. 100–105). The Pennsylvania State University.

References

Moore, M. G. (1997). Theory of transactional distance. In D. Keegan (Ed.), *Theoretical principles of distance education* (pp. 22–38). Routledge.

Moore, M. G., Pittman, V. V., Anderson, T., and Kramarae, C. (2003). *From Chautauqua to the virtual university: A century of distance education in the United States*. Center on Education and Training for Employment, The Ohio State University. http://www.calpro-online.org/eric/docs/distance.pdf

Moore, R. L. (2014). Importance of developing community in distance education courses. *TechTrends, 58*(2), 20–24. https://doi.org/10.1007/S11528-014-0733-X

Morris, P. D., & Clark, L. M. (2018). Using NSSE data to analyze levels of engagement of distance learners. *Quarterly Review of Distance Education, 19*(2), 1–13. https://eric.ed.gov/?id=EJ1202181

Morrison, C. D. (2014). From "sage on the stage" to "guide on the side": A good start. *International Journal for the Scholarship of Teaching and Learning: 8*(1) Article 4. http://digitalcommons.georgiasouthern.edu/ij-sotl/vol8/iss1/4

Muljana, P. S., & Luo, T. (2019). Factors contributing to student retention in online learning and recommended strategies for improvement: A systematic literature review. *Journal of Information Technology Education, 18*, 19–57. https://eric.ed.gov/?id=EJ1204794

Murnane, R. J., & Willett, J. B. (2011). *Methods matter: Improving causal inference in educational and social science research*. Oxford University Press.

National Center for Education Statistics (NCES). (2016). *Digest of education statistics, 2016. 52nd edition. February 2018*. Retrieved from https://nces.ed.gov/pubs2017/2017094.pdf

National Center for Education Statistics (NCES). (2019a). *Fast facts: Distance learning*. Retrieved from https://nces.ed.gov/fastfacts/display.asp?id=80

National Center for Education Statistics (NCES). (2019b). *IPEDS* [Data sets]. Retrieved from https://nces.ed.gov/IPEDS/

New London Group. (1996). A pedagogy of multiliteracies: Designing social futures. *Harvard Educational Review, 66*(1), 60–92. www.academia.edu/2804125/A_pedagogy_of_multiliteracies_Designing_social_futures

Niemiec, C. P., Lynch, M. F., Vansteenkiste, M., Bernstein, J., Deci, E. L., & Ryan, R. M. (2006). The antecedents and consequences of autonomous self-regulation for college: A self-determination theory perspective on socialization. *Journal of Adolescence, 29*, 761–775.

Ouyang, F., & Scharber, C. (2017). The influences of an experienced instructor's discussion design and facilitation on an online learning community development: A social network analysis study. *The Internet and Higher Education, 35*, 34–47. https://doi.org/10.1016/j.iheduc.2017.07.002

Pierce, C. (1970). Offensive mechanisms. In F. B. Barbour (Ed.), *The Black seventies* (pp. 265–282). Porter Sargent.

Polly, D., Allman, B., Casto, A. R., & Norwood, J. (2018). Sociocultural perspectives of learning. In R. E. West (Ed.), *Foundations of learning and instructional design technology: The past, present, and future of learning and instructional design technology*. EdTech Books. https://edtechbooks.org/lidtfoundations/sociocultural_perspectives_of_learning

Postman, N. (1999). *Building a bridge to the eighteenth century: How the past can improve our future*. Alfred A. Knopf.

Riggs, S. A., & Linder, K. E. (2016, December). *Actively engaging students in asynchronous online classes*. IDEA Paper #64. www.ideaedu.org/Portals/0/Uploads/Documents/IDEA%20Papers/IDEA%20Papers/PaperIDEA_64.pdf

Roddy, C., Amiet, D. L., Chung, J., Holt, C., Shaw, L., McKenzie, S., Garivaldis, F., Lodge, J. M., & Mundy, M. E. (2017). Applying best practice online learning, teaching, and support to intensive online environments: An integrative review. *Frontiers in Education, 2*, 59. https://doi.org/10.3389/feduc.2017.00059

Rodgers, C. R. (2020). *The art of reflective teaching: Practicing presence*. Teachers College Press.

Rodgers, C. R., & Raider-Roth, M. B. (2006). Presence in teaching. *Teachers & Teaching, 12*(3), 265–287. https://doi.org/10.1080/13450600500467548

Sanford, D., Ross, D., Rosenbloom, A., & Singer, D. (2017). Course convenience, perceived learning and course satisfaction across course formats. *E-Journal of Business Education & Scholarship of Teaching 11*(1). https://files.eric.ed.gov/fulltext/EJ1167321.pdf

Schön, D. A. (1983). *The reflective practitioner: How professionals think in action*. Temple Smith.

Schön, D. A. (1987). *Educating the reflective practitioner: Toward a new design for teaching and learning in the professions*. Jossey-Bass.

Schroeder-Moreno, M. S. (2010). Enhancing active and interactive learning online—Lessons learned from an online introductory agroecology course. *North American Colleges and Teachers of Agriculture Journal, 54*(1), 21–30. www.jstor.org/stable/nactajournal.54.1.21?seq=1

Schwartz, S. L., Wiley, J. L., & Kaplan, C. D. (2016). Community building in a virtual teaching environment. *Advances in Social Work, 17*(1), 15–30.

Schwieger, D., & Ladwig, C. (2018). Reaching and retaining the next generation: Adapting to the expectations of Gen Z in the classroom. *Information Systems Education Journal, 16*(3), 46–54. https://files.eric.ed.gov/fulltext/EJ1179303.pdf

Shah, D. (2018). By the numbers: MOOCs in 2018. *Class Central*. www.class-central.com/report/mooc-stats-2018/

Smith, D., & Ayers, D. (2006). Culturally responsive pedagogy and online learning: Implications for the globalized community college. *Community College Journal of Research & Practice, 30*(5/6), 401–415. https://doi.org/10.1080/10668920500442125

Song, D., Rice, M., & Oh, E. Y. (2019). Participation in online courses and interaction with a virtual agent. *International Review of Research in Open & Distance Learning, 20*(1), 43–62. https://doi.org/10.19173/irrodl.v20i1.3998

Stevens, D., & Cooper, J. (2009). *Journal keeping: how to use reflective writing for effective learning, teaching, professional insight, and positive change*. Stylus.

Trippany Simmons, R., Rush-Wilson, T., & Haizlip, B. (2016). Respecting diversity in an online environment. In C. J. Sheperis & R. J. Davis (Eds.), *Online Counselor Education: A Guide for Students* (pp. 153–170). SAGE Publications.

van Popta E., Kral, M., Camp, G., Martens, R. L., & Simons, P. R. (2017). Exploring the value of peer feedback in online learning for the provider. *Educational Resource Review, 20*, 24–30. https://doi.org/10.1016/j.edurev.2016.10.003

Vygotsky, L. S. (1978). *Mind in society: The development of higher psychological processes*. (M. M. Lopez-Morillas Cole, A. R. Luria, & J. Wertsch translators). Harvard University Press.

Wasserman, E., & Migdal, R. (2019). Professional development: Teachers' attitudes in online and traditional training course. *Online Learning, 23*(1), 132–143. https://files.eric.ed.gov/fulltext/EJ1211174.pdf

Wenger, E. (1998). *Communities of practice: Learning, meaning, and identity.* Cambridge University Press.

Wiggins, G., & McTighe, J. (1998). *Understanding by design.* Association for Supervision and Curriculum Development.

World Economic Forum. (2020, October). *The future of jobs report 2020.* www3.weforum.org/docs/WEF_Future_of_Jobs_2020.pdf

World Economic Forum. (2021, January). *The global risks report 2021.* http://www3.weforum.org/docs/WEF_The_Global_Risks_Report_2021.pdf

Xu, D. & Xu, Y. (2019). *The promises and limits of online higher education.* American Enterprise Institute. https://files.eric.ed.gov/fulltext/ED596296.pdf

Zeglen, E., & Rosendale, J. A. (2018). Increasing online information retention: Analyzing the effects of visual hints and feedback in educational games. *Journal of Open, Flexible and Distance Learning, 22*(1), 22–33. www.learntechlib.org/p/184660/

Zimmerman, B. J. (2008). Investigating self-regulation and motivation: Historical background, methodological developments, and future prospects. *American Educational Journal, 45*(1), 166–183. https://doi.org/10.3102%2F0002831207312909

Index

AUTHOR INDEX

Allen, M., 89
Allen, R. M., 65, 125
Allman, B., 63
Amiet, D. L., xiii
Anderson, C., 89
Anderson, L. W., 19
Anderson, T., xii, 2, 9, 82, 87, 88, 196, 210
Archer, W., xii, 9, 82, 87, 88, 196, 210
Ayers, D., 124

Bandura, A., 200, 212
Beaunoyer, E., 65, 125
Beckett, D., 5
Bernstein, J., 87
Berry, S., 5, 126
Bettinger, E. P., 5
Bialowas, A., 5
Bigatel, P., xiii
Bista, K., 65, 125
Black, G. C., 5
Bloom, B. S., 19, 20
Bloomberg, L. D., xiii, xiv, 42, 62, 63, 89, 107, 110, 126, 130, 168, 208, 209
Blumenfeld, P. C., 85
Bolliger, D. U., 89
Bond, C. H., 133
Boud, D., 188, 210
Brookfield, S. D., 90, 188
Budhrani, K., xiii, 7, 58
Bunton, T., 89

Camp, G., 61
Campbell, P., 89, 200
Casto, A. R., 63
Cervero, R., 116
Chan, R. Y., 65, 125
Cherney, M. R., 89
Chung, J., xiii

Clark, L. M., 3
Clark, R. C., 44, 146, 207
Cleveland-Innes, M., 89, 131, 198, 200, 205
Cole, A. W., 89
Conceição, S. C., 168
Cooper, J., 62
Cope, B., 21
Cranton, P., 43, 215
Croxton, R. A., 126
Cutri, R. M., xiii

Damary, R., 107, 124
Deci, E. L., 87
Dewey, J., 57, 58, 59, 187, 188, 196, 197, 201, 211
Dirkx, J. M., 90
Draeger, Jr., R., 89
Dupere, S., 65, 125
Dweck, C., 113, 114, 202

Edwards, R., 5
Egbue, O., xiii, 168
Ellis, H., 5

Featherston, M., 89
Fisher, V. C., 89
Fox, L., 5
Fredricks, J. A., 85
Frey, W. H., 122
Fry, R., 4

Garivaldis, F., xiii
Garrison, D. R., xii, 9, 82, 87, 88, 131, 196, 198, 205, 210
Grantham, G., xiii, 89, 107, 110, 168, 208
Gratz, E., xiii
Guitton, M. L., 65, 125

Haizlip, B., 117
Hattie, J., 144

Index

Holt, C., xiii
Holton III, E. F., 42

Kalantzis, M., 21
Kaplan, C. D., 60, 126
Karchmer-Klein, R., xiv
Kegan, R., 43, 215
Kennan, S., xiii
Kentnor, H. E., 2
Keogh, R., 188, 210
Khan, A., 168, xiii
King, A., 107, 201, 211
Knowles, M. S., 42, 43, 96, 193, 194, 201, 212
Ko, S., xiv
Kral, M., 61
Kramarae, C., 2
Krathwohl, D. R., 19
Kumar, S., xiii, 7, 58

Ladwig, C., 4, 41
Lave, J., 59, 196
Lehman, R. M., 90, 168
Lennon, L., 89
Linder, K. E., 126, 168
Lodge, J. M., xiii
Loeb, S., 5
Looney, L., xiii
Luo, T., 5
Lynch, M. F., 87

Madden, J., xiii, 168
Major, A., 168
Markova, T., 107, 124
Martens, R. L., 61
Martin, F., xiii, 7, 58, 89
May, J., xiii
Mayer, R. E., 44, 146, 207
McGahan, S. J., 58
Mc Kenzie, S., xiii
McLean, A. J., 133
McTighe, J., 17, 214
Mena, J., xiii
Mezirow, J., 43, 188, 197, 214
Migdal, R., xiv
Mohr, S. C., 168
Moore, K. D., 18
Moore, M. G., xii, 2, 5, 85, 109, 204, 214
Moore, R. L., 126
Morris, P. D., 3
Morrison, C. D., 107
Motel, L., 89
Muljana, P. S., 5

Mundy, M. E., xiii
Murnane, R. J., 107

Nicholson, H. D., 133
Nicolini, K. M., 89
Niemiec, C. P., 87
Norwood, J., 63

Oh, E. Y., 3
Ouyang, F., 58

Palkie, B., xiii, 168
Paris, A., 85
Parker, K., 4
Peck, B., 89
Pierce, C., 117, 207
Pittman, V. V., 2
Polly, D., 63
Postman, N., 204
Pryadilina, N., 107, 124

Ragan, L. C., xiii
Raider-Roth, M. B., 210
Redmond, B. F., xiii
Rice, M., 3
Riggs, S. A., 126, 168
Ritzhaupt, A., xiii, 7, 58
Roddy, C., xiii
Rodgers, C. R., 87, 189, 210
Rosenbloom, A., 4
Rosendale, J. A., 5
Ross, D., 4
Rossen, S., xiv
Rush-Wilson, T., 117
Ryan, R. M., 87

Sanford, D., 4
Scharber, C., 58
Schön, D. A., 188, 211
Schroeder-Moreno, M. S., 9, 187, 200
Schwartz, S. L., 60, 126
Schwieger, D., 4, 41
Shah, D., 3
Shaw, L., xiii
Shelton, K., 168
Simons, P. R., 61
Singer, D., 4
Smith, D., 124
Song, D., 3
Steimel, S., 5
Stevens, D., 62
Sumner, J., 168
Swanson, R. A., 42

Taylor, E. S., 5
Timperley, H., 144
Trippany Simmons, R., 117

Usher, R., 5

van Popta, E., 61
Vansteenkiste, M., 87
Vygotsky, L. S., 59, 63, 196

Walker, D., 188, 210
Wasserman, E., xiv

Weber, N. L., 89
Wenger, E. C., 59, 196
Wiggins, G., 17, 215
Wiley, J. L., 60, 126
Willett, J. B., 107
Wilson, L., 116

Xu, D., xi
Xu, Y., xi

Zeglen, E., 5
Zimmerman, B. J., 46

SUBJECT INDEX

Accessibility, 65–72
  Accessibility resources (Appendix B)
  addressing, 124–126
  defined, 66, 193
  ongoing supportive engagement strategy, 100
  Strategies for Ensuring Accessible Course Materials, 69–70
  tools and formats, 67
  underserved communities, 65–66
  Universal Design for Learning Framework, 67–68
  web, 66
Accommodations. *See* Learning accommodations
Accountability
  of instructor, 119
  of learners, 48
Achievement learning, 131–132, 198
Active learning, 8, 44, 193
Adapted levels of Bloom's Taxonomy, 19, 20
Adult learners, 5
Adult learning principles, 7–8
  andragogy, 42–43
  and course content, 42–44
  defined, 193
  transformative learning, 43–44
Adult learning theory
  andragogy, 42–43
  defined, 193–194
  transformative learning, 43–44
Affective engagement, 85
Alone learning, 99
Americans with Disabilities Act Amendments Act of 2008 (ADAAA), 66
Americans with Disabilities Act of 1990 (ADA), 66
Analyzing, knowledge dimension, 21

Andragogy, 42–43, 194
Annotated Research Resources, 81
Announcement tool, 45–46
Applying, knowledge dimension, 21
Architectural Barriers Act of 1968, 68
Architecture of engagement, 126, 168
Assessment of learning, 14, 29
  defined, 194
  formative, 35–37, 97–99, 202
  and grading, 151–153
  guidelines for effective, 37–38
  measures, 38
  methods, 30–34, 194
  properties of effective, 30
  rubrics for, 30–34. *See also* Rubrics
  summative, 35–37, 213
  testing, 37
Asset-based teaching, 113, 115, 147, 149
Assignment, 24, 26
  completion, 139
  defined, 194
  feedback on, 96
  presentation, 140
  signature, 56, 212
Asynchronous discussion forums, 127
Asynchronous tools, teaching, 45–46
  advantages and disadvantages of, 46
  asynchronous-synchronous balancing act, 48–51
  defined, 194
  objectives achieved through, 50
  usage of, 46
At-risk learners, 103, 194
Audio feedback, 149
  application, 150–151
  defined, 194–195
  guidelines for, 149–151
  tools, 147, 148

Index

Audio material, transforming teaching material into, 51–53
Auditory learners, 94, 195
Autonomy, learner, 180–181

Backward design, 17, 18
Balanced feedback, 140, 143
Behavioral engagement, 85
Best practices, educational, 13, 195
Bias
   cultural, 8
   implicit, 111, 189–190, 203
   pro-Western, 8
Blended learning, 3, 195. *See also* Hybrid course
Bloom's Taxonomy, 19–20, 21, 195
   rubric based on, 34
Boilerplate feedback, 146, 195

Capacity building, 118
Center for Advanced Research on Language Acquisition (CARLA), 124
Center for Excellence in Universal Design, 68
Chautauqua Correspondence College, 2
Classroom management plan, 92
Coaching-based orientation, 111–112
Cognitive effort, 19
Cognitive engagement, 85
Cognitive overload, 63. *See also* Scaffolding
Cognitive presence, learners, 88–89, 195
Co-learner, 126, 174, 180–181
Collaboration tools, 59, 196
Collaborative learning, 58–63, 196
   constructivism, 58–59
   facilitation strategies, 59
   group activities, setting up, 60
Communications
   defined, 196
   and discussions, 104
   electronic, 2
   email, 91
   nonverbal, 138
   verbal, 138
Communities of practice, 59
Community of Inquiry model, 87, 88, 89, 196
Competencies, 22, 196
Conceptualizing, knowledge dimension, 21
Constructivism, 42, 58–59, 196
Continuous content, 64
Contract, learning, 95
Correspondence education/learning, 2
Course content, 14, 196

accessibility, 65–72
adult learning principles and, 42–44
alignment with course learning outcomes, 24–26
clear and intuitive, 54–55
collaborative learning. *See* Collaborative learning
course syllabus and, 55–58
creation of, 41–72
design and sequence of, 54
development of, 78–80
equity, 65–72
inclusion, 65–72
instructor participation plan, 55
multimedia principle and, 44–51
organization and presentation of material, 53–58
prior knowledge and, 64
relevancy of, 53–54
scaffolding, 63–65
transforming teaching material into audio and video content, 51–53
value of, 53–54
Course delivery, 59, 197
Course design, 13
   backward, 17, 18
   defined, 197
Course development process, 72, 197
Course guide, 56, 197. *See also* Syllabus
Course learning outcomes (CLOs), 14, 22–24
   alignment with vision, 18–22
   course content alignment with, 24–26
   defined, 197
   development of, 17–26
   in sequence, 22–24
   specific and measurable, 24
Course material, 35, 197
Course module, 55, 207
Course navigation, 13, 26, 72, 208
Course Outcomes Map, 24–26
Course syllabus. *See* Syllabus
COVID-19 pandemic, 4, 65
   and asynchronous learning, 46
   online learning during, 2–3
   and Universal Design for Learning framework, 67–68
Critical reflection, 188, 197
Critical thinking, 41, 43, 197–198
Criticism, 134
Critique, 43. *See also* Feedback
   balance of, 143
   defined, 198
Cultural bias, 8

Culturally responsive teaching, 123–124, 198
Culture
　defined, 124, 198
　regional differences in, 124
Culture, for online learning, 13

Deep learners, 132, 198
Deep learning, 131–133, 198. *See also* Significant learning
Dense content, avoiding, 64
Developmental feedback, 144–145
Dialogue, and rapport, 48
Differentiated instruction, 198
Differentiation, 53, 198
Digital divide, 66, 199
Direct assessment, 38, 199
Disabilities, 66
　defined, 199
　invisible, 66
Discussion boards, 45, 199
Discussion forums, 60–61
　asynchronous, facilitating, 127
Discussion groups, synchronous, 128–129
Disembodied learning, 5
Disengagement, for learners, 13, 199
Distance education, 1–2. *See also* Online learning
　current landscape of, 1
　defined, 199
　growth of, 2–3
　history of, 3
Diverse learners, 3–5
Diversity, 13, 122–123, 178–179, 199–200

Education of the Handicapped Act of 1975, 68
Educative process, 57
Electronic communications, 2
Emotional presence, learners, 89–90, 200
Empowerment, learners, 10–11, 200
Encouragement, 116
End-of-term evaluations, 97–98
Engagement
　affective, 85
　architecture of, 126, 168
　behavioral, 85
　cognitive, 85
　defined, 200
　disengagement, 13
　email communication and, 91
　learner's, 9, 85–87, 150
　motivation and, 85, 87
　multimodal. *See* Multimodal engagement

onboarding, strategies for. *See* Onboarding engagement
ongoing supportive, strategies for, 99–102
strategies for, 91–96
through presence, 110–112
Engagement cycle, 81–83
Engagement indicators (EIs), 167–169, 200
Equal access, 66
Equitable assessment, 38
Equity, and course content, 65–72, 200
Equity-minded classroom, 101, 201
Evaluation, 21, 29. *See also* Assessment of learning
　defined, 201
　end-of-term, 97–98
Exclusionary practices, 116, 201
Experiencing, knowledge dimension, 21
Experiential learning, 188, 201

Face-time technologies, 95, 201. *See also* Synchronous tools, teaching
Facilitator, instructor as, 9–10, 201
Feedback, 72, 96
　addressing growth academic mindset, 137
　balanced, 140, 143
　boilerplate, 146, 195
　defined, 201–202
　delaying, 138
　developmental, 144–145
　ensuring teaching presence, 136–137
　frequency, 138–139
　guiding principles for, 139–146
　incorporating technology to provide, 147, 149
　individualized, 136, 203
　informational, 144, 204
　learners' perceptions of, 133–134
　lecture *vs.* interactivity, 137–138
　meaningful/individualized, 139–140
　as medium of instruction, 130–134
　multimodal, 149–151
　prepare to provide, 135–139
　Samples of Feedback Commentary (Appendix I)
　Satisfactory Versus Unsatisfactory Feedback Samples (Appendix H)
　Streamlined Feedback Toolbox, 141–143
　streamlining, 145–146
　substantive, guiding principles for, 139–146
　timeliness, 138–139
　Tips for Providing Engaging Written Feedback: A Brief Cheat Sheet, 135–136

Index

tone and presentation, 138
toolbox, streamlined, 141–143
value of, 96
video, 115, 149–151
written. *See* Written feedback
Feed forward, 144–145, 202
Feed up, 144, 145, 202
Fixed mindset, 113, 202
Flexibility, ongoing supportive engagement strategy, 102
Formal welcome letter, 92–94
Formative assessment, 35–37, 97–99, 202
Frequency, of feedback, 138–139

Generation X, 4
Generation Z, 4, 41
Grade/grading, 19, 29, 202
  assessment and, 151–153
  culture fair, 29
  guidelines, 151–152
  practices, 152
  rubrics, 30
Group activities, 60. *See also* Collaborative learning opportunities
Growth academic mindset, 112–116
  addressing, 137
  defined, 202–203
  instructor mindset, 113–114
  justification, 152
  learner mindset, 113
  strategies for enhancing, 114–116
Growth trajectory, 111, 203

Hidden disabilities, 66
Humanize, online learning environment, 110–111
Hybrid course, 3, 203. *See also* Blended learning

Implicit beliefs, 189
Implicit bias, 111, 189–190, 203
Inclusion/inclusivity, 13, 123
  addressing, 178–179
  course content, 65–72
  defined, 203
Inclusive pedagogy, 123, 203
Indirect assessment, 38, 199
Individualized feedback, 136, 203
Individualized "just-in-time" guidance, 97
Informal welcome video, 94–95
Informational feedback, 144, 204
Institute for Higher Education Policy, 168
Institutional learning outcome (ILO), 22–24, 37, 204

Instruction. *See* Online instruction
Instructional/course materials
  designing and developing, 76–80
Instructional design (ID), 204
Instructional strategies, 44, 204. *See also* Online instruction; Teaching strategies
Instructors. *See* Online instructors
Integrative Instructional Model, 26
Interaction, 8, 58, 204
Interactivity, 137–138
International learners, 107
Introductory meeting, 95–96
Invisible disabilities, 66

Journals, 62–63, 130, 204
"Just-in-time" guidance, 97

Knowledge
  defined, 204–205
  dimensions, 21
  usable, 43, 215

Learner
  addressing, 117–118
  adult, 5
  at-risk, 103, 194
  auditory, 94, 195
  autonomy, 180–181
  cognitive presence, 88–89
  disengagement for, 13
  diverse, 3–5
  emotional presence, 89–90
  empowerment, 10–11
  engaged, characteristics of, 86
  engagement, 9, 85–87, 150
  growth mindset, 113
  international, 107
  monitoring, strategies for effective. *See* Monitoring, strategies for effective
  online, 3–5
  online learning experience, preparation for, 90–91
  perceptions of feedback, 133–134
  social presence, 87–88
  support to be successful, 95–98
  teaching presence, 89
  use of technology, 182–183
Learner-centered approach, 19, 205
Learner mindset, 113, 205
Learning, 2
  achievement, 131–132, 198
  active, 8, 44, 193
  assessment of. *See* Assessment of learning
  barriers to, 7, 51

Learning (cont.)
  deep, 131–133, 198
  defined, 205
  experiential, 188, 201
  online. See Online learning
  outcomes. See Course learning outcomes (CLOs)
  problem-based, 19, 210
  significant, 18
  surface, 131–133, 198
  transformative, 43–44, 214
Learning accommodations, 66–67, 100, 205
Learning community
  defined, 205
  development of, 126
Learning contract, 95, 205–206
Learning environment, 110–111
Learning management systems (LMSs), 29, 61, 90
  best practices, 91
  defined, 206
Learning objectives. See Course learning outcomes (CLOs)
Learning outcomes, 14
  course. See Course learning outcomes (CLOs)
  defined, 206
Learning preferences, 44, 206
Learning strategies, 181, 206
Learning theory, 43
  adult. See Adult learning theory
  defined, 206
Learning trajectory, 22
Lecture, 137–138

Marker points, assessment, 36, 37
Massive Open Online Course (MOOC) movement, 3, 206
Mastery, 37
Mentor, 107, 207
Metacognition, 57, 207
Microaggressions, 117, 207. See also Oppression
Midweek Motivation, 116
Milestone planning, 71
Monitoring, strategies for effective
  communication and discussions, 104
  track progress, 103–104
Motivation, 98
  defined, 207
  and engagement, 85, 87
  ongoing, 115–116
Multicultural learning environment, 124

Multiliteracies, pedagogy of, 21
Multimedia principle, 44–51, 146, 207
Multimodal assessments, 38, 207
Multimodal engagement, 149, 165–166, 208
  diversity, addressing, 178–179
  engagement indicators, 167–169
  inclusivity, addressing, 178–179
  learner autonomy and empowerment, 180–181
  nurture working relationships, 171–173
  sense of community, creation of, 176–177
  teaching presence, ensuring, 170–171
  trust, establishing and maintainng culture of, 183–185
Multimodal Engagement Cycle, 81–83
Multimodal feedback, 149–151, 208
  learner engagement, 150
  preparation, 149–150
Multimodal learning, 208
Multimodal teaching, 146–151
  audio and video feedback tools, benefits of, 147, 148
  strategies. See Multimodal teaching strategies
Multimodal teaching strategies
  culturally responsive teaching, 123–124
  diversity, 122–123
  facilitate group work and collaboration, 127–130
  inclusion, 123
  learning community, development of, 126
  unequal access to technology, 124–126

National Center for Education Statistics (NCES), 222
New London Group, 21
Nontraditional learners, 4–5, 208
Nonverbal communication, 138

Onboarding engagement, 91–96
  classroom management plan, 92
  formal welcome letter, 92–94
  synchronous introductory meeting, 95–96
  welcome video, 94–95
Onboard learners. See Onboarding engagement
Ongoing motivation, 115–116
Ongoing supportive engagement, strategies for
  flexibility, 102
  trust and transparency, 100–102
  visibility and presence, 99–100

Index

Online classroom, 45
Online dialogue, 131
Online instruction
  defined, 208
  designing and development of, 13–16
  materials. *See* Instructional/course materials
Online instructors
  and asynchronous tools, 45–46
  challenges faced by, 7
  as coach, 107
  competencies, 22, 196
  engagement, 9
  engaging, characteristics of, 86
  as facilitator, 9–10
  "guide on the side," 9, 119
  and learner empowerment, 10–11
  as learning partner, 119
  as mentor, 107
  mindset, 113–114
  participation plan, 55
  as reflective practitioner, 187–190
  role of, 7–11, 44, 167–168
  "sage on the stage," 9, 107, 137
  tasks of, 7, 13
  voices, 15–16
Online learners, 3–5
Online learning. *See also* Distance education
  challenges of, 5–7
  during COVID-19 pandemic, 2–3
  culture for, 13
  defined, 2, 208–209
  diverse learners and, 3–5
  nature of, 6
  overview, 1
  technology and, 3, 5, 8
  tools, tips for selecting and evaluating, 49
  traditional learning *vs.*, 3
Online Learning Consortium (OLC), 168
Online learning context, 186, 209
Online learning experience, 90–91, 209
Online learning landscape, 1–3
Online learning tools, 49, 209
Online Support Resources, 81
Opportunities
  collaborative learning. *See* Collaborative learning opportunities
  reflective, 56–58
Oppression, 209. *See also* Microaggressions
Organization, of course material, 53–58
Outcomes. *See* Course learning outcomes (CLOs); Institutional learning outcome (ILO)
Outcomes Planning Map, 22–24

Pandemic. *See* COVID-19 pandemic
Pedagogy of multiliteracies, 21, 209
Peer dialogue journals, 62–63, 130, 204, 209
Peer learning, 209
Peer mentoring, 209
Peer review, 61–62, 209–210
  facilitating, 129
Performance rubric. *See* Rubrics
Persistence, 54, 210
Planning
  for assessment of learning, 29–38
  Outcomes Planning Map, 22–24
Positionality
  defined, 116, 210
  guidelines for addressing, 117–119
  power and, 116–119
Positive relationships, 108
Power
  guidelines for addressing, 117–119
  and positionality, 116–119
Practical drivers of online teaching, 7
Preassessment, 38, 210
Preassessments, 38
Presence
  cognitive, 88–89, 195
  concept of, 87
  defined, 210
  emotional, 89–90, 200
  engagement through, 110–112
  ongoing supportive engagement strategy, 99–100
  social, 87–88, 212
  teaching, 9, 89, 136–137, 170–171, 213
Presentation, of course material, 53–58
Problem-based learning, 19, 210
Program learning outcome (PLO), 22–24, 37, 210
Progress assessments, 38, 210
Progress tracking, 103–104
Pro-Western bias, 8

Rapport, 48
  defined, 210
  dialogue and, 48
Real connection, 95
Reflection. *See* Critical reflection; Reflective practice; Self-reflexivity
Reflection checkpoint, 11, 27–28, 39–40, 73–74, 81, 105–106, 120–121, 154–156, 171, 173, 175–176, 177, 179–180, 182, 183, 185–186, 191–192
Reflective journal. *See* Journal
Reflective opportunities, 56–58

Reflective practice, 187–189, 211. *See also* Implicit bias; Self-reflexivity
Reflective practitioner, instructor as, 187–190
  defined, 211
  reflective practice, 187–189
Reflective questions, 11, 168, 186
Reflective thinking, 188. *See also* Critical thinking
Regional differences, in culture, 124
Rehabilitation Act of 1973, 66, 68
Relationships. *See* Teaching relationships
Relevancy, of course content, 53–54
Resubmission, 152, 211
Rubrics, 30–34
  advantages of, 32
  based on Bloom's Taxonomy, 34
  Basic Rubric Template, 31
  defined, 211
  features of, 30, 31–32
  Sample Grade Justification Rubric (Appendix K)
  Sample Grading Rubric (Appendix J)
  sequential developmental, 33
  types of, 33–34

Safety, 118
Sage on the stage, 137, 211
Scaffolding, 31, 63–65
  defined, 211
  dense content, 64
  guidelines for effective, 64–65
  minimizing cognitive overload, 63
  types of, 64
  zone of proximal development, 63
Screencast, 51, 151, 211
Segmentation principle, 63
Self-determination theory, 87
Self- directed learning (SDL), 212
Self-efficacy, 113, 212. *See also* Autonomy; Motivation; Persistence
Self-reflection, 11, 190, 212
self-reflexivity, 11, 212
Self-regulated learning, 46
Sense of community, 58
  creation of, 176–177
  defined, 212
Sequential developmental rubric, 33
Setup cycle, online instruction, 13–16
  Setup Cycle: Designing, Developing, Delivering Online Instruction, 15
Shared experience, 63
Signature assignment, 35, 56, 212. *See also* Assignments; Summative assessment

Significant learning, 18, 212. *See also* Deep learning
Sit and get approach, 174, 181
Social presence, of learners, 87–88, 212. *See also* Presence
Sociocultural factors, 4, 123. *See also* Diversity
Strategies for supportive engagement
  flexibility, 102
  trust and transparency, 100–102
  visibility and presence, 99–100
Streamlining feedback, 145–146
Student-centered, 212–213. *See also* Learner-centered approach
Substantive feedback, guiding principles for, 139–146
Summative assessment, 35–37, 213. *See also* Assessment; Formative assessment
Support, balance of, 143. *See also* Onboard
Supportive engagement, strategies for. *See* Onboarding engagement
Surface learning, 131, 198. *See also* Achievement learning; Deep learning
Syllabus, 26, 55–58, 213. *See also* Course guide
Synchronous activities
  creating, 47
  guidelines for effective, 128–129
Synchronous discussion groups, 128–129
Synchronous introductory meeting, 95–96. *See also* Introductory meeting
Synchronous tools, teaching, 46–48. *See also* Face-time technologies
  advantages and disadvantages of, 47–48
  asynchronous-synchronous balancing act, 48–51
  defined, 213
  objectives achieved through, 50
  usage of, 47

Taxonomy of Educational Objectives Handbook: Cognitive Domains (Bloom), 19
Teachable moments, 101, 213
Teacher-centered, 48
Teaching. *See also* Course delivery; Pedagogy of multiliteracies
  asynchronous tools, 45–46
  material, transforming into audio and video content, 51–53
  multimodal strategies. *See* Multimodal teaching strategies
  synchronous tools, 46–48

Index

Teaching presence, 9, 89, 136–137, 170–171, 189, 213. *See also* Presence
Teaching relationships
  benefits of, 108
  building, 211
  development of, 108–110
  growth academic mindset. *See* Growth academic mindset
  nurture, 171–173
  overview, 106–107
  power and positionality, 116–119
Teaching strategies. *See also* Instructional strategies; Online instruction
  defined, 213
  multimodal. *See* Multimodal teaching strategies
Teaching through empowerment, 213–214
Technology. *See also* Apps; Learning management system; Learning tools
  defined, 214
  face-time, 95, 201
  incorporating to provide feedback, 147, 149
  learners' use of, 182–183
  and online learning, 3, 5, 8
  unequal access to, 124–126
Timeliness, of feedback, 138–139
Time-management skills, 96–97
Tips for Selecting and Evaluating Online Learning Tools, 49
Track progress, 103–104. *See also* Monitor; Progress
Traditional learner, 5. *See also* Nontraditional learners
Traditional learning *vs.* online learning, 3
Transactional distance, 5, 214
Transformative learning, 43–44, 214. *See also* Adult learning theory
Transparency, 111. *See also* Strategies for supportive engagement
  establishing and maintainng culture of, 183–185
  ongoing supportive engagement strategy, 100–102
Trust. *See also* Strategies for supportive engagement
  creating environment of, 115
  establishing and maintainng culture of, 183–185
  ongoing supportive engagement strategy, 100–102

Underrepresented groups, 8, 214
Underserved communities, 65. *See also* Accessibility; Underrepresented groups
Understanding by Design (UbD), 17, 214. *See also* Backward Design
Universal Design for Learning (UDL), 67–68. *See also* Accessibility
  core guidelines, 68
  defined, 215
  principles of, 68, 69
Usable knowledge, 43, 215

Value, of course content, 53–54
Verbal communication, 138
Video conferencing tools, 61
Video feedback, 115, 149
  application, 150–151
  defined, 215
  guidelines for, 149–151
  tools, 147, 148
Video material
  tips for creating, 52
  transforming teaching material into, 51–53
Visibility, ongoing supportive engagement strategy, 99–100
Vision, outcomes alignment with, 18–22
Visual learner, 215. *See also* Auditory learner

Watershed moment, xii
Web accessibility, 66
Web-conferencing tools, 61
Welcome learners. *See* Learners
Welcome letter, 92–94, 215
  Sample Welcome Letter (Appendix C)
Welcome video, 94–95, 215
Working relationships. *See* Teaching/working relationships
Written feedback, 135
  defined, 215
  tips for providing engaging, 135–136

Zone of proximal development, 63. *See also* Scaffolding

About the Author

Dr. Linda Dale Bloomberg is founder of Bloomberg Associates, ILIAD (Institute for Learning Innovations and Adult Development) and Advanced Learning Solutions, and a cofounder of Columbia University's Global Learning and Leadership Institute. She previously served as senior researcher for the South African Human Sciences Research Council and National Institute for Personnel Research, focusing on change management, diversity initiatives, and workplace learning. Since 2013, she has worked with Northcentral University's School of Education as associate director of faculty support and development and full professor of education. In this capacity, she coaches and evaluates online faculty, develops curriculum for graduate research courses, and serves as dissertation chair and subject matter expert for online doctoral candidates. She also serves in an advisory and leadership capacity for the university's community engagement platform and was a founding member of the University's diversity committee. She consults to numerous research and nonprofit advisory boards, and was invited to serve on the Future Talent Council, Global Advisory Board for Faculty and Staff Development, and as Mentor in Residence for SAGE Publications. Dr. Bloomberg presents regularly at national and international professional conferences on topics related to qualitative research, online learning, and professional development for online pedagogy, and is the author and editor of numerous publications in these fields. She received her doctorate in adult and organizational learning from Teachers College, Columbia University, and holds master's degrees in counseling psychology and organizational psychology from the University of Witwatersrand, Johannesburg, South Africa.

In this book, Dr. Bloomberg distills over a decade of experience in teaching in a multitude of online contexts including coaching instructors to teach online. She has also been researching best practices for online instruction since 2003, when she began her doctoral dissertation, studying the development and facilitation of online learning communities. Witnessing and experiencing the rapidly evolving contexts of online learning, she began writing this book in 2019. With the advent of the COVID-19 pandemic, she became even more committed to producing innovative material that could be swiftly shared and become immediately useful and usable in multiple online educational contexts, thereby creating online offerings that will engage and support diverse adult learners.